The Message

The Message

Robin Brockman

Blitz
Editions

To Jane Fuller

This edition was published in 1996 by Blitz Editions
an imprint of Bookmart Ltd.
Desford Road.
Enderby Leicester LE9 5AD

ISBN - 1 856 05362 8

Printed in the UK.

Chapter One

Something that didn't exist came to call on Catherine Frazier that night and when I arrived soon afterwards she was so pale and terrified it sent a chill through me. Anything that affected Catherine that way, I knew had to be quite out of the ordinary.

'Thank God it's really you,' she sighed. 'Come in quickly.'

Really me, I thought and why had she used our private code phrase telling me to come armed?

I'd duly turned up heeled, though it was pretty rash, with a legally owned 9mm Browning holstered under my jacket, illegally loaded and ready. She shut the door and locked it as soon as I cleared its frame.

'What the hell happened?' I said. 'You look like you've...'

'Seen a ghost? I should be so lucky.' She smiled nervously and flapped a hand at the sideboard. 'Pour yourself a large one.'

Noting that she held a glass of straight Scotch of her own, I walked across and reached for the bottle. No, I realized Catherine wouldn't look the way she did now over seeing a ghost. She half believed in ghosts, had spent most of her adult life hunting them, along with other phenomena like UFOs, Big Foot, Earth energy sources in stone circles and all that. She'd have been ecstatic at the prospect of finding proof of the after-life. I was also sure that no mortal mugger or rapist would have affected her this way either, not the tough, independent self-defence-trained Catherine I knew and unfortunately still loved.

'Tell me why you rang in such a state of... agitation?' I filled my glass with a healthy measure, though as an American my taste runs more to bourbon, added a finger more and turned to her. She was a tricky one. I didn't want to shame her into denying her fear, clamming up or minimizing things.

'I was visited,' she said with an effort, 'by Men In Black.'

'What has the colour they wore got to do with it?' I snapped at her, surprising us both. At the back of my mind was a strange sense of unease and I felt my hand grow wet before realizing it was shaking so badly my whisky was spilling. 'Sorry, I guess you've got me spooked, too. Your saying our code for carrying a gun: East of Whitechapel'...' It came from an old Sherlock Holmes movie: 'Watson, never go unarmed east of Whitechapel', and we had cooked it up during some trouble we'd had years before with a bunch of American zealots. They had been out to get Catherine for trashing on T.V. their belief that UFOs were the work of Satan.

'Hell,' I said, 'using the code made me figure you didn't even think the phone was safe, or that you were being held even as we spoke.'

'Men In Black are a known, unsubstantiated phenomenon,' she told me, trying to sound professional, clinical. 'I was not thinking clearly. A gun might not even be any use against them, if they exist.' Now her shaking returned so violently that it gave the lie to her attempt at composure. 'What do I mean if they exist?' her voice cracked.

Setting my drink down I went over and took her in my arms in as brotherly a manner as I could. For about eight years now our relationship had been platonic, as if the brief marriage in our early twenties had never happened.

For all that while, we had been very close and yet seldom able to get along.

'Ever have a nightmare come in and sit on your sofa?' she asked.

A flip, supposedly comforting and dismissive remark stuck in my contracting throat. Somehow I couldn't even say a simple 'no'.

'They are said to come to people who have seen or have been abducted by UFOs,' Catherine went on. 'Or people researching such cases.'

'Why?' I asked automatically. 'Who are they?' It was pure reflex, a verbal knee-jerk. Inside, I was absolutely sure I didn't want to know.

'To dissuade them, put the frighteners on them.'

'We're not talking about some government conspiracy, are we?' I asked, hoping this was the case, but once again with a weird sort of déjà vû.

'No, not in this instance, something far stranger. Something I was always sure was an illusion or a hoax until... Oh Jesus...' She began to cry at last and I held her tighter.

'They always come when someone is alone,' Catherine explained after she had calmed down a little. 'Most often at night. Sometimes they pose as official persons but they can be quite open about who they really are, as well. Who they allegedly really are.'

'And that is?'

'Aliens.' She smiled and shrugged, but a look of worry and wariness came over her again in an instant. 'Beings from another planet or dimension. They are usually described as strange, not quite human... almost parodies or poor approximations of humans.'

I was waiting, letting her give me all this, hoping she'd get some of her sceptical nature back. I particularly wanted to hear what had happened to Catherine herself but I thought it best not to rush her.

'They deliver vague threats and insist you stop talking about or looking into an incident involving UFOs or alien contacts.'

'Why are they called Men in Black?'

'Because they are almost always wearing black.' She ran a shaky hand through her long brown hair. 'I mean they dress in these old-fashioned black suits, ties and hats...'

'Sort of sinister Blues Brothers,' I ventured. In contrast to my earlier instinctive reaction, I was unable to take it all very seriously now.

'No, more like 1950s F.B.I. men or movie gangsters. Their clothes look oddly brand-new. People say they drive old-style shiny new cars. Their threats are very gangland too.' She took a long pull at her whisky. 'They'd be comical if only...' Closing her eyes she fought off a howl of despair, anger and bewilderment.

'Something you were pretty convinced was nonsense came right in here and...'

'Yes,' she nodded slowly. 'They rang first, of course, and arranged it.'

'They what?'

'I wouldn't have let them in otherwise or anyone else in London that I didn't know. It was to see if I was alone as well, I suppose. They told me they had information about a case I'm working on and in a way, they did.'

'What do you mean?'

'They warned me off it. They said if I continued investigating...' Holding her glass in both hands, she drank deeply again then tried to toss her head dismissively, but once more the fear in her eyes betrayed her. 'They said if I continued, I "wouldn't be so pretty any more." Very "B" movies, isn't it? And they've succeeded already, I dare say. I must look a complete wreck.'

She didn't. Oh, she was a mess all right but the tear-streaked face, dishevelled hair and pale, drained complexion only made her all the more alluring to me. Normally she was a beauty, dauntingly so, more stunning now at twenty-nine than at eighteen, when I'd first met her. I found myself needing, as I periodically did, to remind myself that she was impossible to live with and that I was, too.

A white heat of passionate determination however, all very macho to be sure, suddenly stirred in me. Nothing would frighten 'my' Catherine like this ever again and no one who tried would get away with it, whatever planet or dimension they came from.

'Tell me just what happened,' I said through clenched jaws. 'As if I were a policeman and these guys ordinary heavies. And Cathy, don't worry. Nobody's going to hurt you while I'm around.'

She smiled indulgently, rolling her eyes, but behind it all I could see both true gratitude and some comfort. I guess hearing me mouth this sort of stuff was part of why she rang me. It was the kind of thing we all like to hear from a friend when we are feeling small and running scared. It wasn't like her to admit it, though. Oh, no.

'Thank you, Shane,' she said a little too sharply. 'Or is it Philip Marlowe?'

'Damn it, who rang who?' I growled in exasperation. Did everything between us have to lead to this sort of crap?

'I'm sorry,' she patted my arm. 'All these years researching and pursuing phenomena and now one is pursuing me. God knows I'm shaken, and it really is awfully good to have you here beside me.'

'The best big brother a girl ever had,' I said smiling thinly, trying to keep even a touch of irony out of my voice. Heaven forbid she should find out that I still felt for her the way I did, that a part of me, even reluctantly, wanted her back. 'Now tell me about these guys, as I say, like you were reporting this to the police.'

'There were three of them,' Catherine began after bracing herself and downing the remainder of her drink. 'I should have described them as 'persons' in black because one, and it's very rare, was a woman. Sort of a woman.'

'Sort of a woman? You mean an alien transvestite? '

'No, just not quite put together properly. Not even as close to being realistically human as the two men.' She got up and headed for the sideboard and the Scotch.

'Describe them.'

'The men were about my height, 5'5', 5'6' and the woman 5 feet at most. All three were pale, practically chalk white. They seemed to have lipstick on. Their faces were virtually featureless and always totally expressionless. They appeared rather... well, frail, rickety even, but not in the way very old people are. More as if they were both weak and structurally unsound, inexact. As if a child had built them. The woman's breasts were oddly low on her chest, her legs somehow poorly joined to her hips. They all spoke English perfectly but in an absurd accent.' The neck of the bottle rattled against her glass.

'Hair colour?'

'The men had none under their broad-brimmed hats, the woman wore an obvious wig. They all had trouble walking and they seemed to fade in energy quite markedly while here. They barely had strength to leave, when they finally did.'

I stepped over to the window and looked down to the street below. Both sides of the pavement were visible, as was the road for a hundred yards each way.

'Did you see them leave the building, maybe get into a car?'

'No. As soon as my door closed behind them a weird glow shone beneath it. That lasted only a few seconds and I heard no sound of them on the steps or using any door in the building.'

'Doesn't mean it didn't happen...' I paced around the room trying to think. 'Tell me exactly what they said.'

'I can't tell you exactly.'

'Try.'

'They wanted me to cease any involvement in the case I'm investigating. To do everything in my power to suppress the information concerned, and to convince the contactee that it was all a purely psychological hiccup on her part. A symptom of overwork and mental stress.'

'Did they say or even hint at why?'

'Because it's too sensitive. They implied that far too much had been, and might still be, revealed. More than they could allow, by a very long way.'

'About them?'

'Not specifically. Whatever they protect, I imagine.'

'Did you believe them? Did you believe their threats?'

'I believed everything, more or less, except their threats.'

'What was it that was so frightening, then?' I was too baffled to play cops and robbers. Security was my field, not detective work. 'I'd have thought you'd relish such an encounter. It sounds like you could have taken on all three in a stand-up fight and won easily. You don't take their threats seriously...'

'M.I.B.s never carry out their threats.'

'So all right, it was freaky, but that stuff, or trying to find it, is meat and drink to you. Why did they rattle you so badly? If you scared easily, or even just normally, okay, but you don't. So why...?'

'They knew everything. They knew the impossible to know. They knew me better than I do,' Catherine shouted. 'Not just facts about the case, things only my client and I should know, things she would tell no one else, which I've told no one, but personal things. As if I'd been closely watched all my life, every solitary second.'

I was lost for words and just sat beside her and took her hand. We were silent that way for a long time, thinking, growing more frightened and confused. On one level I didn't believe in any of it. On another, I was eerily as certain it was true as I'd have been if it had happened to me. My faith in Catherine Frazier's mental stability and her veracity was absolute. I just had to accept the entire thing.

'You'd better tell me about this case,' I said at last.

'I mustn't,' she blurted out, wide-eyed, then went on more calmly. 'No, I mean I can't. I've agreed with the contactee to keep it all very private, at least for now.'

'I'm not just anybody...' I began hotly, but stopped myself. I didn't want to sound possessive or presumptuous. 'But you've already involved me and surely tonight's events are going to have to prompt a different way of dealing with this business.'

'I suppose you're right.'

'And you shouldn't be afraid to talk to me about it because of these characters in black,' I added for good measure.

'I've defied them in that already...'

'Not really. Not if you don't give me any information about your investigations, your client as you call him.'

'Her. She's a very important...'

'Whatever.' I waved my hand. 'In the circumstances she'd hardly expect...'

'I'm not talking about their general warning. You see, oh I'm sure I would have rung you anyway, but as it was they didn't simply terrify me, they bloody well made me angry and I couldn't let them dictate to me, no matter how shaken I was. Their scaring me even backfired... it's good to have you here..., but...'

'I'm glad you called, it's good to be needed,' I assured her. 'But don't take me for granted. I have to know...'

'You don't understand what I'm saying.'

'Then spell it out, will you?'

'They, the M.I.B.s, told me not to... not to inform you. Not to involve you. You specifically, by name.'

My stomach turned over and I just stared at her. Perhaps I'd been wrong and she was crazy after all.

'Come on,' I managed finally. 'Why me, for Godsake?'

'They wouldn't say, but it seemed even more vital to them than anything else.'

Chapter Two

I slept that night on Catherine's couch and the next morning she made a few mysterious phone calls. Only afterwards did she agree to take me to the woman whose strange experience had sparked everything off. By now, in the cold light of day, I wasn't buying any of it. Catherine was back to her self-possessed norm, but still convinced something quite extraordinary was going on and that, like it or not, we were both in it up to our necks.

'It's like no other case I've ever seen or read about,' she kept telling me as we drove out of London and deep into the countryside.

'How's that then?' I asked with a yawn. I was prepared to play along to some degree because she had been so genuinely and profoundly afraid the night before. Even if it was all in her mind, she was in trouble. Hauling me into it, I reasoned, might have to do with her still loving me but not admitting it, even to herself. God knows I identified with that.

'The position of the person, the contactee - the calibre of her intellect apart - and the dire necessity of keeping it quiet are all unique enough.'

'Are people who report seeing aliens and flying saucers usually losers then?'

'No, but they are mostly troubled or lonely people, people who might gain something from it, even if only some attention, some company. Most are just what you'd call ordinary folks and almost always the whole thing can be explained by natural occurrences from swamp gas to weather balloons, auto-suggestion to paranoia, overactive imaginations to hoaxes. Heaven knows I've tried to find just a single instance that was probably not one of those things and never have. The best any of us usually get is a case where you quite simply don't know for sure.'

'And this one?'

'Different all the way down the line.'

'How?' I waited and then added a bit tersely. 'We are going there; surely you can fill me in on some of the background and let her tell me what she will later. So she is rich...'

'Not rich. She's... Look, UFO abductees and others who say they have had contact with aliens generally give the same kind of accounts, full of sci-fi imagery, of advanced technology that is really only a shade ahead of our own. They describe humanoids spouting pseudo-religious or ecological philosophy. They tell of examinations involving things being stuck in their navels. Many analysts believe much of it has more to do with unconscious birth memories and half-forgotten movies than anything else.'

'So this woman doesn't fit the usual profile,' I said, trying to sound seriously interested. ' She's rather bright...'

'She's a member of the bloody government,' Catherine growled in frustration, detecting my disbelief. 'And yes, I know that hardly means she can't be a crackpot, but ambitious junior ministers are very unlikely to report seeing aliens or pink elephants even if, like the rest of us, they think they have now and then.'

'There has to be a first time,' I pointed out, trying to hide my amazement. 'It's a growing phenomenon or modern psychological trend.'

'The woman is not seeing things and is honestly more worried about this getting out than about going mad.'

'Okay, okay.'

'They also delivered a lecture but not the standard variety and, for once, they may have actually given concrete information. That is the most mind-blowing thing of all. I can't tell you how unprecedented it is.'

We drove in silence for a while and then I got her to explain how she had heard about all this. It seems the minister had met Catherine's mother at some constituency meeting, or fund- raising function, and had hit it off well enough to carry on quite a long chat. The subject of the doings of their offspring came up and Catherine's field of endeavour was noted and joked about. Anyhow, many months later the woman had, I gathered, encountered creatures from another dimension or whatever and, very confidentially through her mother, she contacted Catherine.

If I expected to meet someone odd, eccentric or on the edge of a nervous break-down, I was disappointed. Truth be told, that is exactly what I'd hoped. But I could not dismiss the word of the strong and confident woman who greeted us at her country home. With Parliament in recess, she was among her constituents, holding what they call surgeries. There was no security around, I noted, as we drove up and she met us at the door, conducting us to her study at once.

With a plain, sharply alert face surrounded by black curly hair, the junior minister stared at us intensely with pale grey eyes and then sat her slightly chubby, middle-aged frame on the edge of her desk. Frowning, she listened to Catherine tell of her adventures with the Men In Black.

'And they not only warned you away from this matter but mentioned your, er, ex-husband as well?' She thought a minute. 'And you have heard of these fellows before?'

'People around the world have reported being intimidated by them, but no evidence of their existence has ever been found. I always assumed them to be fictitious or figments of people's imaginations.' Catherine shrugged.

'Until now.'

'You are quite excited about this business, are you not, Ms. Frazier?

'Well, yes. It is like nothing I've ever come across before.'

'And you have made this sort of thing your life's work.'

'I have been studying the paranormal since leaving university, yes. You know all this from our earlier meetings.'

'Of course.' She just eyed us some more and I began to grow a touch uncomfortable. Her doubting tone worried me. Was Catherine inflating the whole thing? Was she farther gone than I feared?

'I'd very much like to hear exactly what happened to you, ma'am,' I said, hoping now that it was convincingly weird, for Catherine's sake.

'Yes,' she said, smiling thinly and sat stony-faced again.

'You understand that aside from my own name coming up, I am worried about Catherine.'

'Indeed,' she said. 'Perhaps you are.'

I did not like the 'perhaps' one little bit.

'What are you trying to say?' I demanded. 'Are you implying that you haven't reported anything unusual to Catherine, that she has made it all up, that she has simply blown it out of proportion? Or something else?'

'I am implying that she may very much want certain things to be true. That it is possible to create in one's own mind...'

'And did you do so, as well?' I asked angrily.

'I don't blame you for suspecting this,' Catherine sighed. 'I have been in the same position countless times.'

'I also asked you to tell no one about our meeting.'

'Last night obviously changed things.'

'Apparently,' the politician stroked her ear thoughtfully. 'After we spoke on the phone this morning I have begun to wonder... '

'If you even saw what you did?' Catherine asked resignedly. 'If it was an illusion or delusion?'

'If you are not rather too keen on a spectacular case, Ms. Frazier. I'm wondering if it is advisable at all for someone in my position to risk being involved with someone in yours. Certainly, to speak of it in front of a stranger, who for all I know is a reporter from some tabloid...'

I'd had enough. A poor night's sleep on a short sofa, seeing someone I love scared out of her wits and being badly shaken up myself, and now this. I lost it.

'Goddammit, I'm not going to stand here and be insulted by a parliamentary hustler or have Catherine accused of being a fraudster or a fruitcake. You started this, lady. You're the one seeing little green men or whatever and I've been dragged in only to get this crap thrown at me. For your information I own and run a large security firm. The last thing I want is to be known to be mixed up in a mess like this. Or to be selling stories to newspapers. Discretion is a major part of my living and a damn sight better a one it is than chequebook journalism might provide.' I hauled out my wallet and tossed my identification on her desk. 'And as to causing political mischief for ideals, no I don't much like your party, but hell, I can't even vote in this country and I won't ruin my business to score a minor victory for the opposition.'

She was somewhat taken aback by this onslaught, but she carefully examined my credentials, you can be sure.

'I'm sorry,' she smiled finally. 'Would you mind taking off your jacket, however?'

I'd left the Browning and holster locked in the glove box of the car in case she had Scotland Yard boys on hand, so I complied without a qualm. I knew what was coming next. She felt the jacket and patted me down, feeling for wires. Cathering opened and showed her bag and lifted her jumper away from her slim waist.

'You will understand my caution when you hear my story,' she said, satisfied at last. 'I do apologise for all my suspicions. The whole thing has been very startling, to say the least. Forgive me.'

Catherine and I made conciliatory noises and I had hopes of a cup of tea or something, but it was not to be.

'Let's see if we can find you two some wellies out by the back door and we'll take a walk. My family are away, luckily, but they come in all shapes and sizes.'

'You're not afraid your house is bugged, are you?' I asked.

'No,' she laughed. 'But it wouldn't surprise me. I want to show you where it happened.'

'Good,' said Catherine, then to me. 'We were in London when we met before, so it will be my first chance to see it, as well.'

I wasn't at all prepared for what happened next.

We went through several fields, over a stream, in and out of a patch of woods, then began to climb a high hill, my borrowed rubber boots pinching my toes. An old black labrador, its muzzle quite grey, followed along, rarely venturing very far from us.

'It was evening and growing a little dim, but not too much so,' the junior minister said, breathing a bit hard from her exertions. 'Suddenly Percy shot past me and up the hill, bounding like a young dog. When I crested the hill,' she went on, 'he was sitting in the centre of the top staring straight up.'

We reached the top ourselves just then and Catherine gasped. Crowning the hill was a perfect circle of ancient stones.

'You never mentioned the stones!'

'I didn't think to. In the dusk, though I knew where I was, I didn't really notice them and then other things took precedence.'

I raised my eyebrows questioningly and she went on.

'I walked over to the dog and followed its gaze up into the low, thick clouds above us and saw nothing at first. Then a small light seemed to appear, shining through. It grew and penetrated the clouds with rapidly growing strength until Percy and I were completly bathed in it, but oddly never blinded, though I could not, or maybe just never tried to look outside the circle of light...'

'How big was that?' Catherine asked.

'Oh, fifty feet around, at a guess.'

'Roughly the circumference of the stone circle.'

'Why, I suppose it was, yes!'

'What happened next?' I prompted.

'The light surrounded the dog and me, not shining down now, glowing more brightly than ever until I could see nothing, though at no time did my eyes hurt, or even close or squint. Even as it was going on I noted that. When the light faded slightly I was able to see forms in front of me. Human sort of shapes and one stepped forward, spreading its arms. Not little or green, I'm afraid, not big or quite any other colour, either. It seemed the light was behind them now and I could not see details about them.'

'How did they move?'

'What do you mean?'

'Were they clumsy or what?'

'More graceful than otherwise, I'd say.'

'As to their shapes, were they like science fiction aliens, or ordinary people? How did they stack up against ordinary human bodies?'

'I'm not all that sure. I think they did have smallish bodies and large heads and maybe the large black almond eyes.' She shrugged. 'But somehow, I'm not sure.'

'Is this when the being addressed you?'

'Yes, and the first words out of her... it was a distinctly female voice... were an apology for troubling me and an assurance that I need not be afraid.'

'Is that usual?' I turned to Catherine.

'Not unheard of, but not usual, no.'

'Then I was told what a sorry state the world was in generally, and given a formula they said would help clean up the environment, and the name of somebody in Paris.'

'In Paris?' I exclaimed, having to fight back a laugh. 'France or Texas, ma'am?' I could not help but smile.

'They did not say, but as the name was a Monsieur Georges Travier, I can only assume the former.'

'I see. Did they say why? Were you supposed to contact him?'

'No. They said he would be the next person contacted by them. I was only to see that the formula was placed in the right hands, and lastly, on what seemed a very personal level, to remember that life is temporary, to prepare.'

'Prepare for what? Death?'

'Obviously.'

'Anything else?' I wondered. 'What was the general feeling you got from them? Were they playing it straight?'

'Yes, and the overall impression I was left with was that they were genuinely concerned about us. That what they told me and the formula itself were vitally important to humanity. On the whole I was left with an overwhelming sense of embarrassment about the state of the environment, and I'm no more or less green than the next person, but I felt about the same as I would if my home was filthy and the Queen, the P.M. and the U.S. President were coming to dinner in an hour.'

'Did you have any loss of time, consciousness I mean? There were no examinations by extra-terrestial doctors, nothing like that?'

'No, not that I'm aware of. It seemed to happen in 'real time' and only about ten minutes or so, at that.'

'How was the formula passed on?'

'Verbally, but I suppose a picture of it was planted in my head and some technique employed to cause me to remember it exactly. In fact I still remember it. Would you like to hear it?'

We nodded and she reeled off a great deal of mathematical and scientific babble.

'Doesn't mean anything to me. I imagine you have given it to someone who might understand it.'

'Yes,' she nodded. 'It is being tested now, though the scientists doing so hold out little hope that it can achieve what I said "my friend the inventor" claimed it would.'

'Which is, exactly?'

'Burn clean in internal combustion engines, both petrol and diesel, reduce even plastic rubbish to ash in furnaces, render nuclear waste safe.'

'All that, eh?'

'A simple, cheap, water-based, intensely hot burning fuel. Yes, I know it sounds very far-fetched.'

'The idea of burning nuclear waste... aside from the other things...' I was very close to laughing again and later, when they started back for the house, I lingered on the hilltop. Catherine was going to hypnotize the minister in an attempt to gather any lost, or only unconsciously remembered information. For some reason the dog stayed with me.

After several deep breaths, I gave an unchecked guffaw and wiping tears of mirth from my eyes, I shook my head and took a closer look around the place. While I'd listened to the minister, Catherine had searched as well, but found no signs of a flying saucer having landed or hovered above. None of the usual faked, or reported but later missing, or simply unexplained burn marks or matted down grass that often accompany cases like this.

Wandering to the middle of the circle, I looked up as the dog lay at my feet. I didn't see anything there either, in the clear blue sky. With another shake of my head I started away and then the lazy old dog suddenly began to bark and leap around. Turning, I looked up again but there was nothing and that is when I heard, or thought I heard a voice distinctly say, though from where I couldn't tell: 'Deliver the first message.'

Whipping myself around in a full circle, I searched for the source of the voice, even looking at the dog, who was once more lolling about, weepy-eyed and slow. For one thing, I knew it was not the voice the minister had heard. This was a man's, and though there was no one about for miles, and on that bare hilltop nobody could have hidden nearby, I could not credit an alien contact in it. No, the more I reasoned, as I started back for the house and the cup of tea I'd insist on getting even if I had to make it myself, the more I began to believe it had been my own voice. Oh, inside my head, I knew I had not just spoken out loud and not realized it. It was rather as if inspiration had struck an artist or philosopher or scientific thinker. That is what I felt had literally happened anyway, on one level. I was indeed inspired with the idea that I must help Catherine look into this, find out what could be learned from it and, perhaps, partly against my better judgement, thereby get her back.

I had pretty much convinced myself of this notion when I entered the kitchen and found the two women at the table with the kettle beginning to sing on the stove, though somewhere at the back of my mind a strange unease had begun to creep in. An instinctive suspicion, an intuition of trouble ahead and a thing unremembered. An important thing, like leaving the house and wondering if you've forgotten to turn off the oven, multiplied by a thousand.

Seeing Catherine's lovely face, excited and intrigued, dispelled my doubts. Winning her again, as much more than just a pal, was all that mattered. How could I doubt it?

'Did you do it?' I asked, meaning the hypnosis. I must seem much more interested in all this than I have been up to this point, I thought.

'Yes,' Catherine nodded slowly.

'Turn up anything new?'

'Only a vague reference to something I had forgotten before,' said the minister. 'Something they had seemed to mention quite matter-of-factly, about everything making complete sense in the context of what they called the "First Message".'

Chapter Three

I didn't tell them about the voice and tried desperately to minimise it in my own mind. However, after dropping Catherine off at her flat, where she insisted I need not come up to check the place for intruders, I slowly grew nervous as I drove home. Sensing trouble long before there was anything to see, I began to glance expectantly into the rear view mirror. My mouth went very dry and, though feeling foolish, I stopped to unlock the glove compartment where the Browning was.

It was while I was stationary that I finally noticed the shiny, black 1950s Cadillac behind me, also sitting at the side of the road, engine running. In the darkness of the interior I could not make out the faces of its occupants, but a shiver ran through me. When I moved off, so did they and a crazy panic gripped me. I had to lose them.

Having once taken a defensive driving course for bodyguards, I was confident, but that kind of driving attracts attention, breaks the odd traffic law and being stopped by the police with a loaded gun in the car would have been highly ill-advised. I kept telling myself this and that lots of people in London had old Caddies done up in pristine condition. By lots I meant probably way less than a thousand, however, and few if any would be as black as a funeral director's limo.

Screeching around a corner, I realized that I had been speeding badly for some time, taking turns without signalling, changing lanes the same way and going in large circles, doubling back on myself. I couldn't seem to fight off the urge to shake the sinister car from my tail and yet, whatever I did, it was still right there two or three cars or car-lengths behind, never straying farther or coming nearer.

At last I shouted 'Get a grip!' and eased over to the side of the road, on a quiet residential street, breathing hard and seething with anger at my stupidity. A hundred feet back, the Caddie was waiting. 'Right!' I growled, opening the glove box, extracting the Browning from its holster and the shoulder harness wrapped around it. Stuffing the pistol into the back of my waist band, under my coat, I jumped out of the car and walked rapidly toward the Caddie.

The engine revved suddenly as I came closer and the big car started moving, coming at me, burning rubber, building speed. God, I thought, they're going to run me down. As if in a nightmare I still kept going forward, couldn't get my legs to respond, turn, leap sideways. Only feet away the Cadillac swerved and sped along the street, disappearing around a bend.

Shaking and weak at the knees, I stepped over to the kerb and sat down, muttering curses under my breath. What the hell was going on? Was I nuts or was my life actually headed into the Twilight Zone?

Staring out into the road, I noticed, not with alarm but relief, that there were no tyre marks where the Cadillac had taken off, as I remembered it. Had I imagined the whole thing? Had Catherine and the minister's stories got me that mixed up, excited or paranoid?

Getting back into my car, I determined to give it no more thought. I'd see Catherine about our trip to Paris in a day or so, as planned, but otherwise, for the time being, forget about the whole thing. I had plenty to do to clear the decks at work if I was going to take several days off to help her out. Lord knows I was long overdue for a break. Building my business had taken every minute of the last few years, it seemed. Paris with Catherine, on any pretext, would make for a grand holiday, if we could keep from bickering. Our honeymoon had been in the French capital, after all.

Parking on the street beneath my flat, I noticed that the lights were on and another wave of anxiety nearly hit me, but I successfully choked it back. Rushing to Catherine's side the other night, I'd obviously forgotten to turn them off. That was when I realized how tired I was, how little and poorly I had slept the night before on that damn sofa.

Guiltily too, for normally I pride myself on safe and responsible gun handling, I took out the Browning, pulled back the slide and locked it to the rear, letting the chambered round eject into my lap, removing the magazine before letting the slide forward again, then flicking the cartridges out of the magazine into my pocket. Putting the empty magizine back in, I let the hammer gently down on the now unloaded gun, tucked it and the holster into a plastic bag that had long been residing on the floor, and wearily got out of the car.

I yawned as I let myself into the flat, thinking only of locking the gun in the safe and going to bed. I was also admonishing myself for letting my lingering, half-denied passion for Catherine carry me away so far as to impair my judgement and common sense. I mustn't allow her excitement, fears and hopes, her odd interests and half-beliefs, half-suspicions to affect me, too. I had to keep my head and protect her from anything real, or more probably imagined, that troubled her.

Stepping into the living room, I froze. Arranged upon my couch were three chilling oddities of nature, if they were natural. Nasty, pasty-faced and deathly pale, broad-brim-hatted little Dr. Joseph Goebbels look-alikes, inasmuch as they looked like anyone or anything I'd seen before. Long black coats, not Gestapo leather but cloth, cut in a style 40 years out of date, all new, clean as a whistle and eerie as hell.

I have no doubt that I was as drained of colour as they were as I gaped at them, trying to gather enough breath for a curse, a question or a dash for the door. Glancing curiously around, security being my trade, I saw no signs of forced entry. The door had been locked from the outside. The place is a studio, and I could see all the windows too, unbroken, double glazed and screwed down tight with lockable catches.

'Who are you bastards and what do you want? How did you get in here?'

They ignored my questions, simply staring back at me with their steely eyes.

'You will sit down and listen, if you know what is good for you. If you have any regard for Ms. Frazier,' the one in the middle finally said, sounding a lot like Peter Lorre. You'd think that would seem comical but the effect was the reverse. I sat in the armchair, not taking my eyes off the unholy trio.

'Why would you wish to harm Ms. Frazier or me? Who are you?' I asked, putting on all the innocent confusion I could muster.

'I am sure you know. She has certainly told you.'

'Told me what? Are you from the police, the military?' I asked with concern. 'Is she in some sort of trouble over pestering them for information about her crazy UFOs?'

'We are not at liberty to say,' the one in the middle of my couch said. 'She must stop her present investigations at once.'

'What investigations?'

'She has told you,' he said simply.

'I never let her talk to me about that stuff. It bores me and I can't take it seriously but she was frightened by something the other night and wouldn't even try to tell me...'

'You were told everything by her and the minister of transport. You were asked about a message also, from a source you could not identify. You vaguely think you remember seeing beings... people like us before. Do not attempt to recall anything else, or you will very much regret it. Do not assist Ms. Frazier, or inform her of our visit. Convince her you are certain this entire matter is a fraud. It is of course. It makes no sense. Remember you lost her once before because of these fantasies. She will once more ask too much of you, risk your very sanity, jeopardize your career.'

'What do you mean I lost her before because of...' My head was swimming, that whole awful period of my life was a blur. I had drunk too much and blotted much of it out, but we had just grown apart, Catherine and I. She was really far too independent to be married so early, and I didn't know what I wanted in life. Suddenly my U.S. Air Force career had begun to bore the pants off me, too.

'I got kind of messed up and confused back then,' I admitted, more to myself than them. 'And hit the bottle pretty hard, maybe even went a little crazy, but what has that got to do with all this?'

'Be frank with yourself. None of this nonsense is worth the considerable trouble it will cause. The risks it will involve to your lives and other people's. To your happiness. Remember this however, as you wisely did... remember this and only this. It is your duty to keep certain secrets, to avoid promoting panic and unrest. It is your duty also to protect Ms. Frazier from herself. From her delusions and dangerous interests.'

'What secrets?'

'Secrets best kept even from oneself,' the middle one said, while the other two just stared at me still, unmoving, not even seeming to breathe. 'We will go now but you must help us up.' In unison they each held out their hands.

'No,' I blurted out involuntarily.

'You cannot wish us to stay.'

I stood and approached the couch slowly, sick at the idea of touching them. Reaching out for the scrawny, clay-like hands of the first one, my flesh crawled and I drew back a moment before gripping the icy, frail appendages and hoisting the small body three feet into the air. It was so light I was astounded, and when it landed I almost expected it to shatter. More carefully I pulled the others to their dainty feet and they shuffled, turning to the right as if in formation. Then, still shuffling, walking like mechanical toys, they started for the door.

Running ahead, I opened it, and stood with my hand on the knob as they filed past and delicately negotiated the short set of stairs down to the outside door of the block of flats. Following a yard or so behind, I watched them climb, with difficulty, into the Cadillac now waiting at the kerb in front of my building. It drove away slowly.

A neighbour, coming in just then, gave me a funny look, asked if I was expecting someone, and went on upstairs, puzzled by my blank expression. Surely he would have seen them get into the car and drive off.

Back in my flat, I sat once more in the armchair staring at the empty couch, trying to come to terms with what I had just seen. A ton of semi-memories flashed past my mind's eye and only confused me more. They, whatever they were, had been right. There was something... but what? I couldn't get at it. Couldn't, in computer terms, access the infomation from my own brain.

How long I sat wrestling with this I can't say, but I was interrupted by a knock at the door. Looking up, I could see that it was wide open. I'd left it that way in my daze after the Men In Black had gone. Two modern, large, more human-looking similar types now stood at the threshold. Mormon missionaries, I thought, or someone else to hassle me.

'May we come in?' one said, doing so before I could respond.

'If you don't mind, I'll close the door,' said his pal, slamming it and flopping onto the couch where the M.I.B.s had just been. The first guy prowled round the room, examining objects disapprovingly.

'Guy with your money ought to have a bigger place,' the wanderer observed. 'Security work pays. I guess if I fuck up and have to leave the service I can always...' The tone was familiar from a thousand movies. Intimidation as snide and exaggerated interest, revealing an unsettling knowledge of the victim's affairs. The accent was genuinely middle American and nasal. He had stopped speaking abruptly because I had discovered the bag still in my hand and pulled the 9mm Browning.

'Shut up and sit down beside him,' I heard myself saying. 'Keep your hands on your knees.' I watched him hasten to comply, eyes like saucers. 'I've had just about enough of this shit.'

'Hey, be careful...'

'I told you to shut up. Left hands only, one at a time and slowly, get out some I.D. You first,' I indicated the ex-wanderer. He very delicately reached into his inside breast pocket and using two fingers extracted a wallet which he tossed over to land at my feet. 'Now you.' The other guy did the same. 'Now stand up and, by the collar, pull each other's jackets down to the elbow and leave 'em there. Reach for anything and you're Swiss cheese.' They did as instructed. 'Do a slow twirl and sit.' They were not wearing any pistols.

'Look,' the lounger began.

'Lift your trousers up from the knee,' I barked, ignoring him. No ankle holsters. I had not expected any weapons but I wanted to be sure. Even before I opened their wallets and glanced at their I.D. cards I knew they were U.S. Air Force security. I'd once been much like them years ago and knew the type. They were not allowed to go armed outside of American bases.

'What are you doing here?'

'You can get into a lot of trouble waving guns...'

'Not me,' I stepped over and reached under the desk. 'I have a panic button linked to the local police. As I store several guns here legally, they will come quickly. Being into the field that I am, I have many friends in the Metropolitan police. They won't like it that a couple of my presumptuous countrymen have come round, out of bounds, to strong-arm me. I don't have to shoot you guys to totally screw up your day... week or year. The tactical firearms unit will come round and stick H&K submachineguns in your ears and hear how I caught one of you at my gunsafe while the other kept me talking, only looking for papers maybe, but breaking plenty of British laws.'

'They wouldn't believe...'

'Let's see, shall we?' I made as if to press a hidden button. I had alarms, but no panic button but they couldn't know that.

'No, wait.'

'It would be embarrassing to say the least and not at all what your superiors had in mind.' I watched as they reluctantly agreed. 'So suppose you tell me what they did have in mind, eh? Who sent you, by name rank and job title, and why exactly? You have ten seconds to make good sense, starting now.'

'We weren't sent. Just came to look up an old friend of a friend.'

'Yeah and check employment prospects for when we

get out...'

'I don't know a soul in the Air Force any more, so cut the crap. You don't have work permits for the U.K. and I don't hire here for my offices in the States. I'm calling the cops. Let them sort you assholes out.'

'We were told to warn you off this business with the Brit. minister and the formula. Tell you not to stir up any trouble over that or anything else.'

'How would you people know...?' It was strictly reflex, asking that. The scientist had said something, or the minister's house really was bugged. Then someone quite terrestrial had followed me here or my visit with Catherine had been noted at the minister's house. This information had been passed to the Air Force, who still did not trust me, and I was sent these characters.

'Stirring up what trouble?' I asked.

I'd never really known why I had got into difficulty with my U.S. Air Force superiors, or why I had been forced to leave after my first enlistment was completed. There was nothing on my record, my security clearances were never revoked, my discharge was exemplary but my last assignments had been in backwaters and I was unofficially told no promotions would be forthcoming. End of the Cold War and all that, cutbacks in non-flying junior officers, a big shot with an unexplained grudge against me, that kind of thing.

'You'd know more about that than us,' the guy who thought my flat was too small insisted genuinely.

'Well,' I growled at them, 'I damn sure don't!'

'But you gotta know they wouldn't tell us, don't ya?', the couch potato whined.

'Yeah,' the other one confirmed. 'They just said for us to get you to can it, leave off any more involvement with the Brit. government minister or the Frazier woman. They want you to know it would be a lot better for all of you to drop the whole thing. You're supposed to stop the two of them going any farther with it, too.'

'Says who?'

'Not our own boss, I'm sure. Major Stanson, U.S.A.F. Security Police, Mildenhall. He won't even know.'

'He got it from some place else see, and not directly either. Pretty high and he didn't much like it.'

'Get the hell out of here,' I said, throwing them their wallets, minus their military I.D. cards. 'I'll keep these until I'm sure I won't get any other visitors.'

'Wait a minute...'

'I'll know your family's addresses and Stanson's in an hour, with my contacts. I'll have people on you like flies on shit until you can't scratch without me knowing. I'll see each of you busted on something even if it breaks me and if you get nasty, I'll get nastier and with more back-up. You'll all be virtual prisoners on that base for the rest of your tours in the U.K. Now get out.'

They went, and I slammed the door behind them with a kick, then bolted it. That's when the phone rang. More of the bastards, I thought. M.I.5 this time probably.

'Yeah, what do you want me to stop doing?' I yelled into the phone.

'Pardon?'

'Catherine, sorry. I er... just got a call from er... Sharon.' This was a recent ex-girlfriend she knew still gave me grief now and then. 'What's up? You okay?'

'I'm fine. But listen. It's utterly incredible. The formula works. The lab confirmed it. At least, that is, in a lawn mower. A fuel so simple the chemists said they could have made it at home. I rushed over and saw for myself, after the minister rang to tell me. The lab is here in London and they just did it as a lark, didn't expect anything, thought it was a joke, every-day materials... I don't understand it all, but if it works in small petrol engines maybe it will also do the other things claimed of it. But most importantly to me, this is the first time ever that information imparted from so-called aliens has panned out, that their supposed advanced knowledge really proves to be advanced and of practical value.'

'Oh, God help us!' It was the personal implications that had me ready to pass out on the spot. From somewhere inside me a terrible need to find out more, remember more, began to grow.

'God help us? Can't you see that this is good? Proof at last and it is positive, it's beautiful. Don't you see..?'

'Cathy, look...'

'Are you still up for Paris on Friday?'

'No, Catherine,' I said through a dry-as-dust throat. 'No, not Friday. I think we had better go tomorrow.'

CHAPTER FOUR

When I think of a Frenchman I'm usually guilty of imagining some small, dapper gentleman with an eye for the ladies and great taste in food. Georges Travier was more on the lines Gerard Depardieu, and was in fact a burly, gruff construction worker made good. He was not at all the kind of man you would expect to be seeing otherworldly things, and between his work and his hobbies it's hard to figure out how he found the time.

Along with being a highly successful property speculator, Travier was a renowned treasure hunter and had travelled the globe searching for elusive fortunes he didn't need and, occasionally, finding them. Any profits were sent to charity or channelled back into his next venture. Because he was divorced with grown, independent children, he had the freedom to indulge himself and he'd been doing just that for quite a few years.

Catherine and I had had surprisingly little trouble finding the Georges Travier we apparently needed, my contacts in Paris proving very useful along with his own high public profile. The only problem had been what to say when we rang him.

'I believe,' Catherine had said in her decent French after introducing herself, 'that you have recently had a paranormal experience.'

After a bit of explaining about how and exactly what we knew, we were in a taxi from the railway station heading for a meeting without even checking into a hotel first. Naturally I kept looking over my shoulder, but nobody seemed to have followed us from London, though I got no comfort from that. The Government could always find us eventually, if they wanted to, and the Men In Black apparently knew every thought we had, let alone every move we made. I had employed no evasive manoeuvres. We'd just got on and off the shuttle like everyone else.

At the left-bank address Travier had given us on the phone we paid off the taxi, hoisted our bags, entered the old building and started climbing an endless staircase. The flat we were looking for was typically near the very top and, breathing hard, I reflected, looking over the rundown state of the place, on how I wasn't the only successful guy around who lived in seemingly inappropriate quarters.

'Here we are,' Catherine said with relief as we arrived at the uppermost landing and dropped our weekend bags. The only door, directly in front of us, was half opened and, knocking, she pushed it slightly and put her head in. 'Monsieur Travier? Ahh!' she let out a stifled scream and I rushed past her into the bare and smelly apartment.

Sprawled on the floor in the middle of the empty room was a body clad in a dirty white boiler-suit, a moan emitting from it as I hurried in, glancing cautiously from side to side. Whoever had done this was gone, I hoped. Then, suddenly turning over, the body was intact, active and wielding a crowbar.

'Just in time, Monsieur,' he cried, ignoring my astonished expression. 'Take this and help me with this floor board.'

'What? Eh? Okay,' I shrugged, feeling the adrenalin flow come to an abrupt halt inside my system. Kneeling, I took the tool and watched Travier pick up a flashlight.

'Madame Frazier,' he said over his shoulder. 'Thank you for coming.'

As I pried, Travier peered under the board into the

space beneath and groaned again, shaking his head.

'Nothing,' he sighed, then sat up and looked more closely at us, noticing our bags. 'Have you no place to stay? How horrible. We will solve this problem at once.'

'No, we have simply failed to find a hotel before meeting you,' Catherine explained in French, then switched to English, as Travier had just used it. 'Somehow, there is a sense of urgency about all this, don't you feel?'

'Ah, yes,' he frowned and nodded. 'Yet in many ways they are taking their sweet time, my friends. This was a whim,' he took the crowbar and waved it sadly. 'I have really come to make this place a little more comfortable. That to me seems urgent.'

Catherine and I exchanged a puzzled look and stood there like lumps for a moment while Travier got up and went over to another spot on the floor where some obviously rotten boards had been pulled up already.

'That one suddenly struck me as strange.' He shrugged. 'And my instinct to explore took hold.'

'Shall we...?' Catherine began in French.

'Speak English, I have worked in your country often and it will be easier, no?'

Catherine's French was pretty rusty I guess, not that I was really able to tell.

'Could we find somewhere to sit and talk?' she smiled thinly, a touch annoyed. There wasn't a stick of furniture in the once grand and now dingy flat. 'We are very keen to hear about your experience with the extra-terrestrials...'

'But Madame...'

'Mademoiselle.'

'Does that count for divorcees?' I wondered. 'And wouldn't some French equivalent for Ms. be more to your liking?'

'Oh, shut up...'

'What extra-terrestrials?' Travier asked, raising his voice.

'I was given to understand that you believed you had seen...' Catherine began, then stopped herself. 'Forgive me. I'm jumping to conclusions.'

Brother, I thought, have we got the wrong man after all? Was there a mix-up when they talked on the phone a while ago?

'I saw something under the water, not out of the sky.' He held out his hands in wonder and spread them. 'What is more, I heard it speak as clearly as we do now, but of course in native French.'

He's cracked, I said to myself, and we are on a wild goose chase.

Catherine was nothing daunted and soon got Travier to come out to a sidewalk cafe with us and tell his improbable tale. I went inside to telephone my office and have them start trying to find some other man named Georges Travier and to be more specific in regard to the nature of any unusual experiences he may have had. After all, people think they witness paranormal phenomena every day, while we were on the trail of something quite particular and unique.

Back out at the table they were deep in conversation, but Catherine's notebook sat in front of her, the page unblemished, her pen untouched. Nothing useful, I thought. Nothing relevant.

'I am consumed by it, as if it were a passion,' Travier was exclaiming as I sat down. 'I have put everyone who works for me onto it. Opened up all available properties, contacted the people who already dedicate themselves to this work. The priest is magnificent, but his work is only here in France and even that is spit in the ocean. It is a matter of funds as well as logistics, funds above all.' He threw his hands in the air in frustration. 'There seemed to be a promise and it has not been fulfilled. I wait and do what I can....' His voice tailed off and he appeared lost in thought. 'That one flat draws me to it, I don't know why. So I work there myself all I can.' He paused again and smiled broadly at us. 'Maybe now that you are here something will happen.'

'Perhaps,' said Catherine.

'Say that you will stay here with me, help me with the work on it, be there if...'

'Of course,' she agreed without hesitation and it was all I could do to resist kicking her under the table.

'Look, Catherine, hadn't we better...?'

'Don't you fancy a spot of DIY?' she smiled wickedly.

'I will bring sleeping bags, a camp stove, more brushes and tools...' Travier enthused. 'I feel very strongly that this is...'

'What if someone needs to get in touch with us?' I asked. Crashing on a floor in a sleeping bag in the company of an eccentric Frenchman was not the kind of Parisian adventure with Catherine I'd had in mind when we left London.

'My mobile phone, that is how you found me.' He punched my shoulder. 'You can give anyone the number, eh? What could be more simple?'

At the flat we were alone, sitting on Catherine's suitcase waiting for Travier to come back with the gear we needed to set up camp in the place. God knows he had plenty of it from all his treasure hunting expeditions.

'Reminds me of some of my own hunting trips,' Catherine observed.

'Come off it,' I scoffed, my mind elsewhere. 'You've never shot anything but pistols at paper targets when I took you to the range. Never been on a photo safari either.'

'Different kind of hunting and not under the stars.'

'Ah,' I returned to the present. 'Ghost hunting. Hanging around allegedly haunted houses.'

'Quite,' she said. 'Which more often than not are still occupied by the living and somewhat better appointed than this. I usually have a comfortable chair and a heap of recording equipment and cameras. Sometimes even a bed.'

'You have only yourself to blame,' I reminded her. 'This is a waste of time. What if we are put onto the real guy? We'll have to leave this...'

'I'm sure this Travier is our man. The real one.'

'Tell me again what he claims happened to him,' I said resignedly.

'Apparently he was on a practice dive off the coast of Cannes a few weeks ago. Alone, which he says he is foolish to have done, but it isn't the first time. His air supply was running low, but he had enough to get back to the surface and to his boat, as well as his reserve. That is when it happened. In shallow water, with the hull of the boat quite visible above him.'

'Right.'

'The crew saw these weird lights in the water and watched them for several minutes until they disappeared, without thinking too much of it. Then they waited and Travier did not show up even after his air would have been exhausted. He would have been on reserve, which meant trouble, so someone quickly put on tanks and went down. They didn't see him, searched the area he was meant to be in, which was pretty near; no odd currents around, sea clear and calm as a mill pond, miles to shore, too far to swim.'

'Okay, okay, I get the picture.'

'He came back up just as they had radioed to report him missing and almost certainly drowned. He had been gone for ages while they searched, couldn't have been on the suface without being seen and yet still had nearly a quarter of a tank of air and his whole reserve. The lights had been seen again just before he came up.'

'So they say, I'm sure.' I held up my hands and wiggled them. 'This sort of unexplained or made-up stuff happens all the time. You know that better than I do.'

'What Travier saw and heard does not, however.'

'Abduction by sea monsters?' I laughed. 'How does any of this relate to what we might expect after what we know already? What the minister saw and the UFO connection? I think you are clutching at straws or...'

'Unidentified Submarine Objects are an established, often reported phenomenon and quite related to what we may be looking for. Not that we have a very strong U.F.O. connection anyway. We have to keep an open mind. Nothing has been specifically identified, recognised or described along those lines yet. We must not fix our parameters or have preconceived notions.'

'What does he say happened down there?' I sighed, resting my chin in my palm. 'Was it an abduction scenario with a nautical twist, or what?'

'Like the minister, he was surrounded by the light but not blinded by it and as it faded slightly there were beings circling him, floating in a way but not swimming. He realised that he was no longer swimming either but perfectly still, though weightless. Something compelled him to lift off his mask as if to see better, which underwater is illogical and there was air on his face. He spat out his breathing apparatus and turned off the tank, staring in wonder at these glowing shapes around him. One came forward and chided him good-naturedly for diving alone.'

'You've got to be kidding!'

'It's what Travier said,' Catherine assured me. 'It was a man's voice, or thought projection and he asked Travier to relax and listen to what they had to tell him.'

'How did Travier feel? Was he scared? What sort of vibes did they give off?'

'He was excited and in awe but not frightened. Far from it. He says a sense of danger would have been unthinkable in the company of those beings.'

'It is true,' Travier's voice boomed from the door as he came in, loaded with equipment.

'Let me give you a hand,' I said after recovering from the shock of his sudden appearance. God, I was jumpy over all this for some reason.

There were still camp beds and paint and thinners and brushes and scrapers and hammers and nails down in his car, which took several trips to bring up. Catherine had no qualms about playing the little woman, I noticed, putting the kettle on the portable gas stove and leaving the carrying and climbing to us. Somebody had to stay in the flat though, I supposed, given the way Travier expected action at any moment.

Once we were settled in, drinking tea and resting on our cots, Travier took up his own story where Catherine had left off. There he was, many feet under water and breathing normally, surrounded by wondrous benign beings, in the middle of some kind of bubble, it seemed.

'They asked me about my properties, the unoccupied ones, awaiting development or more favourable times to sell. I thought for a moment that I had died and my sins were being listed before judgement but it was all very friendly. They asked if many other people did the same with more property and then told me that it was very important that homes must be found for everyone. They made me feel ashamed, but I did not think that was their purpose. They kept telling me that there was room for everyone and that I must help to arrange this, everywhere. Yes, everywhere on Earth. I laughed, yes, I tell you

I laughed and said I would gladly give all I had but...' Travier sighed and shook his head. 'That is when they told me they would help, that sums would be made available.'

'Just like that?' I asked. 'I mean in French, okay, but in those sort of terms?'

'Exactly.'

'And when it was all over,' I persisted, 'when you were back in the boat, and the excitement about the seeming miracle of your air tanks was past and you were alone for the first time, what did you feel? What do you feel now?'

'Certain,' he said without hesitation, then gave a shrug. 'But of course I also think, and what I think is that I am mad. That I must have nearly drowned maybe and had hallucinations. That this is all very noble and holy but impossible and nothing new, in many ways. Am I not right, Catherine?'

'There is nothing new in life-changing visions, in moral lessons coming from real or imagined other-worldly messengers,' she admitted, a hint of discouragement detectable in her voice, as it had been in Travier's.

'This is not as with your friend in London, is it?' he said. 'She was given something solid, information only an extra-human source could have provided.'

'I will hypnotize you and maybe some more information will come to light that way,' she said with determination.

'I have tried hypnosis before and when I quit smoking. I do not believe I can be...' Travier threw his hands in the air, cursing in French. 'It will not work on me.'

They tried anyway and he was right.

'So, this is pretty much like a lot of cases you have investigated,' I pointed out afterward. 'Ones we have all read about from time to time. Creatures come down, or up, and deliver a few high-minded instructions about rectifying the failings of mankind, and bugger off back to wherever, with only one poor bastard's word for it and nothing actually accomplished.'

'But my friend, I am doing something. Not very much, perhaps...'

'Road to Damascus conversions are nothing new, either,' I said. 'I don't mean to belittle what you are doing or what you feel you experienced...'

'You don't know what I feel!' Travier jumped up and began to pace around the room, waving his arms. 'I have not been converted to good works, far from it. I have not been frightened into changing my ways, abandoning ambition in order to sacrifice for my fellow man. No, no, no. I feel humiliated. I feel as if my grandmother were having to sleep in the street while I have a soft bed in an empty palace. I feel above all the complete importance of finding space for everyone and soon. I feel, no, they have given me to understand and believe, that it is of the utmost importance. Life, they made me know, is too short to be selfish. It will not last so long as to make selfishness worthwhile. Am I clear? I know this, they told me frankly and I have no doubt at all.'

'Sorry, I guess I see and yet...'

'No help,' he shouted. 'It is as if a passenger on a train is shown that it will come to a fallen bridge and plunge into an abyss but shown no way to stop it. Better not to know.'

'You are doing what you can...'

'Spit in the ocean,' he said again in frustration. 'It is not just a matter of trying. It is not my soul this is concerned with but the need itself, the complete humiliation of being found out. Our being found so, how is it put,... cheap?'

We sat in silence for some time, our tea long finished and everybody lost in their own thoughts. For my money the guy was a saint in the making, a good practical zealot and the world needed more like him, but his case had none, or certainly few, of the hallmarks that had made the other one so compelling, so singular.

'Why,' Catherine ask Travier after a while, 'does this particular apartment interest you so much? I take it you have many all over France, so why this one and why is it so personal? Why are you here working with your own hands when you might be organizing, raising capital, co-ordinating your efforts with other charities for the homeless?'

'Who knows?' He threw his hands in the air and they fell to his sides with a slap. 'To tell the truth, it has something more to do with my nose for treasure, but still, it is very connected to everything else.'

I fell to studying his rather prominent Gallic beak and suppressed a chuckle. We were going to be in for a long night, maybe several, before Catherine wised up and we headed for greener pastures. Everything had been so clear-cut in London: we'd find this man and things, probably quite fantastic things, would happen, be explained... and here we were stripping paint, for soon he put us to work, replacing floorboards and cleaning walls, up to our elbows in dust.

I was utterly fed-up already and quite prepared to drop the whole thing when, in the still and blackest night, something strange, creepy and totally unexpected happened.

Chapter Five

I sleep light, especially when things like M.I.B.s and slimy security people have recently come to call, so I was the first to hear it. Snapping awake, I lay still in my camp bed, trying to identify the sound. We had closed the shutters against the streetlights and city noise and only several unpleasant, dim yellow streaks of illumination crept in.

Either side of me I could hear the steady breathing of Catherine and Travier. With a chill, ears straining, I realized that there were voices, low, urgent, frightened, ugly voices coming from the next room. The room could only be entered through the one we occupied; it was on the top floor and a crack cat burglar would have been unable to climb into it even if the window hadn't been latched from the inside.

I had not been able to bring any firearms with me to Paris, but just then it didn't seem to matter, something told me this was not an ordinary danger, that these were not fleshly enemies. The voices grew louder and I mustered the courage to move, picking up a flashlight and sending the beam around the room. The front door was secure and I knew no one could have sneaked in and past us. Weak at the knees, I started to get up and found I couldn't. I was shaking too much.

'Pssst, Catherine. Georges,' I whispered. Both were out of reach or I'd have gladly shaken them rather than speak and perhaps bring myself to the attention of whatever was in the next room. Somehow, I knew absolutely that it was evil.

'Quoi?' Georges stirred after an eternity. Why did I

long for Catherine to be awake instead of the big, tough Frenchman?

'Shhh, listen!' I hissed. 'Do you hear it?'

'What... it is in the street below, go back to... Yes, mon Dieu. Come on,' he growled, scrambling to extricate himself from his sleeping bag.

'Wait,' Catherine whispered with assurance. 'Wait and listen. Try to identify what you are hearing.'

'Voices,' I said in a low, hopefully calm tone. 'Men's voices.'

'Yes,' she said. 'And furniture moving, glasses and bottles clinking around. How many voices?'

'Several,' Georges estimated. 'Speaking German.'

With an involuntary shudder I realised he was right.

'We agree,' Catherine said with excitement in her voice, but no fear, 'that there is nothing in that room, no furniture, no glassware, no drink and that several Germans could not have got in without waking us?'

'But of course.'

'Sure,' I stammered.

'Then what we have here may just be a nice old-fashioned haunting,' she said gleefully. 'I'm going to do a little experiment, if nobody minds.'

'Be my guest,' Travier whispered.

'Like what?' I wanted to know.

'I'm going to make a noise.'

'Oh hell.'

In the dim light I saw her lean out of her bed and search around on the floor, then sit up and fling something at the wall, her shoe I figured. There was a loud smack and we froze, holding our breath. The voices and noise from the other room continued. Staring at the door, slightly ajar as we had left it after working in there, I could see flickers of light beneath and around it. All along they had been faintly there, as if a television were on.

Well, that was it for me. Emboldened or just plain mad at being frightened, I sprang up and charged. Anything that scares me quickly causes one of only two responses. I run away or I go after it. Behind me Catherine was calling again for me to wait but I ignored her. I was going to find out what was in there if it killed me.

Crashing in head first, I saw a sinister hologram image of a plushly furnished room, a large wooden table and seven or eight German officers in World War Two uniforms standing around it. Almost instantly, they vanished. Falling against the wall I slid to the floor, shaking, my eyes wide open and staring into the now pitch-black darkness.

At once Catherine and Travier were beside me, she stroking my face and him flashing a torch around. Carefully they lifted me to my feet and helped me back to my camp bed. In a daze I watched Catherine return to the door and make a great and perplexing fuss of leaving it just the same degree opened as it had been before.

'Let's have the light on in here,' Travier said. 'And make some tea or coffee, eh?'

'No,' Catherine insisted, getting back into bed. 'The light would spill into there and change things. Just relax, let things settle down.'

'But why?' Travier asked.

'It might happen again,' she said. 'Did you see anything at all, darling?'

'I... I,' Darling, I thought. Did I look that shaken up? 'I saw Nazis,' I stammered. 'High ranking officers, just for a split second, then they disappeared.'

'Marvellous,' Travier gasped. 'This place was used by them in the war. The quarters of some real fat cats. But how...?'

'Recording ghosts,' Catherine said. 'I think they must be recording ghosts.'

Chapter Six

Early the next morning I left them making lists of everything we had done the day before, every chemical we had used such as in the paint or cleaning fluids, making notes about the position of everything in the flat, its doors and the degree of light spill, particularly in the 'ghost room'. I had to get out, buy some fresh bread and make a few calls in private.

From the phone in the cafe I talked to my French contacts and then the London office, only to learn that no one else in Paris with the name of Georges Travier, or even a similar one, had had anything like a strange experience recently. I got the impression that they all thought I was going around the bend.

With a few baguettes under my arm, the morning papers and some milk, I returned to the building on which all our hopes seemed to centre. Just inside the door they were waiting.

My blood froze for an instant and then I got control of myself. These flimsy M.I.B.s were not going to push me around, whatever they knew, wherever they came from.

'A word with you, sir,' said the middle creature, standing in my way on the stairs, an oddly old-looking sort for one of his kind, from what I'd been lead to expect. The brim of his hat was well down over his face though, and the others just hung in the shadowy background either side of the door, where the light didn't go.

'Get lost, you little creeps,' I growled. 'I've got nothing to say to you.' Giving him a slight shove, I tried to brush past him but he didn't budge. A bit perturbed, I gave him an elbow to his small shoulder, pretty hard, and it rocked him back, but before I could move the others were on me, pulling me back and kidney-punching, throwing me to the floor and putting the boot in hard. Big, young, strong men in dark hats and coats, as solid as brick walls.

'Halt!' cried the small old one, before barking several more commands in German.

I was lifted up dazed and rushed out the door on their broad shoulders, tossed into a van waiting on the street and hit on the head with a blackjack to calm me down. A 9mm/k Walther PP was pressed to my temple.

'We only wish to know a few things,' the old guy cooed. 'And do not suppose that you will not tell us,' he laughed.

They had ways, etc. I had seen the movies. God, I had read the histories, now and then met the victims. Give me ghosts over this anytime, I whimpered inside my head. What could these Nazi animals want from me?

We seemed to drive around in circles for a long time until we stopped. The back doors of the van were opened and I was hustled from an alley into the basement of a deserted-looking building. Almost inevitably I was tied up at the wrists and the ankles, low near the foot, and thrown on the dirty floor. They had not found the boot knife I wore. Hell, in their arrogance they had hardly searched me. Anyhow, curling up into a ball, I knew it wouldn't be long before the fun and games began.

One of the intellectual pursuits of my conscientious youth had been the study of the German language. Not only did my grandparents come from there, but it seemed good preparation for what I thought would be a long career in the U.S. Air Force, often stationed in places like Frankfurt. Enough of my German remained, despite assignments mostly in the U.K. and U.S.A., for me to understand more or less what these guys were saying to each other. It seemed that once I'd told them what they needed to know, and had fulfilled any other usefulness, I was to meet a hasty end. There would be no question about it, no messing around or time wasting. The younger ones looked a touch pale at this, but agreed.

'It is always easier that way,' the old one told them with a wise grin and a glint in his eye. They nodded earnestly and with determination. 'But leave his face intact in case we need to employ him as a decoy or in some play-acting. Most probably we will kill him right here in this basement, however.'

Following a prolonged preliminary kicking, I was lifted up to sit in a chair, and a bucket of cold water was thrown over me, which in the unheated basement was more than bracing, and then question time ensued.

'What is your connection with Travier?' the old Nazi asked from the corner while a young brute lingered inches away.

'Who?' A punch to my gut rocked me a split second after I'd spoken. 'Wait,' I gasped when I could gulp some breath. 'Listen. You've confused the hell out of me. What do you expect? I only met the guy yesterday. His name isn't etched on my mind. We are going to rent a flat from him. What is this all about?' It was obvious they didn't know or didn't care about everything else that was going on. They had their own agenda.

'We are investigating a crime,' the old one smiled. 'We are private eyes, as you might say. Forgive the rough treatment but we are up against dangerous French gangsters. For all we know, you are one of them.'

'I see,' I said, determined to play the naive American. 'Well, my wife and I just want an apartment in Paris. M. Travier has various properties...'

'Are you unaware of his other activities, his treasure hunting, his theft of archaeological finds?' the aged Nazi hissed soothingly. 'He is a very sinister figure.'

'I didn't know. I guess Catherine and I had better leave him alone.'

'Why did you and Travier spend the night in that long empty, unfurnished and dirty place? Surely that is odd?'

'I... we... we were helping him improve it, decorate...' The fist landed with painful and loud effect against the lower left side of my back. From the corner of my watering eye I saw the thug shake his hand and wince a little. Before I could take any comfort from that, I realized he had started looking for an object to hit me with next time. The old man came over and sneered at me, nose to nose.

'That flat is not for rent or for sale. It is one of his properties awaiting extensive renovation. So it is not possible...'

'He must have lied to me...' I started. A broken mop handle crashed down on my neck and back. The jerk had found something to save wear and tear on his hand, alright.

'Why has Travier suddenly become a philanthropist, virtually retiring from business? Why is he spending so much time "decorating" that particular flat? Tell us and we will let you go, with no further pain.'

I had no doubt of that.

'How can I tell you what I do not know,' I said slowly, as if his English was bad, rather than just heavily accented. Then I shut my eyes in anticipation and my hair almost stood on end. Idiot! Convince them you know nothing and you'll be dead all the sooner. 'Okay,' I quickly blurted out, as if to head off the expected blow. 'Maybe we can come to an arrangement.' My brain was reeling, trying to pick up the pattern all this had been taking, make some informed guesses and lie with enough accuracy to stay alive. I had only one chance and that would need time and a degree of relaxation on their part.

'An arrangement?' The old man smiled thinly. 'Perhaps.' It was the smile that said you were just going to be moved to a more comfortable work camp, that co-operation would help gain better treatment for the others, the voice that explained you would only be taking a shower. Why waste time with force or risk resistance when a bit of subterfuge might create very useful though ill- placed trust?

'Let's each put one card on the table at a time,' I said. 'Because if this is just some crazy revenge thing on your part or a kidnap plan, for instance, I can't help you and you can't help me. For now, I need Travier and I can't afford to help you kill or ruin him, just to save my pretty face.'

'What about your pretty neck?' the old Nazi asked. 'Will you die for Travier or your own greed?'

'The stakes are that high, are they?' I said with a sly grin. 'Then maybe you know enough to be of use.'

'The stakes are very high indeed,' the old guy nodded. 'There is much to be gained for those who are co-operative. Much to lose for those who are not.'

'It goes back a long way,' I told him. Had I seen that face before on a younger man? Maybe even on a younger ghost? I knew from what Catherine had said the night before, that recording ghosts are not supposed to be walking dead spirits but emotionally charged events that, it is believed, may be somehow photographically preserved, occasionally replaying when conditions are spontaneously right. I had to gamble. 'Way back to your youth and the Thousand Year Reich.'

'Again, perhaps. You are only speculating.'

I studied the face and tried to see once more that fleeting ghostly image I'd briefly seen the night before. I calculated the German's age and hoped I had pegged him right as being the youngster in the corner, of lower rank than the others, almost outside of whatever had been going on. That fitted in a lot of ways, too.

'You were not given any of the brandy the others were drinking,' I said. 'You must have been the SS equivalent of a second lieutenant then.'

'What are you...? How do you...?' He stared suspiciously.

I had to fish, like a fraudulent fortune-teller; guess, generalize and improvise, but to keep it up I'd need more from him.

'You had better convince me you have more than some long held, mad obsession with a story you only half know or half remember,' I said, playing a high hand. 'Before I give any more.'

'Very well,' he sighed. And I'll be damned if he didn't begin to tell me, though on reflection it should not have been a surprise. Of course he wanted to tell it, especially to someone who might just have some new information, who wouldn't half think he was a crank, to get it clear one more time in his own head now that things were finally hotting up and because as far as he was concerned, I was a dead man, anyhow.

He rambled, and editorialized and ranted a bit and took his time once he got going. I heard a lot more about his years of search and suffering since the war than was pertinent, but I didn't mind. Every minute he talked and they weren't hitting me was a bonus. Maybe I'd be reported missing and found by the police. Maybe Travier knew these particular enemies and where to find them. At least he and Catherine would be warned by my absence. The longer these guys took over me the better chance the others would have.

The gist of what the old Nazi had to say was that a number of officers from all over the German-controlled world had begun to collect funds to create a post-war

war-chest or a retirement nest-egg for their beloved Fuehrer. For the most part they had no illusions about the future. The monies they had been salting away came from sources that even the victorious Allies would not miss or try to trace. Payments and confiscated cash from black marketeers, bribes from other civilians, money from Allied secret services for false or even real intelligence, escape money from captured airmen and commandos, cash for the lives of people such as Jews and political prisoners.

None of it was to do with art treasures or appropriated property. Some apparently came from funds the Nazi government had allocated for other things, things those in the know had left undone, or had accomplished in a different way than had been planned. That, or otherwise convincingly accounted for. 'War damage' covered a multitude of financial sins, just as it did everywhere else in the embattled world.

Though it seemed to be kept from Hitler, it appeared to be official policy and large-scale. The last meeting of the men in charge of the project had been on the eve of the fall of Paris. Because of the nature of the thing, some began to have ideas.

'There were always two kinds of good Nazi,' the old guy told me. 'The thug and the idealist. In this, they were confederates, though the attitude was deplorably defeatist from the start. The idealists intended that the money should help the cause to live on after the war was lost, or aid Adolf Hitler personally. The others expected to get their own hands on it eventually.'

'Which were you?' I asked.

'The idealists themselves came in two varieties,' he continued, seeming to ignore me. 'The loyalists and the pragmatists. Within weeks of our final meeting the thugs in the cabal were all dead. Only months after that, the pragmatists followed. The Allies' courts, natural causes and at least one silly accident accounted for the rest.'

It all sounded pretty far-fetched to me, but remembering what brought me to Paris in the first place soon had me disregarding that aspect of it.

'Legends of hidden Nazi gold abound,' I shrugged.

'Only I survive,' he went happily on, still ignoring me. 'And I was very junior and never fully informed. We were picked men; only Dr. Goebbels knew of this extra work he assigned us, his little insurance policy which he never really expected would be needed. He died without using or passing on the information about the accounts to anyone.'

'Accounts,' I said, smugly bluffing. 'You know about them. Good. You are not talking about treasure maps and non-existent gold at the bottom of some Swiss lake.'

'No,' he smiled again, and it was the most frightening thing he did. The Walther 9mm/k at my temple had been a charming joke beside it. 'Accounts. Interest-bearing accounts. It is the gaining of access to them that I seek. I have become convinced that the key lies in the apartment. The site of the last meeting. I was sent out when the exact nature of the alternative arrangement was discussed. The way to get at the money if the Fuehrer and Goebbels did not survive the war. My superiors had agreed amongst themselves that this would be done.'

'I see.'

'It was the attention paid to the apartment by the famous treasure-seeking Travier that after all these years confirmed my suspicion.'

'And you have searched the place, for a clue, a safety deposit box key, a document, whenever you could sneak in there?' My God, I thought. It all comes down to coincidence. Travier's well publicised hobby, his ownership of the flat and his personal hunch about the place after his underwater vision. Maybe they were both nuts. Maybe there was something in the apartment, though anything actually physical didn't strike me as a very great possibility. It was too simple and too unlikely. They'd never hide something so vital, that they all knew about, in a place they were about to abandon.

One way or the other I only had one option. Stall and wait for an advantage. Bullshitting or bluffing or even trying to tell the truth, which would soon give away my ignorance or expend my very limited usefulness to them, was not the answer.

'Screw you, you Nazi pigs,' I snarled, as if unable to contain myself any longer. 'I wouldn't let you get your hands on this kind of money...' The broken mop handle descended and we were back on familiar ground.

'Oh, you will tell us, my American friend,' the old Nazi smiled turning toward the door. 'You will tell us everything.'

Well, I'd succeeded in two things, at least. I'd convinced them I had valuable information that might take some time and effort to extract. As the old one went out I was pretty pleased with myself. There were only two young lads now and I'd seen no guns on either of them. My victory was short-lived, however, as they set about their task with both relish and vigour.

I've never worked anyone over and that is what we are talking about here, not actual torture, though I'm sure they would have run to that if they'd deemed it necessary. I cannot doubt, though, that it is thirsty work, which was part of what I was counting on, along with the inevitability of being knocked to the floor with regularity.

The old one came back after a while and my heart sank, but soon he went off again and finally, as the sun went down judging by the bit of daylight that came into the basement from a small window, they took a break.

One of them went out for food and some beers. Waiting in agony both of body and mind, I realised that I was being watched too carefully. The remaining guy came near only to give a half-hearted kick now and then until the other one returned.

It would be hours before a new, good chance would come, but finally it did. By then my biggest fear was that I'd be too wasted to move. At last though, after more visits by the old Nazi and many hours passing, the two lads needed another break. It was late now, and they were tired and bored.

I understood from their talk that they didn't much believe in the old man's story, or at least that the money still existed and could be got at. Despite the jeers of their contemporaries in Germany, they were sort of neo-Nazis. In this on spec and for laughs, they had wanted to serve the strange old SS man and to learn a thing or two. Now, however, they were beginning to wonder.

It was dark in the basement outside the circle made by the single naked bulb. I lay on the edge of it. Perhaps feeling a little guilty, the next time the old man came back he relieved them both for half an hour. They dragged themselves off for rest and refreshment and he sat against the wall in a wooden chair, drooping somewhat himself by now. Maybe even a little drunk. The pistol was still in his hand, though.

I was going to have to be savage. I was going to have to be much more ruthless than they expected. It reminded me of how the old Nazi had reminisced about the gangster element of the party underestimating the idealists. The criminal type thinks he will win because he expects others to be more scrupulous, honourable or gullible. The trouble was that even a criminal Nazi was not as ruthless as the idealistic Nazi, though they in their turn had underestimated, as had the militarists in Japan, the savage nature of normally easy-going folk when they are roused and given licence. I was roused and I figured I had licence.

With my back away from him, in the deep shadows, I finally got my bound hands up under my trouser leg, and on to the thin, surgical-steel dagger taped to my calf. There was no way I could laboriously cut myself loose with the old Nazi sitting there, even if he wasn't watching me like a hawk every minute.

'Please,' I croaked almost in a whisper. 'Please.'

'What?' he looked up.

'I'll... I'll...' I started to sob. 'I'll talk.' I said very softly. 'The money is...'

He came over quickly, leaning across me, off balance, his hands, even the one holding the Walther, occupied with my jacket, trying to turn me onto my back. Thrusting upward with all my strength I got the knife well in, under the fifth rib, into his heart.

If I had tried anything less than killing him outright, he would have shot me for certain. As it was, I had to work fast to get out before the young ones came back. Of course I had the pistol now but I hoped to avoid any more violence, any more potential complications.

A complete mess from my beating and even more covered with gore now, I cut myself loose at once and, after certain unmentionable attentions to the corpse, washed perfunctorily in a second bucket of water they'd kept handy to toss over me if I passed out. Then I took the long overcoat of the dead man and left. All the way down the alley I prayed I would not come face to face with the others returning.

What they'd find in the basement was, I trusted, more than horrible enough to put them off their chosen path in life. The word 'Mossad' written in blood beside the mutilated Nazi corpse would also help in this regard. I didn't want them looking me up again, or Catherine or Travier. This way, having got their measure, I didn't think that would happen, which did nothing to dampen my self-loathing.

At the end of the alley, I was met not by two large figures but by three dark small ones seeming to appear from nowhere. Gripping the gun, I froze, facing them.

'Allow me to compliment you on your methods,' said the middle shape in a mechanically familiar voice. 'But let the Sturmanfuehrer's fate be a lesson to you about what happens to people who learn part of a mystery that is none of their business and then make the mistake of snooping into the rest of it.'

Half delirious, I was not sure if I was seeing M.I.B.s or imagining them. Screaming silently, I charged at them, crashing into their tightly packed group and bowling them over like ninepins. Farther along, I looked over my shoulder and nothing was there, no sprawled little bodies, no struggling shadows, no standing figures, nothing. With a shiver I put it all down to my panic and pain and ran on.

It was raining by the time I walked from where I had the taxi drop me to the apartment and by then almost dawn. I'd dumped the Nazi's coat and managed to wash off in the cold water falling from a nearby building's broken gutter. Soaked and bedraggled, I somehow hauled myself up the steps to the flat where I prayed Catherine and Travier would be waiting, safe but wary.

Nevertheless, in my befuddlement I tried the door and, oddly, it opened. My heart went into my mouth. Had there been other Nazis? Had I misjudged the young ones, whom I'd expected to catch the first train for Germany, looking frantically over their shoulders for anyone following, still seeing the old SS man with his bits in the wrong places? My inner revulsion at that struck suddenly and I expected the worst as a flashlight beam hit me.

'Where the hell have you been?' came Catherine's voice from out of the gloom. 'Chasing false leads or French females?'

'Oh God!' I groaned in relief, feeling my way to my cot, stripping off sopping wet clothes as I went.

'Ah, mon ami,' Travier mumbled half awake. 'What a lot you have missed.'

For the scheme to have worked, it would have taken a fair few of them to survive and the right combination of them at that. The Nazi officers had badly miscalculated on that score, though the selfless, dedicated ones probably rigged it to hoodwink and then screw the others.

'By watching from the door, not even breathing into the room so as not to alter its atmosphere, we heard and saw the whole thing. They were never all present at the same time, and the youngest man was sent away once, and again later, not knowing how important it was, with the numbers to post through ordinary means to Berlin. Because we have it all, though, M. Travier can access the enormous funds,' Catherine explained over coffee and croissants the next morning. The Frenchman was off arranging things even then.

'And with this he's going to house the world's poor?' I asked, hardly able to sit up and aching in every part of my being.

'We don't know how much there is, the accounts are all over the world, but a lot went into them, apparently.' Catherine shrugged 'It certainly should go a long way toward setting up a system for addressing the problem of homelessness.'

'So Travier hopes,' I said. 'If he doesn't snaffle it for himself.'

'Early this morning he and I handed over everything

we had to the priest he's been working with, whose life has been dedicated for fifty years to this issue.'

'Good,' I said, ashamed of myself. I had seen Travier's belief in his mission as clearly as anything I'd ever witnessed in my life. Hell, it was one of the things I had to remember when I relived in my head what had happened in that basement. That and Catherine's lovely face. If those bastards had gone to the flat, taken us all or... that was something else I didn't want to think about.

'Are you going to tell me what happened to you yesterday, or not?'

'No big deal,' I said. 'It was nothing. I went on the razzle after establishing that we were barking up the wrong tree, through my contacts. Then I got in a fight.'

'We have very much not been barking up the wrong tree. There is no other suitable Travier in Paris, is there?' I shook my head at her. 'So, stop lying. What happened?'

'This is still nothing like what we expected, what should be happening, and we have no real reson to think there is a connection,' I insisted. 'Even if there were, there sure isn't any discernible point to it all and no further leads.'

She couldn't deny this entirely and just sat eyeing me a moment until Travier's mobile phone rang. He'd left it with her on purpose, as he would be in offices, to facilitate their communications.

'Allo, oui?' Catherine said, though it was almost certainly Travier and not someone trying to call him. He had been in touch with her off and on for hours. For a long time she just listened and then lowered the phone without switching it off.

'After running around here, there and everywhere with important meetings this afternoon, Georges went home for a hot bath only a few moments ago,' she said.

'Well, bully for...'

'While his head was underwater he heard plainly, the name Alexander Halliday and Alba-Kirky, is it, New Mexico.'

I grinned and shook my head but didn't correct her.

'Here, he wants to talk to you.' She handed me the phone looking both smug and wonderstruck all at once.

'Yeah, Georges,' I said into the thing. 'Strange doings, eh?' Chuckling awkwardly, I still wasn't sure what to make of it all. Nothing was the way I thought it ought to be.

'Something...' he paused. 'I am not sure... they seem to want to know when... it is a little confusing for me. Perhaps I did not understand.' He paused again then asked, ' Do you know anything about a First Message?'

Chapter Seven

I hadn't wanted to frighten Catherine, so I didn't tell her about the Nazis. Besides, you don't go around confessing to what might be considered murder. I wasn't intending to notify the authorities of the incident, that was certain. Nevertheless, I had to recover from the beating I'd been given, which included several cracked ribs and some minor internal damage. Going right away to New Mexico was out of the question.

Between what had happened to us already, what we were learning all the time and her suspicions about my lost day and night in Paris, Catherine, though determined to set off at once, was thankfully reluctant to go alone. Her uncle, a former army officer, would be accompanying her. I would stay in London, ostensibly on unavoidable business and then join them later.

What I did not know, never having met the uncle during our brief marriage, was that he had not been in the army for nearly fifty years and had since become a historian, a defrocked Anglican priest and a drunkard. It was just as well. I couldn't have stopped Catherine from going and I wouldn't have got any rest worrying about her.

They took off only two days after we got back from Paris, but it would be a while longer before I'd be fit enough to travel. In the meantime I had a lot of thinking to keep me occupied. All this mysterious stuff about myself and some 'First Message' had to be sorted out, and where that was concerned only a few things could be checked by others and a great deal had to be dredged up from my own mind, out of my personal 'dark age'.

Catherine looked healthy and happy and tanned, and lovely, when I got off the plane in Albuquerque. By contrast, I was a pale, sickly, delicate creature, still moving stiffly and physically reluctant to be anywhere but alone in bed. There had been nothing for it, however. The more I'd been able to reconstruct from my past and the higher the sense of anxiety I'd experienced at not being involved with the search for the other messages, the more I knew I had to be there. I knew absolutely, too, that Mr. Halliday's would not be the last.

'You have been working too hard,' Catherine commented, studying me cheerfully. 'You look like hell.' She took my heavy suitcase and we walked out to her rented car.

'I want you to hypnotize me,' I said, unable to wait for a more appropriate moment.

'Whatever for?'

'Don't ask.' I winced, getting into the passenger seat with difficulty. I had come much too soon, only a week after she had, and I was paying for my impatience.

'Some fascinating things have been going on over here, I can tell you,' she insisted. 'We are going out to Alex's place now.'

'Great,' I said, not really caring, between the pain and my own preoccupations. 'You know me,' I went on, a touch of anxiety assailing me as I remembered Travier's difficulty. 'Do you think I can be hypnotized?'

'Good question.' She nodded thoughtfully. 'I'm not sure. You're rather pig-headed, and not particularly suggestible, it has to be said.'

'How nice.'

'While you have been keeping the world safe for corporate executives,' she smiled. 'I've been helping to bring to light what may well be one of the most important discoveries in the history of the world.'

'Was it like the other two?'

'Yes.' Catherine gripped the steering wheel harder and bounced excitedly in her seat. 'In its way. Of a piece, certainly.'

'Then it wasn't a discovery.' I gave full rein to a jet-lagged yawn. 'It was a revelation.'

'Whatever,' she shrugged. 'The important thing is that a cheap, plentiful, easily grown, nutritious food source that will grow as well in the desert as a rainforest has been provided. It is a fungus, a lot like a mushroom, a cross strain...'

'Where did it come from?' I asked. 'Aliens again or...?'

'Apparently. Or something similar. I'll let Alex tell you.'

'Tell me about him at least.'

'Oh, he's a wonderful man,' she enthused. 'Though until recently, not unlike the type your company protects.'

'We do other kinds of security work,' I pointed out wearily.

'Right, well, he was a big noise in the odious factory farming business.'

'Then he saw the light and became a vegetarian, or a vegan?' I moaned. 'The world has got to eat this mushroom thing instead now? You sure he didn't knock it together in some lab? It's not just that meat substitute you see advertised on TV, is it?'

'Does that grow on metal or wood or paper, with no more moisture than is emitted by human breath, grow so fast you can watch it happen?' she asked accusingly. 'Could it be grown in a bedouin tent in the Sahara desert over night, be eaten and be there just as fully grown and edible the next day?'

'This stuff can do that?'

'Yes. You smear this goo that is a mixture of various

known fungi and bacterial strains and it just happens. It tastes good, too. Alex reckons it ought to go with recipes found in every cuisine on Earth. Apparently one of the problems with feeding famine victims is supplying foods that the given nationality can find palatable. Yankee instant pudding isn't real popular in Somalia, for example. Alex thinks anybody would enjoy this.'

'And it's cheap, you say?'

'Yes and easily transportable,' Catherine assured me. 'A small jar could plant enough to feed thousands indefinitely. It perpetuates itself. You can't harvest it without leaving enough to grow back. It is microscopic and grows like a weed, though controllably. It won't spread farther than intended.'

'Sounds great,' I admitted almost reluctantly, for some reason. Maybe I was jealous of this Alexander Halliday.

He had a big hacienda-style spread out in the desert, with a pool and horses. Oh, I couldn't help thinking, he'd made his pile before he got ideals. Anyhow, who says he wouldn't make an even bigger one selling this miracle food thing?

The airy, well furnished rooms we went through on the way to my guest quarters, Catherine leading me along, very much at home there, were further proof of Halliday's wealth and taste. I saw no evidence of a wife and kids, nor was anything about the look of the place an indication that the guy might perhaps be gay. You see how my mind was working.

After lying down for a bit, I headed out to the pool and espied an aged and corpulent gent with a red nose and a bright pink body in a lounge chair. With relief I went happily over and shook his hand, introducing myself.

'I hear wonderful things about you, Mr. Halliday.'

'Good lord, I'm not Halliday,' the man snorted and guffawed simultaneously in a very British accent. 'I'm

Catherine's Uncle Bill. About time we met, young man.'

Breathing hard, he lay back into his chair as if the effort of sitting up to shake hands had exhausted him. Easing myself into another lounger beside him, I felt pretty spent, as well. So, we were Catherine's protectors, God help her.

'What do you make of all this, sir?' I asked.

'Bill, man, Bill. We were related by marriage once, after all.'

'Right. What do you think, Bill?'

'Rum,' he said.

'A rum business, indeed,' I smiled. 'But...'

'No,' he huffed good-naturedly. 'I feel like a drink. Mine's a rum and coke. Has been since Jamaica. Just inside there.' He pointed at the patio doors. 'Chap keeps a well-stocked bar, I must say. Help yourself too, quick as you like.'

Rising with difficulty, I made my way into the living room and found the bar. I felt like a cold beer but I needed a stiff whisky. The pain killers I was on were inadequate to the task and travelling three thousand miles hadn't been taken into account when they were prescribed. Hardly caring if it was safe or not, I poured a healthy measure, made the old boy's rum and coke and took them outside.

'Now, Bill,' I said, glancing around to see if anyone could overhear us. 'What do you make of all this? Catherine has informed you about the other two messages, I imagine.'

'Oh yes, quite.'

'And?'

'Always suspected there was somebody up there,' He swirled the ice around in his glass and sipped. 'Only the terms of reference, the orientation if you will, seemed up the spout. Rather ridiculous altogether. No logic, not even any real morality.'

'You've lost me a bit,' I admitted. 'What do you think of Alexander Halliday?'

'Intelligent and reliable. Something of a convert. That sort of dedication, maybe more.' Uncle Bill paused in thought. 'Important information has been given him, surely, and the others as well and it's all very strange of course, but it has a pattern. Have to see where it leads.'

'So you think there will be other messages,' I said, glad to see someone else suspected the same thing I did.

'Bound to be. Ten altogether, at a guess,' he laughed softly to himself. 'Yes, ten would be about right.'

I was beginning to realise that Bill was drunk, but at least that might mean another sort of question would get an honest answer.

'Catherine seems pretty impressed with Halliday. I...' I had been attempting to go on in some subtle fashion to wheedle out of him an idea of the likelihood of any romantic attachment when he guffawed once more.

'Rather fancies him, what? The whole business has turned her head, I believe. This set-up, the work, the weather, even, what?'

'Did he get another name when they spoke to him?'

'Oh yes,' Bill nodded, swirling his ice again. 'A Mr. Vikram Patel, in London.'

'London? And she's still here...?'

'Quite.'

He was only in his early forties, looked like a movie star and had had his fortune from birth, but on the whole he was a nice enough guy. He'd come to dislike the factory farming lark, tried to reform it some and then finally quit and took up horse breeding full time, which had only been his hobby until then. That hadn't made him happy either, though, and he'd moved out into the New

Mexico desert, albeit in considerable comfort, and pursued a little amateur archaeology.

'It was an ordinary enough day,' he told me that night in front of a log fire. Bill and Catherine had gone to bed shortly after dinner, during which, other than small talk, only the food project had been discussed. 'I was a little tired but not drowsy,' he went on. 'Sitting easy in the saddle... I'd ridden Shadow, my grey, and tethered her during the day while I did some digging. She should have been both fresh and anxious to get to the stable for her supper. Instead it was hard work just to get her into a walk.'

'Was she afraid of something?'

'No, just oddly lazy,' he smiled. 'Like she didn't want to leave the area.'

'How did it start? Light or what?'

'Yes, I suppose so. First Shadow stopped altogether and all the kicking and even getting off to pull at her bridle, as if I was in some comic movie scene with a stubborn donkey, wouldn't budge her. Then the lights.'

'Where did they come from? The sky?'

'Sort of, but not exclusively. They seemed to emanate from out of the hills and ravines themselves, out of the very cacti and sage brush, gathering around me, shimmering, dancing in a way.'

'Then figures? Human shapes?'

'Sort of. They just kind of materialized in these sort of science-fiction beams. They looked, from what I could see of them, to be aliens. I mean the popular conception of aliens. They had the big black eyes, the little grey bodies but... I don't know what they really were. I mean, I think... ' he trailed off and stared into my eyes a moment.

'What did you think they were?' I asked seeing that he had an alternative theory or instinctive notion about it.

'Spirits,' he smiled a bit sheepishly. 'The spirits of the

ancient native inhabitants of this land.'

'The very ones whose lives you had been investigating with your archaeology?' I smiled now myself. He'd been tired, working in the sun all day, his mind centred on a particular theme. I was thinking I believed he experienced what he said he did. There was no question of that, but his perception of its source seemed suspect.

'Yes, and I know what you're thinking and maybe you're right. It's just a feeling I had, nothing they said.'

'What did they say?'

'That the world was hungry, that the hunger had to be satisfied, abated. They said there was food aplenty but poorly distributed. That greed, racism and incompetence caused these problems.'

'All true enough.'

'Exactly what I told them before asking what they expected me to do about it. At this point, despite being entranced and convinced of their reality, I was also fairly pessimistic about the chances of any help. I certainly had an overwhelming sense of mission even before they spoke, entering and growing within me as they appeared, as if by way of an introduction. I mean, I knew what their message would be before they delivered it. I was prepared to swear truthfully that I would dedicate my life to feeding the world's hungry.'

'So they talked about this even as you knew it, kind of like to make you comfortable, to make it seem more ordinary, would you say?'

'I guess so, but also as a preamble. As you know, they didn't just want to inspire me to work for the U.N. or some other aid agency, and become the Albert Schweitzer of edibles. After I was well primed, which took about ten minutes at most, they told me how to grow the 'manna' as I call it. Said I was to spread the knowledge wordwide, that it could solve the world food crisis literally within months if handled properly.'

'And of course you were delighted but at the same moment afraid you'd gone crackers, right?'

'You bet,' Halliday nodded. 'But strongest of all was an overriding anxiety about getting it all done in time. That this was vital, that the idea of people starving or just going short, while some of the rest of us grow fat, was humiliating and criminal. That...'

'In time for what?' I stopped him.

He looked blankly into my eyes, his mouth open, and after a pause he shook his head and grinned.

'I don't have any idea,' he said with a shrug. 'I just know it absolutely.'

Naturally I asked Halliday if there was anything he had to tell me, specifically. Anything they had said about me. All I got was a pair of raised eyebrows, a shake of the head and a look that said I must be an appalling egotist. Going off to bed with a hangdog expression, I did not explain, though I stopped to ask one more question.

'Has Catherine hypnotized you yet?'

'Yes,' he said, stuffing a pipe in a rather superior, professorial way with a slight nod of his head, as if to add: 'What of it?'

'Was it easy? I mean successful? How did it go?'

'I related the entire encounter under hypnosis virtually as I had while fully awake. No significant differences. A touch more detail, maybe. Nothing else.'

'I mean, was it...?' I stopped myself. 'Goodnight.' It would either work for me or it wouldn't. One way or the other, though, I had to get to the bottom of this 'First Message' business. Halliday's information and his 'manna' were important, but they did little by way of helping to put things into context, indicate where the whole exercise was going.

Between an aching body and an uneasy mind, uneasy

on several counts, I didn't sleep all that well. The sooner I had Catherine put me under to see what might be lurking within my subconscious where these messages were concerned, the better. It had been simple enough to pin down the months of my life during which things had gone awry. Hence, where I'd been stationed at the time and who I would have worked with or known.

This was another reason for my rash journey to New Mexico. Senior Flight Sergeant Jewarski had retired there and if anyone knew the background of the mental crack-up that ended my career and, to a degree, my marriage, he would. He must have gleaned some snippets of information regarding its cause, as well. Jewarski would also be the least likely of anybody I'd served with to be intimidated by authority and clam up about anything sensitive. I don't mean he'd give secrets to the Russians, but he sure wouldn't let big shots shut his mouth to me about my own life.

So, it was with a certain sense of determination that I rose early the next morning, only to find that Catherine was already out. Gone to help Halliday about his labours, according to both the housekeeper-cook and the late-rising Uncle Bill.

'Only instance of her being more excited by someone else's work than her own I've ever been aware of in her entire life,' he commented over breakfast, giving me an arch look, suggestive more of a challenge than a mere observation.

'That so?' I mumbled into my toast, very much conscious that in my own experience of her, his findings concurred with mine. 'She picked one hell of a time to get interested in the world food crisis, just as the most important case of her life has cropped up.'

'Quite,' Bill snorted. 'Can't tell whether she's smitten,' he added with a sweet smile at me. 'Or just broody.'

'If they went off together,' I said, ignoring his obvious probing, 'she must have left the rental car.'

'Yes, she did.'

'Good, I'll need it today. Hope she hasn't got the keys in her handbag.'

'Indeed not.' Bill waged a finger at me. 'The car is in my name, actually.'

'May I borrow it?'

'No can do, old boy. Insurance. Only Cathy and I can drive it, don't you know. Be glad to act as chauffeur, however. Need to get away from Alex's pool and, more to the point, his bar for a while. Such has been my loyalty to both that I haven't left the side of either since our arrival.'

'Okay, thanks,' I shrugged, hoping Jewarski wouldn't become reticent in front of the old Englishman. This should have been the least of my worries, as it turned out.

Chapter Eight

It began not long after we left the house. We were being followed by a van and a sedan, leapfrogging each other. Not MIBs I figured. The cars were too new and the technique too subtle.

'Shall I lose them?' Bill asked after I had been trying not to bring to his attention the fact that we were being tailed or my anxiety over it.

'Not easy out here,' I pointed out, staring ahead at the long straight desert road. 'Not much to be gained by it, either.'

'They know where we are going, then?'

'Yeah, they probably do, if it's who I figure it is.'

Following the directions I'd been given, we drove on to Jewarski's home, a trailer out in the middle of nowhere, at the end of a dirt road. Before we got that far, however, one of the vehicles behind us suddenly sped by and the other disappeared. As they passed us the two clean-cut young men had smiled and given a wave.

'Bastards,' I growled. 'They are going ahead of us, all pretences thrown away.'

'I'll step on it then,' Bill said through gritted false teeth. He was eighty if he was a day, but a pretty fair driver. 'Would they hurt your friend?'

'I don't know,' I said with a growing sense of alarm. 'It's not impossible. I don't know what he knows, how dangerous to anyone it might be... Hell, I don't even know what I'm supposed to have seen, heard or experienced...'

'Can't gauge it, I understand,' he nodded. 'Are you carrying?'

'What? Oh, against my better judgment I didn't go through the hassle of bringing anything over and...'

'No trouble really. Just have the airline lock 'em in the hold. Maybe have a letter from a club or competition, where you say you'll be shooting.' He waved his hand at the glove compartment. Inside it, nestling in an oily rag, I found a big .455 Webley and a dozen rounds of fat, lead-headed ammo. 'It was my dear Papa's and bagged a few Huns in the first war, then I hauled it about in the last show, always scrounging for cartridges. Never trusted the .38, don't you know.' Wrapped up next to it was an utterly mint Luger.

'Jeeez, this is worth a pile.'

'Captured from an SS officer who despite his best efforts was not himself captured,' grinned Uncle Bill wolfishly.

'I got a Walther in similar circumstances,' I mumbled.

'Pardon?'

'I'll explain later,' I said. 'This is our turn-off coming up.'

'And that dust cloud must be our late shadow's.'

A mile or so ahead the other car sped along, due to reach Jewarski's a good five minutes before us. My instinct told me there would probably not be trouble, that the guys in the car were Air Force security or F.B.I and only there to warn or threaten, but I loaded the Webley and put it in Bill's lap, dropped the other six bullets into his jacket pocket and filled two magazines for the Luger with shiny new rounds from a box of 9mm he'd bought locally.

'I'm going to have to take up Classic shooting competitions back in England after this,' I told him. 'Best slow up and stop well short of the place and go in on foot.'

'And if these chaps are police of any sort we are just

here to shoot tin cans,' said Uncle Bill. 'A fine, traditional and quite legal American pastime.'

'That is what the desert is for, after all.'

'Given the turn of events and on sober reflection, ' Bill said regretfully. 'I wish I'd had a small drink this morning.'

Just as we stopped and opened the doors, a shot cracked loudly down at the trailer, which we could only see the back of. Moving as quickly as we could, with caution and Bill's burden of years, we skirted the Sergeant's mobile home and crept around to the front making full use of the cover provided by the requisite wrecked cars, outbuildings and natural features surrounding it.

Before us was a scene to gladden the heart and give one a sense of déjà vu. The two nattily dressed agents of authority sat in the dirt, their hands upon their heads, while Jewarski lounged in a lawn chair dressed only in his underwear and a baseball cap. His own hands held nothing more threatening than a piece of pie on a paper plate.

Tucking away our pistols and singing out before moving closer, we approached, breathing more easily. From a window in the trailer I saw the muzzle of a shotgun aimed above the heads of the two suits.

'Heck, Sarge, if I'd known you had guests, I'd have come another time,' I called.

'Oh, these gents was just leavin'. They don't want I should talk to you, though. They tell me it's a vital matter o' national security.'

'For us two guys who served a couple years together to have a chat?' I asked. 'They must be impostors, enemy spies.'

'Tha's what I figured. After all, this is the U.S.A. for Chrissake.'

'This is my ex-wife's uncle, Bill Frazier.'

'Glad ta meetcha.'

'Charmed, old boy.'

'Want a piece of pie?'

'No thank you, but despite the hour I could certainly use a cold one.'

'You got it,' Jewarski stuffed the remainder of his pie in his mouth and went inside, emerging with two cans of beer and another paper plate loaded for me. I must have looked hungry. It was good peach pie, too.

'If you two know what's good for you...' one of the uninvited pair began.

'And change the habits of a lifetime?' I wondered.

'You won't discuss any events occurring in 1986. Have a nice get together, old home week, whatever...'

'Too much talk. Scare the chickens,' said a woman's voice from the window.

'Just as these gentlemen began their conversation, the wife had to scare a coyote away from the chicken run. It's on the other side of the house but she's got no sense of direction, nearly put a hole in somebody's foot.'

'Need glasses. All Injun got bad eyes,' the woman's voice insisted. 'You go now, may start to look like rabbits.'

The two agents got to their feet, careful to keep their hands visible.

'Be smart and let the past lie,' one of them said to me. 'Why make waves? Don't give anybody an excuse to get rough.'

'Did you get that dearest?' Jewarski asked his wife.

'Yep, so'd the recorder.'

'Shit,' the agent kicked a stone.

'This ain't the first little call guys like you have paid lately,' Jewarski grinned. 'My brother the sheister lawyer is rubbing his hands together over it.'

'Maybe this is bigger than you know,' the other agent

said. 'Just think about it.'

'Is it big?' I asked.

'Would they tell us one way or the other?' he shrugged. 'All I know is that you'll be in trouble if you keep digging, keep running around meeting looneys who talk to spacemen.'

'Thanks, I'll toss and turn over it,' I assured him.

'Okay, we're out o' here.' They walked slowly to their car and got in, driving away with smiles and shrugged shoulders. They had done their jobs, just with a bit less swagger or needle than intended. I also knew that if it was big, then as they warned, despite tapes and witnesses to this sort of thing, somebody more dangerous could get to any of us when we weren't ready and in ways we could not defend against.

'How much do you remember from back then, anyhow?' Jewarski asked after we'd settled down in yard chairs fetched from inside. His wife had wandered up to the top of a nearby hill with a pair of binoculars.

'You two always this cautious?' I wondered.

'Just since a few weeks ago when they started hintin' and then plain saying I ought to keep my mouth shut if you came around, or anybody else, asking the wrong questions.'

'I'm sorry about all this hassle. I...'

'Hell, if I figured it was your fault, I'd be drinkin' beer with the F.B.I. or whoever they were, and running you off instead. No, I've always figured what they done to you was a cryin' shame.'

'What was that exactly?'

'It's obvious ain't it? Some damn thing that whipped your memory out regarding a certain time of your life.'

'Well, yes, but why? That's the real question.'

'No it ain't. That's obvious too. They didn't want you to remember. But it wasn't something they'd kill you over.'

'And yet didn't trust me to keep quiet about, despite...

'You having security clearances up the wazoo, I know,' the Sarge nodded. 'It was weird.'

'Would you mind telling me everything you know?' I asked. 'Of course, if you don't want to, I'll understand.'

'No problem. There's just one thing. You still got a job for me if they start screwin' around with my pension?'

'That offer's been standing for years and always will, whatever happens over this crap,' I assured him.

'Good. I hope it won't come to that, naturally. I like retirement and my kid brother would have their ass if they tried anything dirty but it's good to know there's a fall-back position, if the worst comes to the worst. Another beer, Bill?'

'Don't mind if I do,' the old boy smiled gratefully, the morning sun reflecting off his bald head. 'Thank you very much.'

Jewarski went inside to the fridge and I tried to imagine what he might tell me. Given the time-frame of my blank period, we were stationed at a base on the Eastern Seaboard of the U.S., not doing anything particularly out of the ordinary. I was a very eager and promising First Lieutenant. Fully expected to go far in my field, the fair-haired boy where my superiors were concerned. Then something happened.

Jewarski came out this time with three beers and we unconsciously moved closer together once he sat down, our six knees almost touching as we opened our cans and he began talking. The usually mellow Uncle Bill was more alert and intrigued than I'd ever seen him, except when the shot went off earlier.

'Do you remember anything at all about a General Simons?'

'Nope,' I shook my head, racked my brain for a second

longer, and shook it again.

'I kinda think it all begins and ends with him,' the Sarge said, scratching his chin thoughtfully. 'Always have.'

'He wasn't the base commander, I know that.'

'No, he came down from Washington on some inspection, but was really up to something else. No big deal, I don't think, not at first, or he'd have brought his own people. Instead he sort of adopted you as a kind of aide or protege, you might call it. Don't know if the C.O. put him onto you as the bright star you were, or if you just met the guy in the Officers' Club one night. It was all extra duty, you still did your usual work with us, but it was pretty plain this other stuff with Simons was gonna do your career a lot of good.'

'Simons had connections, eh?'

'Plenty, and he wasn't some jet jockey, but way into the science and technology end of things. Space and all that. More at home with NASA than the Pentagon.'

'Do you have any idea at all what he was up to? A guess even?'

'Not really. All I know is he stayed at the Base Commander's house, played a lot of golf and took you with him on various trips around the area.'

'Any ideas about where?'

'A few but you didn't say much about any of it.'

'Excuse me,' Bill cut in. 'But wouldn't there be some fellow officer you might have been more likely to confide in. And I know Catherine was in Britain at the time but maybe you wrote letters to her that could have clues, if she kept them.'

'I doubt if I'd have written about work even if it wasn't anything of a sensitive nature,' I said.

'And you didn't hang out with anybody. Didn't take to the other officers,' Jewarski said. 'Too competitive with ones in your own line and too bored by the rest, I remember you saying. We got on okay but we weren't what you'd call buddies then. Lieutenants and sergeants ain't, normally. We talked, you had to talk to somebody, but we only got to kinda like each other after you went off the rails. Trouble is, by then you'd had everything about this stuff wiped right out of your head. Then, after returnin' to regular duties, gettin' all screwed up and everything, they transferred you to some dump in Alaska.'

'And sundry other equally pleasant places,' I added.

'We was out of touch until I retired a few years ago and you looked me up with that job offer. It was nice ta hear that you'd made good in the end.'

'So, was I abducted by Aliens? Did the General and I see a flying saucer crash, meet a Russian spy or commit a murder? Why would Simons arrange for me to be brainwashed? I mean, that isn't exactly standard operating procedure.'

'All I know is, that you came to work one night really weirded out after going some place with Simons. I mean weirded out, as opposed to all screwed up like later.'

'I think I follow.'

'I mean really distracted, haunted like, but not half crazy or drunk or abnormal.' Jewarski sipped his beer. 'That happened after you was sent off on some "temporary duty" and came back a basket case.'

'Do you have any idea...?' Uncle Bill asked excitedly.

'All I know is he was mumbling about a moral obligation being greater than military duty, and that what if some secret wasn't even that, wasn't even a national security issue... well then, what was the right course of action? etc.etc..'

'Did I tell you what...?'

'It was all what you call hypothetical,' Jewarski said. 'You philosophized out loud all the time. I hardly noticed really. It only struck me after everything else went on. Hell, I was busy, lately having to do the work of two men on account you was off with Simons or tired or, like then, otherwise mentally occupied.'

'Surely that was not usual?' Bill snorted, glancing from one of us to the other.

'An N.C.O. doing an officer's job for him cause he's not around or distracted?' Jewarski hooted. 'Gee Bill, I bet you know better than that. Bet you was the cause o' some poor Limey sergeant's premature grey hair, in your time. Unless maybe you guys never notice us non-com.s workin' our butts off, like duck's feet below the water line, while everything's all calm-looking up above.'

'Perhaps not,' Bill laughed. 'Well, here's to the backbone of the service.' He and Jewarski raised their beer cans and drank. 'So, what sort of places did this General take him to? Parts of the base? Off the base?'

'Off mostly, I think.' Jewarski shrugged. 'The place that mostly sticks in my mind was this big radio telescope thing run by guys the General knew. Stuff like that. Nothing secret. You found it pretty interesting and talked about it some. One of our men was into astronomy. Anyhow,' he said leaning back in his chair. 'I think that's where you went the day things turned to shit for you.'

CHAPTER NINE

I had a lot of time to think before Catherine and Halliday got home late that evening. Too anxious to wait until she had had a moment to rest, I began to pester her to hypnotize me. This didn't go down very well and something akin to our old bickering began to surface. Uncle Bill was too far into his cups by now to try to intercede and Halliday was disinclined to do so.

I knew part of the problem was her growing attachment to Halliday, his project and the very pleasant life and surroundings he afforded himself. That and a feeling I had that she was going cold on our... quest, for want of a better word. I had never told her about my connection with the 'First Message' and the U.S. authorities' interest in keeping me out of whatever was going on, let alone their threatening insistence that I should not look into my own mysterious missing past.

She only knew about the Men In Black seeing me and my being in on what we had seen together so far. In my effort not to frighten her or involve her in what might turn out to be a dangerous situation, I had kept her too much in the dark. Until I knew what the connection was between the messages and my memory gap, I preferred it to stay that way.

Of course, if she hypnotized me we might find out both at once, but the hypnotic process would not have been compromised. It wouldn't be led by any preconceptions of hers. As far as that went, after seeing Jewarski I probably knew too much myself.

'It would have been better if we had done it yesterday,'

I grumbled. 'There may not be a lot of time and we can't afford to mess around with this, Catherine.'

'All right, all right, but what does that have to do with hypnotizing you?' she moaned. 'Not long ago you thought the whole business was nonsense or a hoax.'

'Let's just say I don't think that now.' I waved my hand in the air. 'I may know something vital.'

At that point I saw a look pass between her and Halliday. They clearly thought I was trying to bring attention to myself. To horn in on the glory, or to just win Catherine's approval.

Feeling kicked in the stomach, I had to choke back both anger and a high degree of mortification because that, in part, was exactly what I hoped to do. A glance at Halliday's smug face ruined all my efforts to remain composed.

'What happened to your fierce independence?' I growled at Catherine. 'This is the most critical case in your career and you are allowing yourself to become totally distracted by one small aspect of it.'

'I don't call the discovery of something that will feed mankind for all time a small aspect of anything!' she shouted.

'Nor were the others small but...'

'I was still wrapped up in my own ego, my own curiosity.' She shrugged and ran her fingers through her long hair with a sigh. 'Now I wonder if it matters, what business it is of ours where these messages come from? Who are we to rush around collecting them like butterfly hunters?'

'It's the WHY of it that needs investigating,' I said. 'The connections. The...'

'What for?'

I detected much of Halliday's Californian, half-assed Buddhist, pseudo-spiritual pop psychology in this. I'd seen enough of him and the books on his shelves to realise he was well into that mentality.

'You know better than that, Catherine.'

'Do I?' she demanded. 'Why, even if these things are gifts from an alien culture, from beyond the stars or from native American spirits, why should we be wary of them, look the gift horses in the mouth?'

'We aren't.'

'The people who receive them are well chosen to disseminate the knowledge...'

'Yes, so they don't need direct help from us.'

'Are you mad?' She shook her head at me. 'Of course they all need help and if a particular goal appeals to anyone it is their duty to get involved. There are no coincidences. Maybe I was meant to come here and contribute in some way. Maybe the whole thing, from my point of view, has led to...'

'Bullshit, you are copping out. This is about a lot more than a few handy hints from extra-terrestrials or the spirit world. It is going somewhere. There is an overall reason for it happening and happening now. People have been polluting the environment for years, homeless since civilization began and certainly starving forever. Why are we getting this stuff at this particular point in time?'

'I don't know, I just don't know, but why should it have to swallow up our lives? Why us? Who are we after all?'

'The ones up to our ears in the damn thing, that's who, and you know it,' I cried, jumping out of my chair to pace around the room while Halliday looked on in bemusement, filling his goddam pipe.

'Are we?' she asked thoughtfully. 'Or are we just the ones who stuck our noses in? Or got roped into it, or led by our own misconceptions and inner emptiness?'

'This is your life's work, Catherine,' I said aghast and

not even much putting it on for the sake of the debate. 'You always called me a sexist when I observed that women seldom have a proper sense of vocation. Oh, they can be dedicated to a career, or cause, or work; they can be brilliant at it, better than most men, any man, but almost never have a higher kind of loyalty to it. You're just giving up out of weakness or fear or because you've convinced yourself, out of insecurity, that you've found something more important.'

'Why don't you go on back to London and find this Mr. Vikram Patel on your own, if you feel so strongly about it?' Halliday suggested mildly. 'And let Catherine make up her mind without pressure.'

'Because I need her,' I said without thinking.

'Ah,' he smiled. 'What if she doesn't need...?'

'I mean for this investigation,' I stammered. 'It is her area of expertise. It's her case, for Chrissake!'

'Then it is her decision...'

'Excuse me,' I said abruptly, going out onto the patio by the pool. His cool, reasonable, yet somehow patently selfish voice was making me livid. I had to get away from him before I said or did something rash.

Outside, I mulled it all over awhile and found no comfort in my thoughts. I was still no closer to getting Catherine to help me unlock any memories I might have of my mysterious doings with General Simons. As to the rest of it, a terrible feeling of abandonment began to assail me. What if she did quit and I wound up in this all alone?

Behind me I heard someone come out of the house. I sent up a silent prayer that it would be Catherine in an apologetic mood, but at once knew it was unlikely. It wouldn't be in character. Sure enough, it was the inebriated voice of Uncle Bill I heard behind me, wondering if I wanted a drink.

'No thanks,' I said wearily.

'Don't fret about this quest thing, old man,' he said sticking his head out the sliding glass door. 'I'm in it with you all the way. We'll get at the true gen somehow.' He went back inside.

Well, I thought that's something anyway. Maybe Bill and I ought to go home in the morning. If Catherine was bowing out of the hunt, then at least she'd no longer be in danger, provided she kept a low profile. The MIBs would leave her alone and, I had to admit it, away from me she was out of danger from the government, or whoever. With a resigned sigh I turned to go in and ring the airport.

'I'm sorry,' Catherine said, startling me. She stood where her uncle had been a moment before, biting her knuckles and smiling awkwardly. She walked up beside me and we looked out over the desert landscape around us and at the blue water in the pool, lighted from underneath. 'I'll have a go at hypnotizing you after dinner, if you like.'

'Okay,' I nodded. 'Look, I don't mean to be...'

'It's all right. Your points are quite valid. It's just that suddenly I don't know what I want anymore.'

'I never thought I'd hear you of all people...'

'I've simply come to doubt the validity of my rather impractical career in the face of something as simple and unquestionably good and useful as Alex's project.'

'Ordinarily I'd agree. But in the circumstances...'

'And this is all very beguiling, I must admit.' She spread her arms to indicate our surroundings.

'In many ways I can't blame you. It's just that now...'

'Look,' she went on uncomfortably. 'I'm nearing thirty and a nice life with rewarding work that you can be sure matters... is attractive. So, I suppose...'

'And is Alex himself attractive?'

'Does that make a difference to you?'

I couldn't answer that, or explain anyway, even to myself, without revealing more to both of us than I wanted to. I stood silently and let it hang.

'I guess you have a lot of thinking to do,' I mumbled, at which she nodded and we went in to dinner.

The meal was an ordeal for me, with Halliday relaxed and holding forth on various subjects, while both Catherine and I were in a subdued mood and Bill contributed little except to spill his wine. I'd never taken to Halliday, wouldn't have even if Catherine had been on the other side of the world. He thought he was a deeply, coolly spiritual guy and that this revelation from wherever was quite a confirmation of this.

To put him in his place a little I spoke glowingly of Travier and the minister, speculating on what great things must surely come from Mr. Vikram Patel's contact with the probable extra-terrestrials. My heart wasn't in it, though, and my mind was elsewhere. A part of me wanted to cry out that I might have the key to the whole thing locked in my head. But I mustn't. We would see soon enough if Catherine could get me into a trance.

Chapter Ten

I woke up on the couch and turned to the others arranged about me in chairs, feeling very expectant. They were just drinking and chatting casually and I propped myself up on an elbow, remembering that for some time I had not gone under, couldn't let go, then nothing.

'What happened?' I asked.

'Ah, you're back among the living,' Catherine turned to me with a tolerant smile.

'So?'

'You went to sleep after a while.'

'And?'

'I mean after a while you just went to sleep. Literally. Before that it just wasn't working. It happens. Not everyone can be hypnotized.'

With a groan I lay back, trying to think of what I had to do next. Find General Simons, of course, and anybody who worked at the radio-telescope at the time of our apparent visit. But if he were behind trying to put me off already, even hassling Sergeant Jewarski, it wouldn't be easy.

Then something snapped inside me as the conversation in the background sank in.

'Yes,' Halliday was saying. 'The TV crew were very interested, surprisingly nice. The report should be on in a minute or so. We'd better turn on the set. Why, Catherine, I bet you look great on TV'

I was up in an instant with my hands gripping the lapels of Halliday's jacket.

'TV' I growled. 'You went on TV with her?'

Catherine and a highly amused Bill dragged me off him, as Halliday explained he'd done all the talking and Catherine had not been identified, she'd just stood beside him. They hadn't wanted to reveal the source of the food until it was FDA approved.

Stepping unsteadily over to the corner of the room, Bill switched on the screen. Twenty minutes into the news programme the story was aired. Sure enough, Catherine only stood beside him, smiling at Halliday and the press, but she was well featured, her lovely face fully recognizable.

'You bloody idiot,' I fumed. 'Haven't we got enough troubles as it is?'

'What are you so upset about?' Halliday shouted at me. 'Calm down or I will have to ask you to leave this house.'

'I'm not going anywhere unless she comes with me.'

'Some crazy people tried to kill me the last time I was in America,' Catherine explained. 'They had the idea that my debunking most UFO claims was dangerous. That my serious investigation of others, and my statements that they were not threatening, were even traitorous. They believed the aliens were minions of the devil and that I was probably in league with Satan.'

'Don't put it all in the past tense or imagine they have gone away. They were never caught, even the ones we shot and wounded,' I said.

'We're not going to have any shooting around here!' cried Halliday.

'Right, we're off to London tomorrow. In the meantime I'm staying awake until Bill is sober enough to stand watch, and you, my dear, sleep with the Luger.'

Halliday blew his stake at that, Bill having brought guns into his house, but I railed back at him so much that he at last saw that there was indeed room for worry, though Catherine laughed the whole thing off. She kept insisting that it had been years ago and there was nothing to be frightened of. She also made it clear that she was not going to London until she was good and ready.

All this set the pattern for the next few days and nothing happened other than Bill swearing to stay off drink until his niece was safely back in the U.K. and me making Halliday buy a rifle and a .38 for Catherine. As the only New Mexico state resident among us, only he could do so, though he hated it like sin. The long gun was only an easy-to-use, benign-looking .30-30 Winchester lever action, and it wasn't really for him anyway.

As the days of Catherine's stubbornness wore on, all four of us going everywhere together, even Halliday's fears eased and he and Catherine began to make a joke of my precautions. She carried the little .38 in her handbag, however, but just for what you might call 'machisma' and because it made Halliday nervous.

It was my idea to ride out to the desert so I could view the scene of Halliday's meeting with the aliens, if that is what they were. I also figured there would be less danger there than on City streets or at Halliday's house.

Bill insisted he was not up to sitting a horse and stayed home and the other two were in a light-hearted mood, making fun of me as a cowboy, but both of them wanted to visit the site once more and Halliday thought he might do a bit more digging near it.

The ride out was pleasant and we picketed the horses and made camp that night on the very spot Halliday had seen his lights and heard his voices. Despite my nocturnal wanderings on guard duty and hours spent just sitting around, hoping for some sign, nothing other-worldly happened. In the morning I discovered that Catherine, who I had allowed to relieve me on watch, had not brought her revolver; it was still in her handbag at home. She had also promptly and with purpose gone to sleep just after I had.

The next day we helped Halliday with his archaeology and returned to our camp-site that evening. Of course, while we were tired and even I was getting less alert and less 'paranoid', they came.

I had started to wander off into the brush to perform a function of nature and glanced over my shoulder at Halliday holding the rifle, looking at it oddly, smiling before he leaned it back on my saddle.

'It is mine, of course. May even keep it after you go, rather than selling it.'

'Sure,' I said. 'Why not, but I'll still carry it while we are out here,' I told him, then went on about my business.

When I got back the tinned chilli-con-carne was bubbling over the fire and the sun was setting. Catherine had opened a bag of tortilla chips and Halliday tossed me a can of beer. All was bliss.

The engine of the jeep roared just over the rise and an instant later they were on us, howling like wild Indians and firing wildly. Behind us one of the horses screamed, and I pulled the Luger and loosed off a magazine at the jeep. A man standing in the open back cursed, dropped his automatic rifle on the floor and sat down hard. Turning sharply they raced out of pistol range and stopped, shouting at one another and watching us warily.

Flat on the ground now, I looked from side to side. Halliday and Catherine were behind their saddles in the traditional manner, one as white as a sheet and the other letting out a string of curses all her own, mostly directed at herself. Re- loading it, I tossed her the Luger and rolled over to grab the rifle. It felt oddly light in my hands.

One of our attackers was hit, I was pretty sure of that, and the others were not some shock troops ready to keep on coming, do or die. They were Good Ol' Boys, family men maybe, convinced perhaps that Catherine was a minion or at least a dupe of Satan, but probably having plenty of second thoughts just now.

After a lot more shouting amongst themselves, the engine revved angrily and they drove off, as I'd prayed they would, firing a few inaccurate parting shots.

Relieved, I started to stand up after they were safely distant, the car noise still fading, when another shot cracked a centimetre from my ear. With a will I tried to burrow into the ground, some instinct telling me this was serious, this was not a lucky shot, not the work of the group of idiots who'd just fled.

Two rapid shots followed and to my horror the unwounded horses dropped as if pole-axed. The one hit first rolled about dying slowly. I wished we hadn't tied them so well. They would have torn loose from the picket rope and run off at the first shot.

From the corner of my eye I saw Catherine crawl toward the wounded horse. A shot rang out and it was still. More rifle shots followed, aimed at Catherine and slammed into the dead horse.

'Everybody stay put,' I whispered.

It was still fairly light so the camp fire didn't make us too visible and would soon die out. We could make a break when full darkness came, if whoever was shooting at us didn't have a night vision scope.

Out near where the shots had come from I heard movement and saw a shape go from one rock to another. I took aim and released the newfangled safety catch which original Winchester 94s didn't have, but suddenly behind me Catherine was firing. The target went to ground.

'He's way out of your range,' I scolded her. 'I could have got him with this...'

'I'm afraid...' Halliday began.

'We all are,' I assured him.

'No, I mean I'm afraid I unloaded the rifle...'

'You what?'

'I unloaded...'

'Okay, okay, where are the shells?'

'I was afraid of you if you got mad or jealous. Afraid of accidents and I didn't believe we were in danger, so...'

'All right, but where...'

'I threw them out there somewhere.' He indicated the darkening desert around us and my heart sank even as I uselessly worked the lever action and saw that he was telling the truth. Even the box of cartridges inside my saddle bag was gone.

The movement came again out there, more obvious now, more confident after the wild shots that had greeted him before. Soon he would realise he could easily stand off, out of pistol range and be perfectly safe. He would be able to find a good spot and pick us off one by one where we cowered on the ground behind the meagre protection of a dead horse or saddles, which wouldn't stop a modern rifle bullet.

Just when I was thinking our only chance might be if we each ran in different directions, bold as brass, the shooter stood up. Coming toward us, he stopped about a hundred yards off and even stood on a rock to check on Catherine's position.

Jumping up, I aimed the empty rifle and he ducked, but when no shot came he resurfaced and rested his rifle on the rock, aiming at me.

'Go away,' I yelled, still bluffing, keeping the useless Winchester trained on his chest. 'You're an easy target. Go away and I won't shoot.'

'I don't think so,' he said, emerging, more sure of himself than ever now. Clearly I was talking too much and not shooting. 'Sound travels far out here. I heard Mr. Halliday.'

'I was conning you,' Halliday screamed.

'I'd feared that, but now it is obvious. That, or you

haven't got the balls to fire.' The guy walked a few yards closer and put the crosshairs of his telescopic sight between my eyes. 'You can't say you weren't warned,' he said, working his bolt action then putting his finger back on the trigger. 'Goodbye.'

Catherine stood up and began firing carefully at him, her shots coming close enough to make him flinch and duck once, but soon the Luger was empty and he shook his head and laughed.

With the sling wrapped around his left arm, he settled his sights on my head again, took a breath, let half of it slowly out and began to squeeze the trigger.

In that split second I saw all this, saw the beauty of the dusk, knew he had light enough to kill me and the other two, regretted my failings, wondered fearfully if there was an after-life, and then saw the lights, and thought he'd fired and I was dead.

All around us the lights appeared in the milliseconds it took him to pull the trigger, but looking down his scope, perhaps he didn't notice.

Frozen as I was, still kneeling and pointing the empty rifle, I found I was not afraid to die. The lights were beautiful and I even had time to smile.

Suddenly a long blue flame erupted from the Winchester. It bucked in my hands and rocked me so far back that I fell flat on my rump. The flame seemed to shoot through the air with a sizzling crack, striking the muzzle of the sniper's rifle, going right down the barrel of it, with a great flash, exploding the round in the chamber and those in its magazine.

Screaming in horrified wonder, the sniper himself stood surrounded in the blue glow and dropped the ruined gun, desperately flailing at his flaming arms. All I could do was stare disbelievingly. I'd never seen a miracle before.

Chapter Eleven

With wet, makeshift bandages we wrapped up the sniper's burnt hands and arms and made our way to the jeep he had hidden a mile or so away. It was a struggle to keep him quiet until Bill and I were alone with him. Shocked and awed and grateful, he wanted to tell us everything he knew.

When Halliday and Catherine were out of the room I let him talk. It wasn't much and it wasn't anything I hadn't expected. Apparently there were those in high places who wanted me stopped, wanted me never to find out what I once knew. Some of them, a small minority, those who'd privately sent the sniper, wanted me stopped at any cost.

'They've been monitoring the Soucer Satan nuts for a while,' the sniper explained with gritted teeth. 'And used their planned attack as cover for my supposedly more effective one. It was nothing personal on my part.'

'What is it they don't want me to remember?'

'I sure don't know,' he said through his pain as we waited for an ambulance at Halliday's place. 'And I got the damnedest feeling that they didn't know either.'

We gave the ambulancemen a story about a barbecue gone wrong and let the guy go. My concern now was to get Catherine, Bill and myself safely out of the United States.

We needed to meet the Mr. Vikram Patel that Halliday had been told was to hear the next message, of course, and I needed to get to my own company's nerve centre to start some investigating. I also had to organize proper security for us and try some new tack for getting into my subconscious. I knew in my soul that none of us would be safe, that nothing would make sense or be accomplished until what they called the 'First Message' was recovered.

Regardless of the final dangers in New Mexico I had recouperated from my Paris ordeal, but God knows we were all exhausted after the long flight back to London. We parted at the airport. Catherine and Bill, who was going to stay with her for a while, were driven home by one of my men for protection.

Another, my deputy, gave me a lift home for the same reason and to brief me on business matters and the short search for Vikram Patel.

'It was like Travier all over again, only easier,' he had said.

By now I discerned a pattern and it did not surprise me. Finding the new message receivers would never be the problem, never be the mystery. Whoever was sending the messages would make it easy.

I called Catherine to tell her about Patel and to see if she and Bill had got home okay, then spoke to the man who had driven them. There had been no evidence of a tail.

At her insistence I gave her Patel's telephone number, obtained by my people by devious means, and she rang him at once.

She was very lucky to catch Mr. Patel in London. He didn't live there but was visiting from India, doing some business and seeing relatives.

His contact with the alien beings had taken place before his journey began and unless we went to India, he said, we could not see the scene of it ourselves. He would gladly meet with us, though, despite his limited time.

For me it was good to see Catherine eagerly back on the case. The miracle in the desert had galvanized her into a renewed fascination and determination to follow the series of phenomena to the end. The interest in Alexander Halliday and his specific task had proved to be fleeting and more indicative of a stage in her life than a desire to change everything or give up anything.

Realizing that almost made me hopeful and would have done so wholeheartedly, if it hadn't also worried me on another level.

Anyway, Patel invited us to dinner at his sister's home as soon as he heard what we had to tell him. Our finding him had not been difficult, for already he was making a name for himself with the British media.

So far, however, his claims were being viewed with more curiosity and amusement than serious study. He remained, nevertheless, both unperturbed and undaunted.

For our part we tried to avoid reading anything about Patel's work that day, preferring to hear about it and how he obtained his knowledge, from his own lips.

All we knew, could not help but know, was that it had to do with mass hypnosis and thought projection. These things alone, aside from the apparent source of Patel's information, were enough to have Catherine dragging me off to meet him the very night of the day we got back to London.

Thus, we were out and on the move again after a fairly quick turnaround and hence very worn out when we got to Patel's sister's place that evening.

Bill had stayed behind at Catherine's flat, too beat to emerge soon, but we were followed in another car by two fresh protectors, who remained outside, not the least bit conspicuous as it turned out, among the lurking press. For good or ill, we were photographed going in.

'I'm afraid we may not be safe people to know,' I felt constrained to confess after the introductions were over.

'Miss Frazier warned me of this on the telephone. And I her,' the tall, dignified, sixtyish Patel smiled. 'It must be of little concern, for doubtless there is no shortage of enemies already. A few more will make no difference.'

'I guess not.'

'Perhaps yours will stumble over mine and mine over yours,' he smiled.

'Hope so,' I laughed.

Patel's sister came out from the kitchen to meet us, then disappeared again. His brother-in-law was at his own sister's visiting their children, who had been moved there to get them away from the general tumult and media circus.

We were alone in the sitting-room of their North London flat having tea when Patel related his extraordinary experience.

'First let me tell you something about myself,' he sighed. 'I am not wealthy but I do very well. The nature of my business is such that I have many, many people working for me. Perhaps more than some of the biggest corporations in the world. One of the reasons I am not wealthy is that I try to pay the best wages I can, to look after my workers, to educate them and provide medical care.'

Something about Patel told you that this was not bullshit, not some feudal master's version of what a saint he was.

'My family, especially my wife's family, call me an idealist and even a fool. They accuse me of not having got over shaking Gandhi by the hand as a small boy.'

'If anything would do it, that might,' I nodded.

'Do you think this is why you in particular were chosen to receive your message?' Catherine asked him.

'Yes and no,' he shrugged. 'I am not a good man. I do not like religion and I do not allow differences in caste or religion to affect my workers.'

'To me that is good and still idealistic,' I said.

'No, in me it is my own form of intolerance. I frankly dislike religion. All of it.'

'But still...'

'Besides, a bit of assistance to my poor employees is not going to impress anyone. I am not as bad as some but still, by British standards I run sweat shops, use child labour, conditions are not totally safe. I am an exploiter. I feel this too and yet have no shame in it. I do what I do not for ideals, as some people say, but out of practicality.'

It was the only thing he said that I didn't entirely believe, but at the same time I knew what he was getting at.

'Your feeling was that that was the reason...'

'Yes, that only,' he pointed his finger at the ceiling. 'The message was not a reward, not a confirmation of my goodness. I simply know how to deal with large numbers of mostly unskilled people, with the attempt, and really only the attempt, not to take complete advantage of them. Perhaps my plans to come to London shortly also played a part in it.'

Catherine and I were dog-tired after our travels, but wide awake as Patel began to describe what had happened to him. It was in one of his factories, one not far from his home and, as was his habit, he had gathered the workers together to make a little speech about productivity and see if anyone had any general suggestions or complaints. He had nearly finished, had heard a few ideas from a spokesperson or two, and was just about to say his goodbyes and give his usual encouraging words when instead, he began to say something quite else, something he was not consciously trying to say or wishing to say.

'It was as if I had no control of my voice,' he explained to us. 'And after a few minutes of this the factory floor was flooded with a strange light and all the people were simply staring at me as if mesmerized, which in fact they were. The lights descended around me, swirling, and then I heard the voice.'

'A male voice?' Catherine asked.

'Yes,' Patel nodded. 'But not a man's.'

'Could you see bodies of any kind among the lights?' she wondered.

'Vaguely, but they were only there to have something to focus on, I believe.'

'What did they look like?'

'Only one was defined well enough to see. A small, slight figure.'

'What else do you remember?' Catherine asked. 'What were the eyes like? The face, the head?'

'Bright and clear eyes, small and round,' Patel said with his own eyes closed. 'The ears were large and there was only wispy grey hair on the head. The smile of the person, spirit, or god, was very gentle.'

I exchanged a look with Catherine. Certainly this was not the extra-terrestrial type we were used to hearing about. Not that Travier had gone into descriptions in my hearing, but the others had seen pretty much your now standard 'alien' of sci-fi fame.

'A god?' Catherine whispered.

'Who knows?' Patel shrugged. 'I understand that there are comparisons that must be intriguing.'

'Please go on,' Catherine urged.

'The clearest figure,' Patel said, 'told me he hoped I had not minded their controlling my voice, but insisted it would make plainer what they were going to teach me.'

It seems through him they had asked permission of his workers, received unconscious consent, and put them into a mild trance. They had then taught Patel how to do so himself at will, how to show others the technique.

They explained that one hundred willing people were all that was necessary and, lastly, insisted he telephone his sister in London later that day.

'Was there anything else?' I asked.

'Oh yes, but that must come next. You see, when I got home and rang my sister she was very excited. She had just been watching television, a programme taped earlier, when suddenly I appeared, standing in my factory, quite still, apparently listening avidly to some invisible person, asking questions, nodding, smiling rapturously, then thanking someone, saying goodbye to an apparent assembly and disappearing as the taped programme returned just where it had left off, though about ten minutes had elapsed. She feared it was a prophetic vision and that I was about to die, or something.'

'What had happened?'

'My workers had projected my image to London, to the place I had asked them to while my voice was not my own. Since then, doing as I was taught, I have purposely repeated the exercise several times, live and on video tape. Soon it will be done under perfect test conditions and there will be no doubt from any quarter.'

'And the reason they gave, the point of it all?' I asked anxiously.

'Let me simply say that this will replace the television camera, the communications satellite, the fax machine and any number of other such devices. One hundred, or multiples of one hundred, untrained willing people, simply have to free their minds and mildly concentrate. If they wish, I have been told, while doing so they may even think anything else they like. If relaying private matters they remember nothing, if broadcasting a cricket match, for instance, they see and remember as much as they would if fully conscious.'

'The populace of the Third World will put the West and

the East Asians out of business, or at least force them to compete on equal terms,' I cried amazed. 'This in its way is the most revolutionary thing yet.'

'It is not for revolution,' Patel smiled. 'I am a dual national and it is not a coincidence that the second place, and very early on, where I am teaching and discussing this is in a western nation. Unemployment is a global problem, a world-wide abomination.'

'That's the point? Universal employment?'

'Yes. Above everything else the beings conveyed to me the absolute need to give useful, satisfying work that only humans can do well and quickly. The human brain has long been under-used. Now we can tap into some of its power and give important employment to anyone who needs it.'

'A lot of major and minor technocrats are going to need it soon,' I observed.

'And they will have it, but relatively speaking they are few in the wider context. Don't forget the receiving apparatus will still be electronic for some time. I have no idea if it will evolve into mind-to-mind communication, individual or collective. I was not told anything about that.'

'Not one-to-one, a sort of natural internet, then,' I mused.

'I think not,' Patel shook his head. A moment later his brother-in-law came home and soon after that, dinner was ready. The first home-cooked Indian meal either Catherine or I had ever eaten.

Between one thing and another, we hardly noticed the passage of time, with the excellent and exotic dishes, Patel's and the others' conversation, our endless questions and his about the other messages. It was late when we left.

The press had gone home, my two employees were awake but disgruntled, and Catherine and I were suddenly exhausted. She went to sleep in the car and I, on auto-pilot, found myself driving straight home to my place. Only the act of parking and stopping made me realise I had forgotten to take Catherine to her flat.

I honestly feared an accident if I tried to drive her there now, and asking the men in the escorting car to do so would have been a great liberty. They were too weary and it was far out of the way home for both men.

Waking her up I explained, fearing she would think I'd planned this, but she only nodded and gathered her coat and handbag in a daze.

'We need to talk over so much as soon as possible, which will have to be after a night's sleep. Might as well be in the same place when we wake up, and anyway I don't want to disturb Uncle Bill stumbling in now,' she yawned.

The two guys walked us up to my flat, checked it out as we leaned on the door jamb practically asleep already, and wished us a goodnight, only going downstairs after hearing me confirm that I had locked all the locks on the door from the inside. By then Catherine had collapsed into a chair, half dozing.

'I forgot you don't have a bed and a couch like normal folk,' she struggled to her feet. 'Come on then,' she swayed in front of the sofa bed and I went over and helped her remove the cushions and open the thing out. At once she flopped onto it, while I fetched the quilt and pillows from the closet.

'I trust,' she said sleepily in a mock southern American accent, 'that extreme fatigue will assure that we behave as perfect ladies and gentlemen.'

As I kicked off my shoes and threw off my jacket before lying down beside her, I could only agree.

Chapter Twelve

In the morning I did not wake up to a nice, if unconscious cuddle or even the smell of coffee and bacon. We both just sort of fell out of bed at roughly the same time and headed for the toilet. Naturally, I played the gent and let Catherine go first, even giving her a new toothbrush I had in the medicine cabinet. After my turn we went out to a local cafe in our rumpled clothes, still not very well rested but anxious to compare mental notes.

'So,' she asked once we were installed at a table and had tea and toast before us, with large plates of sausage, eggs, beans and chips on the way, 'what were you most impressed with about Mr. Patel's lesson?'

'Well,' I said, scratching my unshaven chin. 'The lesson itself for one thing.'

'Certainly, but aside from that.'

'He didn't see aliens as we expect them to look.'

'That's right, he didn't.'

'First one of the message receivers who didn't,' I observed sipping my tea.

'Ah, that's just it, he isn't.'

'What do you mean? Travier?'

'No, inasmuch as he described the beings he saw, he seemed to think they had the now standard silvery skin, large heads, small bodies and big black, almond eyes. I wish I could have hypnotized him. Anyway the other two said the same, except under hypnosis.'

'Except under... Well, what did they see?'

'Under hypnosis they described much more ordinary human shapes, but not human, not living. They may have been holograms, spirits, illusions. I don't know. I think whoever these beings are... if beings they be, must use some degree of our own input, must draw on our imaginations or something just to be seen. Remember what Patel said about their being visible only so he might have something to focus on.'

'What did you mean, 'if beings they be'?' I asked.

'Only that they may not be separate from the people they speak to. It could all be a trend, a strange brainwave, a bunch of much needed ideas coming into the collective consciousness from human creativity itself.'

'What happened in the desert was outside us, Catherine. Way outside us. Anyhow, other than global worries, none of which are new, why should this stuff surface now?'

'Indeed,' she said, smiling as our food arrived. 'Of course, I am of the private opinion that this is the work, that these are the gifts, of extra-terrestrials. Either ones already among us and trying to be helpful, or ones keeping the usual flying saucers, if they exist, well out of the picture, perhaps lest they confuse things needlessly.'

'Maybe,' I shrugged. 'I find it interesting too, that the only non-westerner so far is the one who didn't see, or believe he must have seen, the regulation alien.'

'Well spotted,' she pointed a loaded fork at me, smiling. 'Though as a dual national and fairly westernized person, Mr. Patel must have seen the image often. However, none of the others were particular believers in aliens, UFOs or...'

'Who knows what any of us believe in, deep inside? What we are haunted by, inspired by. Especially while we're wide awake and safely sitting in the light of day.' I peppered my eggs heavily. 'Take a lapsed Catholic, for instance. Or somebody who swears they are not superstitious. The inner man or woman is prey to far more than any of us realize, let alone admit to.'

'Or the reverse in these cases. Remember, under hypnosis neither the minister nor Alex actually saw the beings as sci-fi aliens.'

'Does that mean aliens look like us, don't look like anything, or...?'

'Maybe we'll see eventually,' she said hopefully. 'Perhaps they simply trigger something in our brains that seems like sight, functions as an image. Down deep it appears human-like, while consciously it reflects what we have come to expect.'

I ate on, suddenly aware of how happy she was, looking into her bright eyes, all excited by the chase, the puzzle, the new knowledge and the fascinating mystery of its sources and its meaning. I realized at the same time that I was just as happy and that much of it for both of us came simply from being together, working together.

An equally sudden guilt hit me in the next instant, guilt over not having been honest with her, and having betrayed the quest. My excuse had been not wanting her to have preconceived notions to lead me with while putting me under hypnosis, but that didn't matter now.

The desire not to endanger her any more than was necessary was invalid too. The danger was already pretty considerable. After all, no one would believe I hadn't told her everything I knew already.

We had no guards that morning, but I was wearing the Browning again out of worry for both our hides. I decided at last that she might as well know all the reasons why.

'I've been holding out on you,' I confessed, putting down my knife and fork, looking her in the eye.

Cocking her head to one side, she stared back at me, trying to tell if I was joking and, if not, what on Earth I could be on about with such emphasis. Meanwhile, I was still trying to figure out how to begin, how to express it and succeeded only in opening and shutting my mouth once or twice.

'I wondered if you'd get around to telling me,' she said, going back to her food with unaltered relish. 'You've waited long enough, God knows.'

'You knew...'

'That something was up? That you had a hidden agenda?' she laughed. 'How could I not've known?'

'Well, it seems that...'

'And then the sniper made no secret about who his target was, remember. And I know you spoke to him while I wasn't present.'

'Of course.'

'Is this to do with why you wanted to be hypnotized?'

'Yes,' I nodded, starting to eat again. 'I hoped some memories might be unlocked.'

'From about eight years ago?'

'That's right. How did you know?'

'I was around. We were married, after all.'

'This must have been before that, or after. I mean while I was in the States and you were at university. I don't suppose I wrote to you about any of it, did I? That period just before Alaska and the bust-up? Did I write anything that could relate to this stuff, or say anything later when we were together again before it all fell apart?'

'That whole time is a blank for you, isn't it?' Now she had stopped eating again, looking very intently at me. Intently and tenderly. 'And not because of the drinking or because you want to conveniently or guiltily forget it.'

'Hell, yes,' I said. 'It is a blur, months of my life, the end of our marriage, leaving the Air Force, plenty... but the blank, the absolute empty space, is just before all that. Sure, you and I were apart, and it already seemed we were not going to work out a way to stay married and each do our own thing. I know I was acting pretty strangely.'

'I always suspected... even tried to talk to you about it, to broach the subject. Your reactions in some ways were so similar to cases I had seen.'

'Jewarski thinks I saw or learned something so secret and freaky, the Air Force or the government itself went so far as to literally wash it out of my head.'

'Abductees say the same, only it's the aliens who do it.'

'So I understand. Did I convey anything to you that might be a clue...?'

'Oh God,' she set down her utensils and reached out for my hand. 'Lots of things. And I heard them, even noted them, tried to delve and dig, mostly out of professional curiosity, and just got angry myself when you laughed, mocked my interests and job, or violently and vehemently rejected the very notion...' Tears began to stream from Catherine's blue eyes. 'I let you down. I, of all people, should have...'

'Forget it. It was too far-fetched and too close to home. Doctors never see symptoms in themselves or their families...'

'Sure they do.'

'Water under the bridge,' I said, giving her hand a squeeze. 'Does anything particular spring to mind that was at all similar to what's going on now?'

'Not really,' she smiled, bucking up a little and reaching for her cup. 'Maybe I'll have to hypnotize myself and try to find out.'

'You see,' I struggled on, reluctant to continue, almost shy about it. 'I seem to know but not remember...'

'What?'

'This "First Message"'.'

She almost choked on her tea.

[illegible]

Chapter Thirteen

Of course Catherine knew there had to be some reason for my being dragged into the whole thing. A reason for the Men In Black who had come to her specifying that she should not contact me. Certainly that had been suspicious, but with all the rest going on and her intention to let me tell her my side in my own time, she'd let it alone. Anyway, it was still a surprise to her somehow, my being directly involved in the messages themselves. Jesus, the fact that I might hold the key to the full mystery nearly floored her.

Neither the British government minister nor Alex Halliday had heard anything of my connection to any of this, but Travier had been strangely inspired to chivvy me along regarding the 'First Message' and it was from him that a new piece of the puzzle soon came. It also gave a clearer picture of the overwhelming forces ranged against us.

Catherine had gone to meet Mr. Patel with an 'escort' from my company. She was determined to hypnotize him and help arrange the next demonstration of his lesson's marvellous possibilities. I went to my office, where the note to ring Travier was waiting.

Within the hour I was on a plane to Paris, but only after a lot of manoeuvring to shake off anyone tailing me. Once in the French capital, I went through more of the same before being picked up by a blue Citroen on a particular corner and being driven to meet Travier and a friend of his in the country. The trip took a long time. The driver was taking his own precautions.

Finally, in a stone farmhouse miles beyond even the

furthest suburbs, I found them drinking the local wine slowly and waiting patiently. The driver was sent outside to keep watch, which only added to the suspense. I was given a glass after the introductions and sat down at a rough wooden table with them.

'Call me Robert, but of course that is not my real name,' Travier's friend said. I'd figured as much.

'Naturally,' I said. 'So, what is all this about? Georges said it was urgent.'

'You two were in similar lines of work, a few years ago,' Travier explained. Catherine had obviously told him a bit about me.

'Tell me...,' the friend began, happily cutting straight to the heart of the matter, though searching for a way to put it.. 'Did you actually understand this reference to a "First Message" when you heard it? Did it make sense to you?'

'Not really. If I ever got one or heard of it, the whole thing has been wiped from my memory. I'm trying to find out what it was now, but...'

'Was it wiped away on purpose?' Travier's friend asked.

'Apparently.'

'That makes sense. But it would appear that you actually heard it, knew it. No?'

'I guess so,' I shrugged. 'What do you know about all this?'

'First, please tell me what you do know, what you can remember.'

'Okay,' I took a breath and gave them everything that I had learned from Jewarski and what little was still in my own head left over from the time it must have happened.

'I see.' Travier's pal, Robert, nodded after a pause, once I was finished. 'There seems to have been something similar that occurred around or exactly at the same time here in France.'

'Were you there?' I asked anxiously.

'No. I only heard rumours of it. Reliable rumours from

within the middle ranks of our security apparatus.'

'Who would have known the whole story?'

'Only someone very senior, from what I can tell. This, you see, has intrigued me for some years,' he smiled. 'I have quietly made enquiries here and around the world, amongst colleagues who might know a little something.'

'What have you found out?'

'Because it is not what might be termed national security, because there are many who do not take it seriously or even believe it, the talk is fairly open, almost light-hearted. It happens, you see, that every major nation you can name has an experience or rumour, or legend or joke along these same lines.'

'Are brainwashings and assassinations attached to them?'

'Sometimes, especially in the less democratic countries, where such things are more common in any case. But I have never heard of anyone except the very high ranking actually having been privy to the knowledge, having heard the message. Perhaps some such people did exist, and they are all dead or silenced in other ways, brainwashed as you say you were. Or, of course, they are dedicated to suppressing the message by their beliefs or loyalty to authority. Who knows? All of that is possible.'

'Maybe there are others trying to remember right now, just like I am.' God, I hoped so. 'Others being admonished by these extra-terrestrials or whatever, the same as me. Being urged to get busy passing it on.'

'Perhaps so,' he frowned and sipped his wine. 'Of this I have heard nothing. Only you, the sole non-general, admiral or senior political leader I have heard of attached to the story, only you have been breaking ranks. As far as I can ascertain only you are trying to find out, remember or track down someone who does know.'

'This wasn't just your hobby, was it?' I guessed. 'Isn't still.'

'Correct. I was assigned to look into it. To see if we

leaked anything. Eventually finding that other nations had similar experiences, I was ordered to see if these countries had leaked anything about it.'

'And they haven't,' I said regretfully, feeling very singled out and alone.

'No, you are unique in all the world, in that regard.'

'Great.' I grimaced. 'And what is the message?'

'I don't know,' he laughed through his nose, French fashion. 'I would never have been told.'

'All right,' I said, more than a little exasperated. The more I learned about this business, the more uncomfortable I felt. 'What is the nature of it? What did they tell you to investigate about the reports, rumours or leaked information?'

'Ah,' he smiled, glancing at Travier and raising his eyebrows at me. 'Direct radio wave contact with intelligent life in outer space. Nothing less than a clear message, a deliberate communication from them, sent to us.'

On the way home, we took the same careful measures to ensure that none of us were followed. My driver dropped me off only after various devious turns and back-tracking manoeuvres and I nipped around on foot and in and out of the Metro before choosing a hotel at random to rest in over night before heading back to London. There was no way that anybody could have tailed me or anticipated my movements. It just wasn't humanly possible.

But there they sat, quite inhuman, waiting in my room. Perched in a row on the edge of the bed like crows on a telephone line, the Men In Black stared at me grimly.

Frozen in the doorway, the key half in, half out of the lock, I stared back at them, breathless and nauseated. It seemed to go on a long time, this staring match before I came in and closed the door behind me. Odd to say, it was one of the bravest things I had ever done, they were so chillingly unnatural.

'Did you have to go and sit on the bed?' I moaned. 'I'm sleeping in that bed tonight.'

'But you can hardly expect to have slept very well tonight wherever we sat,' said the one in the middle.

'You guys make my flesh creep.'

'Let it creep. That is the desired effect. It is a healthy reaction. Trust your instincts.'

'Go to hell.'

'That is not possible.'

'What do you want? Same old thing again, I suppose.'

'Why do you defy us? Surely our demands are not unreasonable. The whole matter of the messages frightens you. Your own people do not want it to come to light. It endangers those you care for.'

'Did it ever occur to you that your very appearance could be counter-productive?' I asked. 'You guys are your own worst enemies.'

'We are your own worst enemies,' the middle one said, slowly shaking his head. 'And we can do nothing about our appearance.'

'Poor old you,' I sneered and then a sudden recklessness overcame me. Exactly who and what were these guys, after all. 'Come on out and let me buy you all some new clothes. Let's hit the night spots, find a good brothel, what do you say?'

'That is not possible either.'

'Then go ahead and make your goddam threats and get out,' I shouted, fed up with them, angry at my own impotence and theirs. Why did they scare me so and why did they actually do nothing? 'Kill me with some ray gun, or whisk me away to Alpha Centauri, you bastards.'

'That is not why we have come.'

'Tell me the message. Or tell me why you want to stop it, you Gestapo-looking little shits. I'm sick of you. Come on, show me what you're made of.'

'It is not we who want to stop you remembering or relaying the message.'

'Yeah, sure.'

'It is you who do not wish these things to happen.'

'Go to hell.'

'Again, I must advise you that that is not poss...'

'Okay, okay. What do you mean...?'

'You know the so-called message. You have not forgotten it. It is you who suppress it. Your authorities helped, agreed, desired it too, but it is your decision not to know it, not to recall it.'

'I don't believe you.'

'That is not important.' With difficulty they stood up shakily. 'We have told you and we must point out that inside you know best. Your choice to forget was the correct and healthy one.' In unison they turned and marched through the door on the left, closing it behind them.

After a moment of shock, I leaped up to yank it open.

'You assholes, that's the bathroo...' It was tiny, damp and empty. Lowering myself to sit on the edge of the bidet, my legs having turned to mush I began to shudder and mutter to myself. It was madness. It was all just simple madness.

The most terrible need to see Catherine hit me like a falling piano. Only she could keep me sane or keep me company in my insanity. Leaping up, I ran from the hotel and with difficulty found a taxi. Despite the hour and my exhaustion, I had to get back to London that night. Heading for the airport, I was determined to get a flight even if I had to rent a small plane and fly myself.

Between one thing and another, recent associations and now this, to spend a night in Paris would have frightened the life out of me. And, as I say, I desperately needed Catherine. The worst thing was, I knew the Men In Black had spoken the truth.

Chapter Fourteen

A complete wreck, having got a late flight and a cab from Luton, I found myself pounding on Catherine's door in the wee small hours. Only the distinctive click of Uncle Bill's big old .455 Webley revolver on the opposite side brought me to my senses.

'It's me, Bill. Let me in. Is Catherine home?'

'No,' he said, opening the door amid grumbling under his breath about the hour. 'She's on Patel's sister's couch. Whatever they got up to went on till late.'

'Shit!' I staggered in and collapsed on Catherine's couch. 'Shit!'

'And that's what you look like,' he helpfully assured me. 'What happened to you then? Anything interesting?'

'Christ,' I moaned, throwing my hands in the air. 'Only the confirmation of my darkest suspicions and fears.'

'Yes.' He eyed me knowingly. 'Always a little harrowing, that.' He'd closed and locked the door and put the gun away and now stood, arms folded, studying me. 'Tea or something stronger?'

'A lot stronger, thanks.'

'Right.' He went to the sideboard where Catherine kept her booze. 'I've cleaned her out but there is this bottle of Greek brandy she's got from somewhere. Shall we try it?'

'Why not?'

'And then you can tell Uncle Bill all about it.'

'Did the mental projection process work under the test conditions?' I managed to ask. 'That's what Catherine was helping Patel with, wasn't it?'

'Indeed,' Bill said as he poured, after giving the drink a

dubious sniff. 'It went swimmingly. She was highly impressed, as were the media.'

'Shit,' I said again. 'Who's looking after her. She sent my guard home, I imagine.'

'Oh yes, but she has my Luger and Patel's brother-in-law is rather handy.'

'That's good,' I took the glass he brought to me and at his second asking I spilled my guts to him about my long day and its several lessons.

'Interesting fellas, these chaps in black,' was all he said before falling silent for a long time. 'Do they ever seem to know everything about anyone else.'

'They knew all about Catherine.'

'Hers or yours?'

'What?'

'Her people in black, or yours?'

'Hers about her,' I said, thinking a minute. 'And mine about me. Why?'

'Nothing. Just that I'm developing a theory about them, that's all. You see, I've been visited as well.'

I set down my brandy and looked at him. He was sober and I could tell he was serious. With Bill I'd learned to make quite certain of both whenever he said anything out of the ordinary, which was pretty often. He didn't seem particularly shaken though, and that was the usual reaction after seeing MIBs from what I could tell.

'When was it?'

'Earlier this evening.' He had me describe my three Men In Black, and fetching Catherine's notes on her own encounter, re-read them aloud to remind us of the appearance of the ones who had visited her.

'What were yours like?' I asked him. 'What is this theory?'

'First let us review,' he said, hitching up his pyjamas and walking back and forth in front of the sideboard where his glass rested beside the bottle of strange brandy. 'Cathy's chappies were like gangsters, after a fashion. One of them was a woman. Your own were similar but leaning toward the Gestapo type more than otherwise.'

'I'd say so, yes.'

'And they were all men.'

'Yep, what of it?'

'So were mine,' Bill said. 'And they too sort of conformed to the dark clad, tough guy motion picture "heavy" image, in a general way. From what I gather, this is the norm, the mean, the starting point, the basic, unadulterated Man In Black. After that they become rather individual, custom-made, bespoke bogeymen, wouldn't you say? They take on aspects... no, instead I'd call it the feel of something we each in our own way especially fear and despise.'

'Okay, I follow you so far.' I stretched out on the couch but felt no temptation to sleep. Something told me Bill had a handle on this. 'What were yours... what was the feel of your MIBs? How were they different, individual to you?'

'They came, or merely appeared, in here as I came out of the shower, starkers and drying what's left of my hair. They were dressed in old-fashioned new clothes, but positively reeking of brimstone. They had reddish faces and though no one else reports any, mine had pointy ears and cat-like eyes to boot. My impression of why these ones walked poorly was that they found it difficult with shoes on their cloven hooves. The legs were bent wrong as well, bovine style.'

'Bloody hell...' I shivered. 'And they said what?'

'To stop helping you, dammit!' Bill exclaimed 'Told me that the information was never meant to be given out and that I was in the gravest danger if I had any more to do with you or the messages.'

'Were you scared?'

'Dust-dry mouth, nearly loose bowels.'

'Right.'

'So,' he went on. 'The feel was of evil, devilishness, of meeting minions of Old Nick himself. Satan's own...'

'Wait a minute. You're begining to sound like the weirdos who shot at us in New Mexico before the professionals got in on the act.'

'I can only say that that's how they damn well seemed,' Bill grunted. 'I'm blowed if I believe flying saucers are the work of Satan, or that these Men In Black are bloody devils. They just simply struck me as being devils, same as they struck you as Gestapo men.'

'So, you think they become what we most fear, in order to be more effective?'

'Perhaps,' he shrugged and fell into an armchair. 'However, I am of the opinion that they are figments of our imaginations entirely.'

'Oh, come on.' I sat up and faced him waving a dismissive hand. 'You can't deny all these concrete messages...'

'Of course not. I only mean the MIBs are imaginary. The very personification, or maybe I ought to say "alienification" of our fears. They appear only to tempt us to shy away from what frightens us. To leave the mysteries alone because we so fear the very mysteries themselves.'

'And we tailor-make them in our own subconscious minds?'

'Exactly. Or to put it another way, there is nothing to fear but fear itself.'

'You're saying that they are fear itself.'

'Yes, and that being so, coming from within as they do, the blighters have us cold. Know us like books, what!'

'Catherine,' I told Bill, 'was speculating this morning about the beings who give out the messages. She suggested that maybe the look of them, at least, may be fed by our imaginations. That they are visually what we expect to see, or want to see. If so, I guess it makes sense that the MIBs might resemble what we very much don't want to see.'

'Especially if we conjure them up out of our own fears.'

'Right.'

'Well, that is my theory,' Bill yawned. 'Funny thing is, as I said, they come as things we fear and despise. They are things that in some part of our selves we are damn well not afraid of, that we are at heart determined to defy, resist and defeat.'

'And maybe they reaffirm what we instinctively feel is right and wrong.'

'That's my opinion.' Bill yawned again and stretched. 'Well, I'm off to bed. Cathy's given me her room but as she's on another couch tonight, make free with that one.'

'I will. Thanks.'

'Goodnight.'

After he had left the room I closed my eyes but for a long time no sleep would come. What if he were right? What if Travier's friend from French security had been right and what if the Men In Black had told the truth? As I dozed off at last, it occurred to me that all this was not only possible but, in a strange way, downright probable.

One way or the other, I knew I had to somehow contact General Simons and learn or re-learn the 'First Message'. The men who worked at the radio telescope back when I was supposedly there could be helpful too. So, I figured as I dropped off, I'd move heaven and earth to find them in the morning, fly anywhere and do anything... that is when the phone started ringing.

Elsewhere in London, in his sleep, clear and deep as stone-carved letters, Patel had been told to whom the next message would be given. He'd rushed in to wake Catherine, who first rang me at home, then her own flat to tell Uncle Bill. The odd thing was there was not just one name, but two.

'This might be the most immediate message yet,' she said. 'These men are, even as we speak, attending the Petra conference.'

'The what?'

'The Middle East peace talks in Jordan. Don't you read the papers?'

'Not lately, for some reason...'

'They're Ahmed Haseem and Doron Samara, the chief Syrian and Israeli negotiators,' she cried enthusiastically. 'This really is big. Well, of course they all have been, but this could really shake things up, make the whole matter far more public and undeniable...'

'And for good or ill, blow the lid off everything?'

'Your end of it as well,' she went on excitedly.

'Yeah,' I agreed, with a cold shiver down my back.

'I've booked our seats on the morning flight to Amman,' she informed me. 'Using your credit card number.'

'Great,' I said flatly. Fear itself, I wanted to remind the still slumbering Uncle Bill, if well founded in fact and physical reality, was quite a reasonable thing to be frightened of. The several other dangers lying ahead were enough to petrify a kamikaze pilot.

Chapter Fifteen

Whatever Catherine thought, we couldn't just take off for Jordan and expect to get to see two guys engaged in vital discussions about the future of their countries. Aside from anything else, I knew the security considerations would be enormous. These men's own mothers would have been hard pressed to get to see them there.

Aside from the Jordanian security and that of the negotiating parties, there would certainly be plenty from the U.S. who were brokering the deal in a big way. Many of them would be hired in, as well as official government people. The chances were that I'd know somebody out of all this crowd. Hopefully someone who could help us get in touch with Haseem and Samara.

In the meantime we tried more conventional methods just in case, ringing the hotel where the conference was taking place, the embassies of the countries involved, press contacts we knew who'd be out there covering the story. Nothing worked, and Catherine was growing frustrated. For my part, I was more concerned with figuring out where to find my General Simons and any of the people from the radio telescope installation who had been around when I'd apparently gone there.

As luck would have it, things began to develop at the same time on both fronts. The retired General had been located in New York State and an old pal of mine was found to be in daily contact with both the Israeli and the Syrian diplomats at the Petra conference. I was torn, unable to decide where I should go first.

'Reason it out,' Catherine said, as she and Uncle Bill

and I sat in a pub near my flat. 'If the authorities are after you, or some amongst them, wouldn't they be watching the General's home?'

'Sure,' I shrugged.

'With all that's going on in regard to this business,' Bill pointed out, 'they might well be positively guarding the bugger.'

'No doubt that's true too,' I admitted. 'But I have to get at General Simons and find out what happened to me back then, what I was supposed to have learned.'

'Charging in hoping for a confrontation won't help if you can't see him, if you get killed or arrested or secretly tossed into some loony bin.' Catherine hit the table with her small fist and grimaced at me. 'Will it?'

'Get some people to do a reconnaissance of the bugger's HQ, old boy,' Bill winked at me. 'If you like I could co-ordinate operations,' he began to chuckle. 'I've a lady friend in New York City I could stay with. That's far enough from the General to allay suspicion but close enough to receive and assess reports from your men.'

'Who is this lady?' Catherine asked, poking her uncle in the ribs.

'An old war-time comrade's widow,' Bill grinned. 'And a chum in her own right.'

'After meeting Haseem and Samara we'd have more of an idea of what is going on,' she said to me. 'This message is so unique. The aliens' apparent first direct hand in human political affairs. The fifth message that could be the last. It could...'

'I still maintain there will be five more, or four if you don't count the lost first one.' Bill stood up, wagging a finger. 'My round. Same again, everyone?'

'Don't forget that among other things he's an ex C. of E. vicar,' Catherine smiled and shook her head after Bill had gone to the bar.

'So?' I raised my eyebrows.

'The commandments, thicko,' she laughed. 'So what do you say?'

'All right,' I sighed. 'Jordan it is. But then, unless we get to the bottom of things some other way, I'm going after Simons.'

If Harris hadn't owed me a few favours from the past, like putting him in the way of getting such prestigious and well-paid work in the first place, we wouldn't even have been able to get a hotel room in Wadi Musa. That's the town beside the ancient city of Petra, on the edge of which was the hotel that housed the conference.

Petra is carved from the rock of the surrounding mountains and hills and was established by the Nabataeans in a secluded valley in Old Testament times. It's one of the most spectacular and intact, ageless man-made places on earth. The premier tourist attraction in the Kingdom of Jordan, but easily reached from Israel and Syria.

It sort of symbolized the mutual benefits of peace. I mean the site drew people to the whole region, adding to the appeal of travelling there, just as places in Israel and Syria did. Enmity and closed borders were not a problem in Mexico or Egypt or Europe. This region was crying out to be seen as a whole, to everyone's advantage.

Anyhow, that was my theory on why Petra was chosen as the location for the conference, among other things; but despite the numerous hotels around there, as I say, we were hard pressed to find accommodation. Anthony Harris, a former employee of mine, fixed us up.

Petra was too important to tourists to close, but the area around the big hotel where the talks were taking place was sealed off and the rooms were given over entirely to the people involved in the conference or protecting the delegates. Harris himself stayed there, while we were put up in an unfinished hotel halfway up the hill toward the village of Wadi Musa. It was owned by the brother of a Jordanian buddy of Harris and not due to open for another week, though our room was comfortable. There were twin beds, to Catherine's relief. All the others that were habitable had Harris's men in them.

Once installed, we sat on the beds and Harris walked back and forth biting his knuckles, giving us worried, sidelong looks. Something was up, but other than dealing with the hotel manager and greeting us amicably, Harris had said nothing much. Now we were alone he obviously meant to, but it didn't seem easy.

'What's up, Andy? Won't you be able to get the message to them after all?'

'No problem there. No, that's not it,' he shook his head nervously. 'You're in trouble, aren't you?'

'I told you I was all along,' I reminded him. 'But once they get the message the negotiators themselves will want to see us, no matter what.'

'The tail that's been on us for so long has been dropped already,' Catherine assured him. 'Not a whiff of it on the drive down from Amman.'

'That's because they knew where you were going,' Harris snorted. 'There was one hell of a flutter in the U.S. government security camp about the time you would have boarded your flight in London to come here. The official "unofficial" word is that you're dangerous.'

'How so? Are we...?'

'You're not supposed to be shot on sight,' he laughed, some of the strain leaving his features. 'It's more in the line of the two of you being potentially embarrassing.'

'And it's unofficially official?' Catherine rolled her eyes. 'What does that mean?'

'That that is what they want to be believed, without seeming to actually say anything at all. On the other hand, the rumour is that they are both afraid of you and curious. They could have stopped you coming this far, if they had wanted to, after all.'

'Have you been approached?'

'Oh yeah, you bet. They want me to report everything you do. Let them see the note or whatever you want passed before I give it to...'

'You told them what we came for?' Catherine asked. 'Who we are here to see?'

'He wouldn't have had much choice,' I told her. 'We can't ask him to screw up his life over this. Get fired for us.'

'I told them what I know, sure,' Harris confirmed. 'That you want me to pass messages to Haseem and Samara. If there was any question of you being a threat to them I wouldn't do it, but there's not. Nevertheless, it's my job to keep the people responsible for these men's safety in the picture. That there's hassle from somewhere high up in the American security apparatus just means I have to be careful how I play this, to do right by everyone, and not shoot myself in the foot while doing it.'

'I appreciate that,' Catherine said a bit begrudgingly.

'You know how grateful I am...'

'You got it coming. Don't thank me. I'm real good at walking tightropes. So, what is this message for the negotiators?'

'Well...' Catherine and I exchanged a wide-eyed questioning look and thought about it. 'Obviously a verbal message would be best, create fewer security problems and be less obtrusive than writing a note to hand over.'

'And it's got to be succinct,' I added.

'Yeah, it'll have to be,' Harris said. 'I'm not exactly in their company for long, I mean they walk by, sometimes say good morning, I escort them for a few metres...'

'Tell them, either or both, that we know about the otherworldly experience they have recently had, the message they have received and that we can shed some light on it. We can explain about others who have...'

'What?' Harris squawked. 'You're shittin' me. Come on, what do you really want me to say?'

'That's it,' I said, more than a little abashed. 'They will know what you are talking about at once, I swear it. And they'll probably be relieved.'

'They will,' Catherine insisted. 'It's very important, despite what it sounds like.'

'This'll teach me to listen to rumours,' Harris gasped, having gone pale staring at us. 'You two really are a couple of fruitcakes.'

'Goddammit Andy, you owe me this,' I started to growl.

'We know how nutty it sounds,' Catherine soothed. 'And we know what an imposition this is. How vital and high-level these talks are, how major a job it is in your career. But if you doubt us, we can put you in touch with several reputable people...'

'All you have to do is whisper it softly in their hearing and they will pick up on it,' I told him. 'They'll jump to hear more, beg to be put in touch with us.'

'Please, you could get me in trouble, get me thrown out of here or made a laughing stock at the very least,' Harris pleaded.

'Doesn't what I did for you stand for anything?'

'Sure, but that was years ago...'

'Oh, so it doesn't matter, it can be written off now...'

'No, I mean you could have gone nuts since then for all I know,' he wailed. 'Look, let me think about this. What the hell is going on?'

'There have been a series of messages from extra-terrestrials, or what seems to be extra-terr...'

'Wait,' he held up his hands. 'I don't want to know.'

'We'll pay you,' Catherine said desperately.

'Andy, if you don't do this we'll find another way, but I won't forget that you let me down. By God I'll...'

'Wait, will ya'. Who said I wouldn't do it?' He waved his hands. 'I just gotta think. I'll have to say from the start that somebody else asked me and I think it's weird and I'll apologize in advance.'

'Fine, fine,' we cried together, jumping up, me to slap his back and Catherine to kiss his cheek.

'Now, I gotta go,' Harris insisted. 'I'll see you tomorrow.'

'Have them ring us here or send for us,' Catherine called as Harris went out.

'Man, is he going to be surprised when he sees their reaction,' I laughed, lying back on my bed. The flight and the drive down in the rental car from Amman had worn me out. I had barely stopped moving since all this began and wasn't completely recovered from my ordeal at the hands of the Nazis in Paris, despite some recuperation in New Mexico.

Catherine flopped upon her bed opposite and proposed a nap before going out to look around and have dinner. It was early evening and Harris wouldn't be seeing the negotiators until the next morning. Once that happened, we figured things would move pretty swiftly. We weren't wrong on that score.

We were in the hotel dining room the next morning having breakfast when Harris came in. He didn't sit down but just stood towering over us, glaring down.

'They looked at me like I was crazy,' he hissed. 'Like I was some outright lunatic at best and totally unprofessional at worst. I was humiliated and one or two other people couldn't help overhearing. We are quits after this, understand? Quits.'

'Gee, Harris, I don't know what to say...' I began in utter dismay.

'Are you sure they understood you. Do they speak English?'

'Yessss,' Harris seethed. 'And they heard clearly and didn't have a clue about any of it. They later asked to have me put on other duties. Do you know what this is going to do to my career?'

'I can't imagine what happened. Maybe they are being cagey, maybe...'

'Why don't you two get out of town before you humiliate anyone else, or get thrown out altogether?' With that, Harris stormed out of the little hotel and left us staring at each other in bewilderment.

'Could the Americans have got to them? Lied about us, warned them off, threatened them?' Catherine wondered.

'I don't know, but I don't see how they could,' I shook my head. 'Would you fail to listen after these strange beings gave you some vital message? Would a few U.S. security men or diplomats matter after that?'

'Maybe.'

'What could they threaten? How would they explain?'

'All right, not threaten but... No, you're right. If they had had a message, no warnings that we were weirdos or dangerous would stop them seeing us.'

'That depends, and they are very busy about important stuff, but Harris would have seen something in their eyes,' I said. 'He's no fool and being observant is part of his job. If he says they didn't know what the hell he was on about, then they didn't.'

'What can have happened?' She ran her fingers through her long hair and rested her chin in her hands. 'Nothing like this has gone wrong with the other people, the other messages.'

'Maybe the Yanks have brought some pressure to bear,'

I sighed, suddenly very worried. 'Or their own governments or all the governments. After what Travier's pal told me, that makes sense. It isn't just one country's big shots worried about what's going on, what we are on to and finding out about.'

'I'm scared,' she admitted and I could only nod.

Jordan is a very nice and civilized country, but I began to imagine it would nevertheless be far easier to pick up a couple of people and arrange for their disappearance here than in the U.K. or U.S.A. Our arrest on some charge or visa hassle could be managed at the very least and take ages to sort out, especially with our embassies conniving or dragging their feet. As it was, I felt in my bones that something was going on.

Nervously we stayed in our room the rest of the morning until Catherine got mad and we went out in defiance. By then I had decided the best thing we could do was to be seen by as many people as possible and we wandered around Wadi Musa greeting everyone we saw, especially the foreigners. Buying fruit and bread and other things for a picnic lunch, we chatted away to all the shopkeepers and told everyone our names and what hotel we were at, where we were from and what we planned to do with the day.

The most gregarious couple the place had seen in years then proceeded down the hill to the entrance to the ancient city of Petra, which was also the site of many of the larger hotels, including the one the talks were being held in. At the ticket window and gate we were in for a disappointment.

By now, having read about it and half being glad we had time on our hands after all, we wanted to see the intriguing and ghostly lost city, with its beautiful Greco-Roman facades carved from stone, the many tombs and the Roman amphitheatre. We longed to climb the surrounding High Places of Sacrifice and explore the huge site at our leisure. It would take our minds off our troubles and kill time while we waited for something to happen for good or ill.

'I am sorry,' the guard at the gate said, 'Petra is closed this afternoon. The negotiators of Syria and Israel are being given a tour, and for security...'

'Those bastards...' I began, just about fed up with the whole thing.

'Will it be open tomorrow?' Catherine enquired politely.

'Oh yes,' he assured us. 'As usual, but we can sell no more tickets for today and people are being asked to leave the site now.'

As he spoke, tourists were streaming out on foot and on horseback, led by the men and boys whose livelihood it was to give people rides to the entrance to the Siq, the narrow passageway a mile or so distant, which leads for another mile through a gorge and into the hidden valley of Petra. Remember the place where Indiana Jones found the Holy Grail in the final movie. That is the Treasury, the first thing you see at Petra coming out of that gorge.

I was in quite a state as we made our way up the steep hill, back to Wadi Musa and our hotel. Angry, bored, frustrated and worried, I kept cursing under my breath and wished we had taken a taxi from back at the entrance. Instead, I'd gruffly dismissed the driver's offers, storming by in a huff with Catherine trailing behind me, lost in thought.

When we were about a third of the way up, hot, legs aching and breathing a bit hard, a car pulled up beside us. Good, I thought, a taxi. Looking up, however, I felt a chill. It was a long black car with tinted windows.

As the door opened I thought, 'These creeps are all we need', but the occupants were very human indeed and very American. I even knew one of them. They were C.I.A. and they did not look pleasant or friendly.

'Get in, you nerd,' the one I knew growled.

'Shove it,' I said, walking on. I was unarmed again, what with all the international travel, and much regretting it.

'Just get in, will you?' he said again.

'Do Haseem and Samara want to see us?' Catherine asked hopefully.

'Are you kidding?' the C.I.A. guy laughed. 'Now get in, or do we have to pull strings to have you deported or something?'

'That might be preferable,' I said. 'What do you want? The last time we were visiting a desert landscape things got a little unhealthy for us.'

'Not so much for you as other people, from what I hear.' He smiled now. 'That wasn't us and the men responsible are being dealt with. We just want a private word.'

'Kiss my ass...' I said, but suddenly three burly men spilled out onto the road from a second car, and in full view of a few pedestrians and a horseman or two, we were bundled into the first car. I fought, mostly to draw more attention to us, but not very much, being afraid of Catherine getting hurt if things got too ugly. The worst was, I figured it might get even uglier once we were at their mercy and off into the desert.

The car did a sharp U-turn and headed back down the hill, turning right, and soon pulled up at the entrance of one or the swankier hotels, near the one the peace talks were held in. Catherine and I went from holding hands desperately to exchanging relieved looks and relaxing considerably.

'Come on,' said my C.I.A. acquaintance. 'Or do you want to be frogmarched through the lobby?'

'Who are we seeing?' I asked. Something told me it wasn't just him who was going to grill us.

'You'll find out.' He led the way inside and to the elevators, refusing to tell us anything before we were conducted into the sitting room of a suite on the top floor.

'Who...?' Catherine tried again.

'Please, just sit and wait. Do you want a Coke or a cuppa coffee?'

This time we chose not to reply and he sat down with a sigh. All the other hefty gents had drifted off when we got out of the car, so we didn't feel particularly frightened any more, just nervous and curious. The vibes we were getting spoke of power and the anticipated arrival of a person demanding of respect if not awe. I'd been patted down in the car and soon a woman security agent arrived and took Catherine into another room for a similar operation.

When they came back the woman left and we waited for about twenty minutes in silence, the C.I.A. guy by now more nervous than we were. I couldn't figure that out until the eminently recognizable visage of the U.S. Secretary of State appeared suddenly at the door, surveyed us critically and swept into the room.

'Thank you for coming,' the Secretary said to us. 'You can go now,' he told our Agency 'escort'.

'We didn't have much choice, sir,' I said, watching the guy leave with a glare.

'Most regrettable,' the Secretary spread his arms. 'Now will you two young people tell me why you are in Jordan trying to bend the ears of men engaged in some of the most important peace talks this century, with nonsense about extra-terrestrials?

'Well, sir, 'I began uncomfortably, but Catherine Frazier cut me off.

'I'm sure that when my grandfather Sir Donald Frazier

was desperately advising Neville Chamberlain not to trust Adolf Hitler in Munich at what really were the most important peace talks this century, he little realised that his granddaughter would be condescended to and browbeaten by a non-elected official of a friendly democracy, in a Kingdom ruled by a Sandhurst chum of my maternal Uncle Tommy. I hardly dare think what my brother Hugh of the BBC's 'Panorama' will make of it.'

Once again silence reigned as they stared at each other. I swear to God the Secretary of State was going a touch pale. Remember I had been married to the woman and even I wasn't sure if all she said was true or not, but it left the clear impression that she was someone to be reckoned with, wasn't overawed and wouldn't let herself be pushed around. I knew her, though, and I knew she was riled and that she was prepared to be difficult and formidable.

'You must understand,' he said after a pause to swallow hard and think quickly, 'that whatever their relative place in history, these talks must be sheltered from unwarranted intrusions, unnecessary distractions.'

'Thank goodness,' Catherine said to me, 'that you are a dual national and entered Jordan on your EU passport, that we are both British subjects and citizens of the European Union, not that this gentleman and his strong-arm men have authority in Jordan in any case. I wouldn't have thought the Secretary of State had extraordinary powers of arrest in the United States, for that matter, let alone the right to blatantly abduct...'

'No one has been abducted,' the Secretary said quickly. 'There is no question of your not being able to leave here whenever you like.'

'Shall we now then?' Catherine said to me, standing up.

'Wait,' said the Secretary with uncertain firmness.

'How do you imagine the press or the Jordanian government would react to a pair of loonies in a security scare at a conference like this? With sympathy?'

'We were nowhere near the negotiators but on a street in front of witnesses...'

'After trying to pass eccentric messages...'

'There is no law against that...'

'Shut up,' I shouted at both of them, surprised at myself. I mean I've been my own boss for years, the employer of hundreds of people and I didn't like being talked to by this man like an errant school kid either, aside from the manhandling by the C.I.A., but this was the Secretary of State of the most powerful nation on earth, and a pretty smart cookie in his own right.

'Please,' I went on hurriedly, 'Catherine, let it alone. You've made your point well. And you, sir, don't think we are so stupid as to believe a man in your position deals with every small distraction of the kind you say we are. What do you want?'

They eyed each other a moment warily and relaxed some, sitting back in their chairs.

'I suppose it might be of interest,' Catherine allowed.

'What do you wish to tell Mr. Haseem and Mr. Samara?' the secretary asked.

'Why do you want to know?' Catherine countered at once.

'Isn't it obvious?'

'What questions could a couple of eccentrics pose to anyone,' Catherine enquired, 'even high level peace negotiators, that they might be of such import as to attract the notice of the American Secretary of State?'

'You tell me,' he smiled.

'Why?'

'Because I may be able to help you. Or to be frank, protect you.'

'We aren't here to ask questions,' I said simply. 'Not so much as we are hoping to be told things by Haseem and Samara.'

'Yes,' Catherine agreed. 'And maybe to answer some questions of theirs.'

'I've spoken to them,' the Secretary assured us, 'and they never heard of either of you, have no idea what you might mean by your message from Harris. Neither does Harris, for that matter.'

'Do you, sir?' I asked.

'Why are you involved? Someone of your standing?' Catherine wondered.

'The vital nature of the talks,' he shrugged. 'And because I'm here, after all.'

'Please,' Catherine rolled her eyes impatiently, but modified it with a smile. It was fairly apparent that the man was on thin ice.

'I was asked personally by the President...' He shrugged again. 'I have no idea myself what any of this has to do with me, my work or the nature of these talks. I know you may somehow be dangerous and that you may be in danger. Why whatever you are doing is of concern to the President is a mystery to me, though. Are you extra-terrestrials?' he asked with a grin.

Out of sheer sympathy and in hope of gaining some understanding in high places, we told him everything we could. Certainly he had heard of some of the incredible things we had witnessed and investigated the advent of, though he had had no more notion of their other-worldly sources than anybody else.

'I don't know what to think,' he sighed when we had done. Then, glancing at his watch, he jumped up. 'I'm late,' he said. 'The others will all be waiting. Thank you for telling me what you have. I'll inform the President, in case he does not know everything already. I am obliged to tell you that he, as leader of the free world, implores you to leave off any further investigation of these matters.'

'But you know we will not,' Catherine smiled.

'Yes, I'm sure of that, Ms. Frazier,' he nodded and bowed slightly. 'I will make enquiries of my own. It may be that this comes under my area of responsibility after all. Remember that you are in danger, and again I have to say that you may be making a big mistake. Doing untold harm to world stability.'

'How?' she wondered. 'We haven't even written about any of this so far. It isn't us receiving the messages or doing the work to develop projects resulting from them.'

'Quite,' the Secretary agreed, heading for the door. 'Nevertheless, it is my duty to remind you that this is the view of the Commander-in-Chief and, I am informed, many other world leaders. God knows why.' He then left, still, I think, half believing we were eccentrics and the politicians themselves, superstitious nitwits.

CHAPTER SIXTEEN

We emerged from the big hotel in a daze but had the sense to take a taxi up the hill this time. Instead of going to our own hotel, however, we had the driver take us to a bar, the only bar in Wadi Musa. It was early evening by now and we not only felt very much like a drink but a serious reassessment of our position as well, given all we had recently learned.

Walking up the steep stairs to the bar, with visions of large cold bottles of Amstel beer in our heads, we noted the reactions of the several off-duty security people around the place. Hostile or amused looks greeted us, even as we were politely guided to some free seats by the Jordanian waiter. The security folks sneered, sniggered and moved tables to avoid us. I'll be damned if Harris himself wasn't in the corner and turned his back on us.

We ordered and drank quickly, distinctly uncomfortable, both of us experiencing a heavy sense of foreboding. It jangled my nerves and I could see Catherine growing jumpy and suspicious. I began to think the best place for us was our room with the door locked, and then the road out of town at first light.

Self-consciously we finished our beers and left, walking quickly back toward our hotel, which was about a third of the way down the hill and at the edge of the village. Just before we got there another car drew to a rapid halt beside us and men leaped out. Wishing I had a gun, I took up a fighting stance and pulled Catherine behind me. This was it, I knew. We'd had it.

'Please,' someone cried, going on in desperate terms to

try to confirm our identities and put us at our ease. It dawned on me that the men seemed a mixture of Arabs and Israelis and two of them a mite aged for bullyboys or assassins.

'Shut up,' I warned Catherine, who had admitted who we were at once.

'It's Haseem and Samara, don't you see?' she said, stepping around me to shake their hands. 'We asked Mr. Harris to speak to you about us.'

Well, they greeted her eagerly and then pumped my hand too, and at Catherine's insistence we stepped the few yards farther on and into our hotel, where the manager brought us tea and we sat in the dining room, all guards at a distance, and talked excitedly.

They had just seen the light, quite literally.

'We were in Petra,' Samara, the Israeli, said in astonishment. 'Up on the High Place of Sacrifice, everyone keeping a discreet distance, except the Secretary of State, who had fallen a few dozen metres behind.'

'It was sunset,' the Syrian, Haseem, continued. 'But this was no trick of the light. We truly saw them, truly heard them.'

'What did they tell you?' Catherine asked.

'To make peace, of course. To make peace at once.'

'They stood there in the shining, beautiful brightness and told each of us in his own language the final bargaining position of the other, the bottom line.'

'They detailed military secrets and economic information about the other's country and assured us of the feasibility of peace, of its mutual necessity.'

'Did the Secretary of State see them?' I wondered.

'No one did. It was as if no time had passed, yet we must have listened to them and talked things over for an hour. It felt like an hour.' Samara looked questioningly at Haseem.

'Yes, yes, at least an hour.' He raised his hands in wonder. 'There were people all around, guards on the other high places, others not fifty paces from us.'

'And no one saw anything,' Samara shrugged. 'No one seemed to. We didn't tell anyone but they all acted normally and, as we say, no time seemed to have passed for them. We have not even spoken of it to the Secretary of State.'

'That might be best,' I observed. 'For now anyway.'

'What do you know about this? Tell us why you have come here,' they insisted.

No matter how much we wanted to question them, we had to answer and I let Catherine do most of the talking. She explained about the other messages, about my having somehow got the first one and lost it, of the possible international conspiracy to suppress the messages and the information they contained, despite their usefulness.

'Did you feel that these aliens, or whatever, were hostile, evil in any way?' I asked the two peace envoys.

They just stared at me as if I had spoken gibberish, or made an indecent suggestion. I glanced at Catherine in that split second and she raised her eyebrows.

'We have been given various descriptions of these beings,' she said quickly. 'A few preconceived or simply popular conceptions may have crept into our terminology. What exactly did you see and did you both see the same things?'

'It's the first report by two people we've had on this,' I said, trying to sound very professional. 'No two so far have been quite alike.'

'We saw angels,' Samara said flatly.

'Angels,' Haseem nodded. 'We are both secularists, both by the notions of our two countries socialists, pragmatists, realists. We saw angels.'

Their faces shone with the wonder of it, more like peasant kids from Portugal or Yugoslavia than a couple of cagey diplomats from the most hostile and notoriously hard bargaining nations in the Middle East. Regardless of what their countries might do, these men were united by what they had seen; they were brothers.

I all but muttered a blasphemy and stared at them now as they had at me moments before. This was an odd turn even after Patel's testimony and, on the whole, I found myself wishing Uncle Bill was with us.

'What did they look like? Did they have wings? Haloes?' I didn't go as far as enquiring about the harps.

'Haloes,I'd say,' Samara confirmed, then looked to Haseem for agreement.

'Yes, I saw them.' He made the shape above his head.

'Did they tell you they were angels?' I went on. 'In so many words?'

'No, it was too obvious.'

'Very much.'

'You had no idea that they were extra-terrestrials?'

'That is what angels are, after all,' Haseem said after a second to think. 'Isn't it?'

'They were not aliens as in science fiction,' the more Westernized Samara pointed out. 'I am certain of that. There was no spaceship, they looked like people, only more perfect.'

'Solid or airy?' Catherine wondered.

The two men compared mental notes and agreed that the beings had been neither one nor the other, neither purely physical nor ephemeral.

'Might they have been holograms?' she suggested.

'They had too much of a presence, I think,' Samara thought.

'They were there, not mere images of something,' Haseem insisted.

'Why did they come to you, do you think? Why now?'

They had been so energized and exhilarated, certain of

the experience and their shared wonder and inspiration, that it was a shock to see them suddenly perplexed, looking to each other for guidance and then to Catherine.

'There have been a lot of peace talks in this region recently and particularly elsewhere, with the whole world in the balance. such as a few years back, Reagan and Gorbachev. Did they see angels?'

'Who knows?' Samara shrugged. 'Maybe. Would they have said something?' He looked at Haseem. 'Will we?'

'The beings themselves didn't say that you must?' Catherine asked a bit surprised.

'No,' Haseem shook his head. 'That is not as with the others? They were all told to make public their messages, were they not?'

'Yes, but theirs were of a more concrete nature. What would you say was the overriding message that you received? Its essence?'

'To make peace, yes, but...'

'To display brotherhood, unity. That this part of the world was divided against itself seemed suddenly appalling, disgraceful.'

'Yes, not that we have our differences, not even that we fight, have fought often. We felt no shame in that somehow.'

'Yes, yes, but without words, they seemed to convey that above all we must get along now, that we must make peace now and see that it is one that can last at least twenty years. That to still be fighting then would be abominable, humiliating.'

'Twenty years?'

'More or less,' Samara said and they both nodded.

'Not forever?' I gaped at them. 'You are not supposed to spread the word of peace and brotherhood throughout the world, end war itself somehow?'

'Not that we were told,' they frowned, exchanging glances again.

'Nothing like that.'

'Just cool it between yourselves for now?' I said doubtfully.

'Display unity.'

'And brotherhood.'

I was strangely inclined to take them to task for the inadequacy of this when the hotel manager came over to say there was a phone call for me from the United States. I left reluctantly, while Catherine began belatedly to do her investigator-of-phenomena routine.

On one level she was, I could not help but note, out of her depth, and so was I. All this was a far cry from looking into ordinary UFO reports or carrying out executive protection. We were both in over our heads.

I wondered half in jest whether this was going to be the President, as I walked to the desk to pick up the phone. I couldn't have been much more taken aback if it had been. The voice was one I found weirdly familiar.

'How are you, son?' General Simons asked jovially after introducing himself.

'Befuddled,' I said, actually having to pause to catch my breath. 'Not dumbstruck, however,' I finally added. 'What happened to us, to me? And why did you disappear and let me go crazy all by myself?'

'Maybe I was going crazy too,' he said.

That knocked me back . I'd never thought of that possibility before.

'I have someone here I think you ought to talk to.'

'Eh, hello?'

'Hello,' I said, my head reeling. Maybe this would be the President.

'I'm Dr. Edward Merimak. I ran the radio telescope installation you and the General visited eight years ago and I'd like to tell you, to the best of my knowledge, what happened that night.'

At the table, when I returned, the three of them were still chattering away and Catherine seemed to be fully taking part in the very peace plan they were preparing to present to their governments. That was their major worry, persuading their fellow countrymen to follow their proposals. To best accomplish this, neither wanted to accept concessions the other one might not be able to get his leader and people to wear.

They were in absolute collusion to find a way to help each other and then sell the whole thing back home as a hard-fought contest. To make it seem the best possible deal that they could get from the tough customer on the other side.

Something about it struck me as highly amusing and it was all I could do to keep from laughing. I was also pretty lightheaded, confused, scared and relieved, not to mention so oddly worn out or wrung out, that I felt almost drunk. It was in that spirit that I made a proposal of my own.

'What do you say we all go to the bar and get a drink,' I said. 'Toast brotherhood and unity, eh?'

Incredibly they nodded, still discussing things, and stood up to follow me out. Between their mutual distraction, inspiration and a certain awe of Catherine and me, they came along like sheep.

'It won't blow your cover too much and it'll be one in the eye for Harris and those jerks we saw there earlier,' I chuckled, conducting them out of the door in the middle of a stream of guards and aides who'd converged as soon as we had got to our feet.

This veritable parade trooped out of the hotel and, regardless of security, due to the short distance, we just naturally walked, so everybody else did too, rather than climbing and crowding into the waiting limousines. I guess we had gone fifty yards and were about to turn the corner to the street the bar was on when the bomb went off.

The flash lit the night and the air became rank and jangled, debris rained, pandemonium ensued and everybody screamed at once. The negotiators were swamped by security men and in danger of being crushed. I lost sight of Catherine immediately and staggered around in search of her. The world had slowed to a snail's pace, however, as it fortunately does for me at such times. She was okay, I soon realised, staring down the street in the direction we had come from; the direction of the explosion. Turning, I saw too that the side of our hotel was missing and I started running toward it.

The first casualty I came to was one of the drivers but he was dead. Beside him lay another, and pulling out the emergency equipment I carried, I started to do what I could. Other than weapons or morphine I had the full kit we use on V.I.P. protection jobs.

The second driver died almost as soon as I started to work, and without pause I left him and carefully approached the hotel itself. There was no time to think, but only to act. Checking for falling masonry, I entered the hotel and found in what was left of the lobby one of Harris's off-duty security team, down and bleeding among ruined crockery and spilled coffee.

Kneeling, I opened his mouth, and suddenly felt hands touching mine from the side. Glancing up, I saw Catherine at my shoulder.

'Clear the airway, stop the bleeding, treat for shock,' I chanted like a mantra and she repeated it, a good disciple. By now people were emerging coughing and dust-covered from the kitchen and the upstairs rooms. Others were pouring in from outside, like us, to help the wounded.

Working desperately, trying to keep emotions, fear and revulsion in check, Catherine and I did what we could for Harris's man. With relief I realised this one would probably make it. Before we could move to help anyone else the place was full and all the wounded were being seen to. God knows there were a lot of first-aid trained people around and even a doctor or two. Soon ambulances began arriving.

The rest for quite a while was a blur. I can recall every detail of the actual attempt to initially treat the wounded, to clear the building and to get the growing crowd back from the unsafe structure. I even seem to have taken charge of several operations where there were enough English speakers around to make a difference.

Once the authorities took over though, which was pretty quickly in real time, we just stood around like zombies, with bloody hands and clothes, the adrenalin running out of us fast and that strange post-action exhaustion setting in. All this was at most only fifteen minutes after the explosion.

Eventually we were found a big room in the very hotel where the negotiators were staying and fresh clothes were brought to us from somewhere. Once we were alone, almost mechanically we fell into each other's arms for comfort and literal support. Then, just as mechanically, we stripped and showered together and went to bed.

There was only a large double bed and we lay in the middle and held each other tight for a long time before a very haunted sleep came upon us. In both our dreams we were together. And in both were in grave danger.

In the morning, still cuddled up and perhaps in need of some reaffirmation of life, nature took its course and we made love for the first time since several months before our marriage broke up. For a while the fear was dispelled. The doubts and the mysteries were put aside. Afterwards, however, there were new ones to go with the rest.

Self-consciously, we showered separately and put on the unfamiliar clothes that had been donated to us. Almost hurriedly we went downstairs for breakfast, to be among others, to get some news and plunge into life again, as if seeking safety there.

Harris joined us at our table and as the silence ended we were grateful to him for it. He thanked us himself for helping his man, who had recognized us and was going to recover.

'I'm sorry about yesterday,' Harris added. 'I was wrong to doubt that you knew what you were doing. I should have realized. Hell, you're one humdinger of a security man too, even when you aren't on duty.'

'What do you mean?' I asked, baffled.

'Getting the envoys out of that hotel the way you did, without panic...'

'I didn't know there was going to be a bomb, for Chris'sake!' I croaked. 'Would I have left the others in the building...?'

'No, of course not, but some instinct sure told you something was up. Good thing too. As it was, the dining room was empty by then, a few hotel staff got hurt in the kitchen, my man and others in the lobby, but nobody else. If you and the envoys and their entourage had still...'

'The drivers...'

'Oh, yeah. The Israeli and the Syrian limo drivers both died. It's a goddam shame. Hamas is blamed, or the Israeli extreme right, ' Harris shrugged. 'Who really knows?'

'I don't even want to guess,' I said, noticing that Catherine had tears in her eyes

'There is nothing left of your stuff,' Harris smiled apologetically. 'Your room was that side of the hotel. The only one finished there at the time and just two floors above the dining room.'

'Our passports were on us,' I thought out loud. 'Money, air tickets, travellers cheques,too. Credit cards ditto. Just clothes and a camera lost , I guess, no big deal.'

'Looks like it was on a donkey,' he said.

'What?'

'The bomb. In a bag on a donkey tied to a tree beside the hotel. A new one on me, I gotta admit. Blew the donkey's ass off, naturally.'

'There was a donkey tied up under our window yesterday,' Catherine said. 'I noticed it when we first arrived. It didn't have anything on its back, though. No saddle or pack or anything.'

'Well, this one sure had something.' Harris stood up and slapped me on the back. 'Keep trusting those instincts,' he said. 'See ya' around.'

'The bomb,' Catherine breathed. 'That bomb...'

'What about it?' I asked when she did not go on.

'It wasn't meant for the envoys. It was meant for us.'

She was right, I knew, and I wondered if someone in America had not known the phones had not yet been installed in the rooms. Someone who had seemed to wish to keep me on the line for longer than I'd felt comfortable with talking long distance, even on somebody else's bill. Someone who would not have realized or cared that the peace negotiators were with us, along with dozens of other people.

'It was Simons who rang me last night,' I told Catherine.

She looked up and into my eyes. She was scared, I knew that as well as I knew I was myself, but by God she was still intrigued and now very angry.

No, she was not about to quit, though in some recesses of my mind I regretted that, even while admiring her. You see, I couldn't quit now, either. Not if she didn't.

'General Simons and a Dr. Merimak.'

'New York,' she said.

Chapter Seventeen

In the end we did not go to New York together. I had to talk her out of it, or rather I thought I did. The peace envoys had given her the next name, and she had gone off to Berlin to investigate, instead. The awkwardness that had grown between us since making love on the night of the bomb may have made her actually prefer that in the end.

For my part, I didn't want her coming with me for the same reason but also because it was going to be dangerous. Anyway, investigating the messages and their recipients was her job. Dealing with Simons and recovering my memory of the 'First Message', was mine.

When I got to New York, Uncle Bill met me at the airport, and aggressively driving his lady friend's car, he took me into Manhattan, cursing other drivers, and behaving like a native. The life of the city along with the work he'd been doing for me had put new energy into the old boy and his eighty years sat lightly on him.

'New York rubs off on a chap, don't you find?' he remarked. 'It is life, it is humanity, it is civilization for good or ill, going full tilt and full circle. Fascinating, exhilarating and scarey as all bloody hell, what!'

'Well, yeah,' I said. 'That pretty much describes it.'

'How is Catherine?' he asked. 'The bomb business worried me.'

'I have people watching her twenty-four hours a day. A very tough woman I mostly assign to female politicians and pop stars is her constant companion. They're in Germany meeting with the latest message receiver. Some computer wizard named Schiller.'

'What did the last chaps tell you?'

I gave him a run-down of it from what I remembered and had heard.

'Of course, I got a long-distance phone call from the General while we were talking and didn't hear everything. Then the bomb sort of ended the possibility of further discussions or any question of Catherine hypnotizing the peace negotiators.'

'Too bad. And what sort of beings did they see?'

'Ah, that was the odd bit,' I smiled. 'They saw angels.'

The car lurched suddenly and we almost hit the one in front as Bill seemed to be having spasms. A coughing fit hit him and his foot went lead-like on the gas pedal.

'They saw what?' he gasped, struggling to right the car and control his breathing.

'Well...' I paused until he was settled down again. 'Angels, or so they said.'

'Angels, eh?' he nodded with a shiver but nothing worse this time. 'Remarkable. Still, I might have known. Yes, yes, it had to come eventually.'

'What do you mean?'

'Makes sense, doesn't it?'

'Hell Bill, none of it makes sense to me.'

'We talked about this in London, don't you know,' he went on enthusiastically. 'How each one of the message receivers has seen something a little different, or certainly felt it.'

'I guess so.'

'Absolutely, old boy. Of course, the first one thought she saw those characters I believe the professionals like Cathy call Greys, the now regulation man from outer-space. The French chappie might have as well, but didn't really describe them as much of anything, did he? Fella was under water at the time, after all, and then again our

American chum seemed to see Greys, but didn't describe them as such under hypnosis and all along felt more as if he was meeting some sort of ancient Red Indian shaman.'

'I remember,' I said, also recalling the sort of books I'd noted on his shelves. 'Halliday and I never discussed his feelings or observations in much detail, but that stuff didn't suprise me.'

'Rubbed each other up too much the wrong way, what!' Bill chuckled. 'Yes, so then we have Mr. Patel and his god, or ghost of the Mahatma, as it sounded to me.'

'So now it's a Jew and a Moslem,' I went on. 'Albeit secular and quite worldly men, seeing some Old Testament angels. Okay, so it's also not a surprise.'

'Don't you discern a pattern, old boy? A trend?'

'Sure, just as we thought in London, people see what they expect to see, or hope to see, or some combination of the two.'

'Ah, but that's only part of it.'

I yawned and stretched in the car seat. Though I was tired, there would be no time for any rest. We would have to move fast, before the opposition could anticipate our next move.

'Right,' I said getting down to business. 'What's the story on the General?'

'Gone to ground,' Bill cried with vigour. 'But we are working on ways to dig him out or,' he leered at me, 'send in a terrier, what!'

'Tell me all about whatever plans you've cooked up.'

'Well, the one I like best,' Bill leered again, 'is what I've come to refer to as my James Bond gambit.'

I made the same mistake as I did with Travier, picturing somebody as something he wasn't. Imagining either a scrawny guy with thick glasses and a pocketful of pens, or an old egghead with a vague look and a funny accent,

I got a wiry, foul-tempered maniac who had been a wrestler at college. This latter while there for his doctorate, I might add. He'd got his B.A. at seventeen. Dr. Edward Merimak was still very young and fit.

With Uncle Bill driving and me struggling as I was with a man one year my junior and a third again my weight, I don't know how we did it, but the kidnap part of the plan went like clockwork. Stopped clockwork for a few hairy moments, but on the whole not bad. God knows our move was unexpected.

In the end the chloroform did the trick. This, combined with high levels of low cunning just to get us in a position to use it, constituted our only assistance.

We had him zonked out in the back of the car and heading into the sticks almost before we knew it, despite the wrestling match. Bill's groundwork had paid off. We'd known Merimak's movements and habits like an old favourite tune and the rest was set up perfectly.

At the rented cabin in the Carolina woods we started on him, not gently, but a far cry from what I'd been handed out in Paris only a few weeks before. We had no desire to hurt him and we didn't really. Just enough to get the point across and convince our prisoner that we were quite mad and fully capable of any wickedness he could imagine.

On the whole, I think we got everything he knew almost at once. However, we also had to lay the foundations for what would come later. To a large extent that was what really mattered, for this was 'all part of the masterplan', as Bill frequently said with a wink.

'Please, I swear that's all I know,' Merimak kept pleading, staring wildly from one of us to the other.

This was very early on. Only the first evening to be exact, and we hadn't tried even a third of our proposed party pieces on him.

'Really?' Bill yawned.

'I swear it's the truth.'

'He swears it's the truth,' I said to Bill in a bored and mildly doubtful kind of way. 'What do you think? Should we believe him?'

'Believe him?' Bill asked amazed, using accents more associated with East End villains than the officers' mess or the pulpit. 'Where would the fun be in that then?'

'You're right, mate, we're just getting started,' I nodded, falling in with his act. 'Hand us the pliers. Might as well do a proper job of it.'

'Too right, me old China, too right,' Bill laughed, leering at the good Doctor. 'This geezer wouldn't really tell the truth now, would he? I mean, he hasn't had enough flamin' incentive, has he?'

'Please,' Merimak screamed. 'I don't want you to hurt me. I've told you everything. And I told you the truth on the telephone to Jordan. I swear I didn't know about the bomb and I'm sure Simons didn't either. We would never harm you, or anyone. I swear...'

'You watch all this bloody swearing,' Bill warned him with a straight face and then a sideways grin at me.

'Tell us the one about the last time me and Simons came to your facility,' I told the doctor. 'That one cracks me up.' I slapped him on the back and smiled cruelly.

'It's the truth,' Merimak insisted, bobbing his head, looking with beseeching eyes from Bill to me and back again. 'As I told you...'

'Suppose he takes it right from the beginning,' Bill suggested. 'See if he changes his story. I don't trust him an inch.' With that he poked the doctor in the ribs. 'What'll we try next, when he lies again?'

'I thought we agreed on the pliers?'

'Right you are, right you are,' Bill nodded, poking Merimak again. 'Go ahead and just see if you can sound convincing.'

'Please,' he bounced in his chair excitedly. 'I'm not lying and I've long resented having been forced to suppress what little I know, just as you have. Stop playing with me, and I swea... I assure you I'll do whatever I can to help you.'

'Okay, we'll see' I said, beginning to feel a bit sorry for him. 'But take it from the start anyway.'

'And remember we've recorded your last version,' Bill said in his normal voice.

'I had begun to monitor the 21 centimetre wavelength, just as the Ozma Project in the 60s did. ' Merimak said. 'It is believed to be the most likely to be used for inter-stellar radio communications, if there should be any. It is simply the least affected by electromagnetic interference. Hydrogen atoms...'

'Cut to the chase.'

'Very well, the long and the short of it is that I began to detect what might have been radio waves from an artificial source, not from quasars or pulsars. They seemed to be generated intermittently by intelligent life. '

'Go on,' I urged him. 'What happened next?'

'Fearing ridicule and being unsure of what I was actually hearing, I told only a few colleagues. When the obvious explanations had been ruled out, I contacted Simons..'

'Why Simons?'

'He was not just both a friend and a communications expert, but also an Air Force officer. As I told you before, the signal seemed to come from deep space as expected, only some of the time, not always, I mean it jumped around. It came from nearer, too. Even from the Earth itself.'

'From where on Earth?'

'Everywhere and nowhere, as I've already told you. It

was always the same frequency but somehow from whatever direction I happened to begin with each night. Obviously the telescope had been used constantly on official projects, mapping, so...'

'Sure, sure, go on.'

'We thought it might be a military thing, or that secret communications already existed with extra-terrestrials or that it might be the Soviets up to no good,' he shrugged.

'Obvious concerns,' Bill smiled with mock gentleness.

'So I privately asked Simons to come down and listen to it.' Merimak swallowed hard, staring at Bill. 'He did so and obviously knew nothing of any military explanations for it. Soon, however, the signals began to be more regular and clear. Intrigued, we also became a bit concerned, though wary of doing anything official yet. That is when he had you accompany him.'

'Okay, I'll buy that, more or less.'

'Finally and most remarkably, the signal seemed at one point, while coming from very deep space, to be sending plain old-fashioned morse code. We were flabbergasted and yet it threw us into ecstasy and near panic. Then a clear precise message apparently came through and, with all of us crowded around, words seemed to be transmitted in English. Simons ordered you to clear the room. You did so, but staying on the inside of the door you must have heard what, if anything, was said.'

'But you didn't hear it, of course?' Bill asked him. 'You were outside.'

'Yes,' said Dr. Merimak. 'None of the rest of us heard it.'

'Just me and Simons?' I said.

'Yes, how many times must I say it?' Merimak howled.

'As many times as we ask you,' Bill told him with a villainous sneer.

'Then what happened?'

'Just what I told you before,' Merimak moaned. 'You two were in there for a very long time and looked quite affected by what you had heard when you came out. Simons nervously began to talk fast, make up obvious excuses. Later, officialdom descended and other radio astronomers. The whole thing was checked out and quietly discredited. We were told to forget it. That we had been hoaxed, that we had overheard a psychological warfare experiment meant to confuse the Soviet Union. I don't know all we were told, but grant money for any unrelated projects we proposed came our way and we got on with our work and did as we were advised. We forgot it.'

'Then years went by...' I said, nodding and raising my eyebrows as a signal for Merimak to continue.

'And suddenly Simons pops up, long retired. He's very nervous and has plenty of official-looking back-up. He won't give anything away but he asks me to speak to you in Jordan by long-distance telephone. That was all. Now you lunatics kidnap me and I've had enough. Please leave me alone.' He sagged in his chair and whimpered softly.

'Simons was so placed in the Air Force and the communications field that he would not have been fooled by this hoax nonsense though, would he? Nor would he have been ignorant of the kind of operations they described to you as secretly going on?'

'That was my assumption at the time,' Merimak shrugged.

'And now, what in your opinion actually occurred?' I asked. 'If you really want to help yourself, quite aside from us, I don't want to hear any bullshit. I don't want to hear what you think I want to hear, or what you think they want me to hear.'

I pulled out a big .45 automatic pistol and pointed it at

his head after dramatically cocking it. The gun was empty, but he didn't know that.

'If I even think you are lying I'll kill you, just like that.' I snapped my fingers. 'You had better give me the straight truth as you really feel it and see it or you will be dead an instant later.'

'Please...' He began going whiter than I had ever seen in a human face.

'Talk,' Bill said, calmly stropping a straight razor on the doctor's tie. It was an old dull one that he had not used in twenty years, when wrinkles and a shaky hand had made it inadvisable to go on shaving with it, but it made Merimak's eyes bulge. 'What do you think happened? What do you think Simons believes happened?'

'A com... communication,' he stammered, closing his eyes tight. 'From beyond our planet or our dimension, and I think Simons believes so too and is afraid of the information getting out.'

'The fact or the content of the communication?'

'Both.'

We let a silence hang in the air as we digested what he'd said.

'Now please...'

'Any idea what the latter was?' I asked, nudging his nose with the gaping muzzle of the big bore pistol.

'No, no idea at all, just that it seemed to freak out both you and General Simons back then and that it still freaks him out now.'

Chapter Eighteen

The James Bond gambit was to get into full swing on a moonless night only days after we had 'interviewed' Dr. Merimak. By then the retired General Simons' large home in the small town of Norwich, New York, had been observed for many weeks by a group of old people Bill had recruited.

They had rented a house across the street from General Simons' big place, which was surrounded by security fencing. From there they could easily watch the guards who patrolled his two acres of well-mown grounds.

Bill himself was back in London by now, doing sterling work from that end. His set-up in Norwich itself was perfect and ingenious. Our spadework with Merimak was visibly bearing fruit. The plan was going to be a masterpiece.

They came for me at 3 a.m. on the morning before I was meant to infiltrate the well-guarded grounds of the house. I was snug in bed and wearing only my pyjamas when they burst in, having taken a sledgehammer to the door.

Flying from under the sheets, I charged at the first one through the door and went for his throat. Fending me off expertly, he hit me in the solar plexus and doubled me up, chopping the edge of his hand down on the back of my neck.

I fell hard but rolled over, kicking at him and another man, getting one in the balls and clutching at the second one's feet, but by now they had been joined by a third man and quickly trussed me up with ropes, bundling me into my own blankets. Kicking and growling, all I could do was curse them.

'Who are you?' I kept shouting. 'Where are you taking me?' They said nothing and gagged me even as I attempted to bite their hands.

Soon after the big, swift, very skilled men had overpowered me, I was dragged outside and thrown into the back of a van. We did not drive far, though some precautions were taken in case anyone had seen the abduction. Going in circles around town and out into the countryside, they made sure we were not being followed. We weren't, of course.

After a change of vehicles, we went back into Norwich and the General's home. I was frog-marched from the garage into the house and down a corridor to the study, where Simons himself sat waiting. The face was familiar from pictures I'd lately been studying because all my conscious memory of him had been erased. He was smiling as I was conducted in and he stood up to greet me.

'Well, we meet once again,' he held out a hand and did not bat an eyelid when I refused to shake, though my hands were tied in front of me, not behind. 'Surely you're not offended by my stealing a march on you.'

'I don't know what you mean,' I snarled at him. 'Let me go or I'll...'

'What?' he shook his head. 'Have me arrested? I don't think so. Besides, who will miss you? You yourself have taken every precaution imaginable to see that all trace of you in America has been lost. The papers you left in your room are false. We have taken them away in any case. We have also removed your burglar tools and other foolish items of equipment, along with photos of me, my house and grounds, and details of my security system.'

'I don't know anything about such equipment,' I lied. The stuff had indeed been all over my room.

'Come, come, your fingerprints are on every item.'

'Then why didn't you have the police pick me up? Or are these the police? Do you own them in this town, or what?'

'You have seen too many movies. These men work for our government and are detailed to protect me.'

'A retired officer?'

'Ex-presidents are so protected and some ex-generals and others, yes.'

'I guess my being arrested properly would have given me the chance to tell my story,' I growled at him. 'You couldn't have that, could you?'

'Indeed not.'

'Why didn't you just try to have me killed again then?' I demanded angrily, glaring at him and the two guards still in the room. He had allowed the other half dozen to retire for the night, excepting the ones out on the perimeter.

'Murder you in my own backyard?' the General laughed. 'We only really located you when you showed up here after frightening the life out of Dr. Merimak. What a bumbler you've turned out to be with the pressure on, though.'

'Oh yeah...'

'We discovered you with ease. Your attempts to use the security fraternity's old boys' network to get a line on my arrangements here gave you away, too. Just as your ex-wife's uncle renting that room for you and acquiring all that equipment did. Your amateurish assault with the old gentleman on poor Dr. Merimak would have only been surpassed by whatever screwed-up solo operation you were planning to attempt on me...'

'Go to hell.'

'What were you going to do? Sneak in here and beard the lion in his own den?'

'Just like James Bond,' I said bitterly.

'Delightful,' the General laughed. 'We'd only have captured you, just as we have now. That is, if you were not harmed in the attempt to get in. You should count yourself lucky that we snatched you when we did.'

'Okay,' I sighed. 'What do you want?'

'To be left alone by you for one thing,' he said simply. 'And for you to stop all this nonsense about aliens and miracle information from space.'

'What happened to us at the radio telescope facility? What did we hear?'

'Nothing but a hoax,' Simons said with a sigh, going on in mild tones. 'A hoax which you took seriously and have been obsessed with ever since. We had hoped you were cured a few months afterward. The Air Force psychiatrists did all they could and you were sent back to duty, but in the end you remained unstable. When in later years I heard that you had made a success of your life, I was pleased and relieved.'

'Touching, very touching,' I muttered.

'I always thought you had considerable ability and promise...'

'What are you going to do with me now?' I looked him in the eye, trying to see into his mind and tell if he was speaking the truth.

'Well,' he smiled, 'we need to find out what you have to say about these other alleged communications you have convinced yourself have occurred...'

'They've happened!' I protested. 'They're facts.'

'We want to help you get back to normal again, too,' he carried on, ignoring me. 'To aid you in returning eventually to the life you led until this condition of yours sadly flared up again.'

'You can't pretend that everything that has been happening is a figment of my imagination, General. You can brainwash me again if you want, but it won't change anything. Oh, I won't be running around finding out more, threatening to make it all public, but it isn't just going to go away.'

'Let me worry about that, why don't you?'

'Why are you suppressing this?' I asked sincerely.

'Suppressing what? A hoax? A series of hoaxes?'

'You know better.'

'The delusions of a former lieutenant and the off-the-wall investigations of a known pursuer of strange phenomena that never check out?' He spread his arms and tilted his head up questioningly. 'Really?'

'These things do check out and you know it.' I said. 'Why else are you trying to have us killed?'

'I never did that,' he said, pursing his lips, giving his head a little shake. 'It wasn't me or any official branch of the government. The mavericks are being rounded up now, don't worry. They, er, like you, believed these reports were true. And they see them as dangerous, but of course aliens, in the form of dangerous enemies or benign benefactors, do not exist. They are not coming... communicating with us.'

'Are you aware that every major nation on earth may have heard what we did that night?' I asked him.

'I am aware that many countries have rumours of the same kind of hoax or mythical contact you believe we experienced, yes. Every country also has an official religion, a set of legends, superstitions, and childish stories of magic and fairies,' he smiled and once again spread his arms.

There was a long pause while he let all this sink in.

'You will stay here for a few days,' he explained finally. 'And then be taken elsewhere. Remember it is for your own good.'

Outside the first stun grenades went off and it was my

turn to smile. More muffled explosions followed and I hit the deck and covered my ears. The General's bewildered features froze, and were only defrosting into a shout of anger at me and orders to his men when Uncle Bill's hired commandos burst in, tossing another stun grenade, flattening the General and the guards who had remained with him.

Within minutes these ex-S.A.S. troopers had him bound, gagged, hooded and moving fast, all the guards hog-tied, blindfolded and mildly drugged. Outside, where I ran with assistance, still stunned myself, the noise of helicopters filled the air and the General, struggling and cursing through his gag, was finally given a shot and put under altogether. As predicted, it had been a masterpiece.

Chapter Nineteen

When he woke up I was waiting for him. Much the worse for a lost night's sleep and being clobbered by the stun grenade, not ready for it, as I had been.

Doing my best to appear composed and confident, I only paused to get him cleaned up a bit, not wanting to waste any time. We couldn't let General Simons stew for as long as we would've liked, though everything had been done that could be done to confuse and disorient him, to cause him to lose all sense of time.

When he came to, he was freshly shaved and dressed in clean prison clothes. Little things in his cell indicated a longer stay there than he had actually had.

Staring at me as his head cleared, he could hear the sounds of prison doors clanging, many feet shuffling along and voices ringing against stone walls.

'We have decided to discontinue the drugs, General,' I lied to him, smiling a friendly smile. 'You seemed to be having a reaction to them.'

'Where am I?' he croaked.

'I hoped you'd say that,' I laughed. 'I love a good cliche now and then.'

The truth was he had only been moved to the house across the street.

Nobody in Norwich ever noticed the comings and goings of Bill's group of senior citizens who were renting the place, nor any disguised additions to their number. No one in town, not even the General's security team, had realized that a small unit of well-trained and equipped young men had been arriving in the town and taking up residence just a few hundred yards from his home.

My room a few blocks away had been bugged, my clothes had been bugged and even my pyjamas had devices sewn into them to make it easy to track me and to listen to any conversations I might have had.

When I was lifted, as we had hoped and expected I might be, our people monitored me all the way. The proposed, intentionally obvious infiltration I'd prepared for, had only been a contingency plan. Our heavy-handed, unsophisticated job on Merimak had also been done largely to deceive Simons as to our methods and capabilities.

Though the lay-out of the General's house was known to us, we still wanted the advantage of my personally speaking with him to give the commandos our precise location. This assured us of taking him quickly and of doing so with the minimum of fuss or injury to his guards.

As hoped, most of the General's men had been stood down following my capture and the snatch had been easy for the excellent men Bill had hired. Sound effects had taken care of the rest. We certainly hadn't used any helicopters.

By now the commandos were out of the country and the old folks, to confuse things deliberately, made complaints and reports to the police of the noises the night before. Soon, they too would quietly depart.

Meanwhile in the basement, with new sound effects helping out, phase two, the interrogation, was about to begin.

'You screwed up pretty badly doing what you did,' I told the General, lounging on a chair in a shadowy corner of his cell. 'And now it's your ass.'

'What?' he seemed dazed still. 'What did you say?'

'Minds have been changed. New directions are being taken. Blame for the past being apportioned'

'I didn't do anything but take orders and conduct myself according to my duty, as seemed best for my country,' the General managed to say after a long pause. 'Who brought me here? What am I being charged with?'

'Murder, treason, God knows what all,' I shrugged. 'You're the scapegoat, no doubt about it, but I can't do anything to help you and I don't much want to.'

'I never murdered anyone,' he gasped. 'As to treason...'

'Two men died outside the hotel in Jordan.'

'I had nothing to do with that,' he exclaimed innocently. 'Washington asked me to phone you there and to have you speak to Dr. Merimak, but I had no idea...'

I could plainly see that he was lying.

'Who did then?' I asked. 'The president? The Secretary of...'

'No, of course not,' he insisted quickly, thinking fast before going on. 'But if a leak occurred, those who want you silenced and this message business utterly suppressed, the real extremists, may have acted independently again.'

'Independently.'

'Yes, and until they are stopped...' he paused as inspiration struck. 'Why in heaven's name do you think I have so much security? I am a target too. We are in this together...'

'I'm not a prisoner!' I pointed out cheerfully. 'You're the only one who's tried to make me one. Just a few short weeks ago...'

'Weeks, my God... All right, but I did not try to kill you,' he said gently. 'Can't you see that all along, by my own lights, and because the government insisted on our silence, that I did what I could for you, that I protected you.'

'How's that?' I smiled. He was not only buying the whole thing, but trying to manipulate me now.

'I persuaded them to try to "brainwash" you, as people call it, to keep you on in the Air Force, to let you alone all these years and not to kill you, especially lately. Some uncontrollable elements have broken the law, ignored orders and have recently tried to eliminate you against instructions. I had you brought in for your own protection as well as for mine, which lowered my security obviously and allowed...'

'Well, thanks a heap. Looks more like you lowered it only after you kidnapped me.'

'That was not the case,' he sniffed. 'Besides, it is now apparent there must have been inside co-operation with whoever has captured me. My men, a few anyway, would defy the government itself, but the rest...'

'Okay, so what?' I prodded him. 'I still don't see how we're in the same boat.'

'We know a secret only a handful of living men in the world are privy to,' he said urgently. 'We are the least senior, the least secure.'

'We? I was brainwashed, remember?' Inside I shivered with excitement. At last I was getting at the truth. 'And anyhow, you are a General...'

'But not a president, a former president or prime minister. Not a king or dictator. Very few other people of lesser rank have long survived, who know what we do.'

'And why is that, would you say?' I yawned and feigned unconcern.

'The world is not deemed ready to hear it,' he said. 'And I can only agree with that judgement.'

'Well...' I got up to leave. 'Could just be you have been wrong. Anyway, the powers that be have changed their minds. Ready or not, the world is going to hear...'

'No, I can't believe that. Not yet.' He held his groggy

head in his hands. 'There could be chaos, mass insanity. For Godsake, just like the Orson Welles radio play...'

'The War of the Worlds?' I asked, fighting the growing anxiety in my voice.

'Maybe later,' he ignored me. 'After people have been given some preparation by the governments.'

'That's starting now,' I lied, again giving him a touch of the spur.

'I don't know what to think any more,' he groaned in confusion. 'But I do believe it should be the world's governments... even the damned UN's choice when and if the message should be revealed, not you or me or your ex-wife or the press.'

'On the whole, I guess the big shots are afraid to keep this secret now, after the other messages have been coming in,' I went on lying. 'Sure, like you they're also afraid of panic, of mass hysteria or whatever, but above all, right now they fear that those sending the messages will be pissed off. The governments figure they'd better come clean.'

'So that's truly the prevailing thought now?'

'Yes, I'd say so.'

'I did warn them of the dangers of these...' he tailed off frustratingly.

'Of course you are associated with the opposite view, even with the extremist General. The one that had gunmen and bombers out doing all they could to suppress the messages.'

'It wasn't just me. I'm being set up, used,' he howled. 'The bastards are selling me out, covering themselves by blaming me.'

'Yep, that is my assessment,' I smiled, starting to go. 'But I'm okay.'

'Why are you here?' he asked suspiciously, all of a sudden. 'What have you got to do with this now?'

'I came to gloat mostly,' I admitted, a little shamefaced, sitting back down again, acting confused now myself. 'They're going to use me against you.'

'That is to be expected,' he sighed, looking keenly at me.

'You really did try to help me, didn't you?' I asked in a lowered voice. 'At the beginning and lately?'

'You bet I did,' he assured me.

'I'm supposed to get you to incriminate yourself,' I told him with my head down. 'It's funny, now they think I'm protected from "above" and they're afraid to do me in.'

'So that's it.'

'The thing in the desert was only the beginning. Weird happenings have covered my tail for some time now. I'm special, they think.'

'Maybe they are right,' he said, looking at me deeply, then a glow entered his eyes as he spoke in hopeful tones. 'You wouldn't let the people who tried to kill you use you now to destroy someone who tried to help you? Even if I was wrong at times, I did my duty, followed orders and whenever possible tried to look after you.'

'You're right,' I admitted reluctantly, in a soft voice. 'That doesn't sit very well. But what can I do about it?'

'Reveal this to the world before they do, spread the whole truth before they lie and frame me and dishonourably use you. Warn the world of the danger, above all...'

'But,' I said simply. 'I don't know, or anyway, remember the whole story, do I?'

'I will tell you,' he said with a heavy sigh.

There wasn't a scrap of evidence that anyone but a group of retired people had used the house for a few months and left it in good order. The cell arrangement in the basement no longer existed and all the sophisticated sound gear had been removed.

The General himself was caused to believe he'd taken a long airplane ride. Drugged afterward, he was dropped outside of town, within walking distance of his home. By then I'd returned to London, with a fictitious but rock-solid alibi for the entire time he had actually been missing.

I was pretty much a zombie by then though, lost in thought and confused about things. I saw Bill and expressed my compliments over his plans, but I avoided Catherine, who was very anxious to see me.

Work suffered and my personal security was lax, despite the fact that not only the extremists but perhaps the establishment itself might now be more determined to get me than ever. Hoodwinked and hoaxed, General Simons for one would certainly be seeing red.

The truth is I was indifferent to the possible, even very likely dangers, indifferent to the quest, which had been, I felt, mostly completed now. My end of it at any rate, which in itself would have been enough to leave me at a loss.

As it was, I had plenty of better reasons to be disconcerted and bewildered. Maybe the General and the powers that be had been right, I kept thinking now, as I contemplated what Simons had told me. Maybe they knew what was best.

Quite aside from public panic or riot or defiance of authority, it was impossible not to feel simply undermined. And sure, I personally felt panicky, felt like running riot with anger and frustration, felt more inclined to defy authority than ever in my life.

Above all though, as I say, I felt undermined and in several odd ways, betrayed. Eventually I knew I'd have to talk to someone and Uncle Bill seemed the best choice. After all, I owed him an explanation. Not that I didn't owe Catherine one too, but somehow I just couldn't face her. Maybe I even blamed her for what was going to happen.

Just seeing Bill, of course, was more than I wanted to bother about, but having decided to do so one evening, I crawled into the bath prior to going out. I'd become pretty grubby of late, staying in, living like an urban hermit.

As I lay there in the hot water, soaking with a wet washcloth over my face, I began to reconsider my situation.

'What the hell,' I mumbled to myself. 'I'll not only tell Bill, I'll tell the bloody world. What does it matter to me?'

'A great deal,' a soft hissing voice replied.

With a jolt I sat upright, tearing the cloth from my face and there they were. One of them seated on the dirty clothes hamper, another on the toilet with the lid down and the talkative one was perched inches from me on the edge of the bath tub.

'No, no, no,' I moaned. 'Not you guys.'

'Surely you did not honestly think we would be far away at a time like this.'

The other two MIBs nodded in agreement with their spokesman.

'Why can't you leave me in peace?'

'Why can't you leave yourself in peace?'

'Is it one and the same thing? Are you my fears personified?'

'Leave these strange matters that do not belong in your life quite alone, and you will never see us again.'

'Is that a promise?'

'An absolute guarantee.'

'I can't unlearn anything. I can't forget what I know.'

'Do you regret not having listened to us now?'

'Maybe.'

'It is not too late to minimise the damage. Try to put

your life back together again. It is not right that you should be troubled or that you should trouble others. You must not think simply of yourself.'

'Get out of here. Why do you care so much? What is it to you?'

'We must guard against the breaking of the rules.'

'What rules?'

'Those that govern the world, make it real, make it logical and keep it running as it is, as it always has been.'

'It's pretty screwed up and always has been.'

'But isn't it this, the eventual loss of these things, that you now regret? The old established ways, the human dilemmas, the challenges, the certainties and normality you believe in?'

'Not all of it, no. Not a whole hell of a lot of it. Quit confusing me and trying to scare me, I'm scared enough as it is.'

'It is your profession to protect people. Should you not protect them now? All of them? Should you not spare them the moral, psychological and physical bewilderment you are now experiencing? The inevitable social confusion and breakdown...'

'Oh lay off, will you?' I cried, slapping the bath water with my fist.

'Be careful,' said the wordy one on the edge of the tub, looking aghast at his dampened trouser legs. 'I would strongly advise you not to get us wet.'

'Oh yeah, and what if I do?'

'I can assure you, you will very much regret it. Very much!'

'I doubt it, you mock sinister little bastards,' I sneered at them struggling to my feet. 'But let's just see, shall we?'

'It is most unwise,' the speaker waved his tiny, pale hands.

I was dancing in the tub by now though, kicking water

at them, bending over to cup it into my hands to throw it at them, splash it at them.

Losing my balance, however, I fell back into the tub, howling with laughter at their discomfiture, landing on my ass in the bath and sending a tidal wave over the edge to cascade across the floor. The laugh was cut short when my head struck the tiled wall . Rubbing it vigorously, eyes tight shut against the pain, I took up the laugh again but on opening my eyes a moment later I realized they had gone.

I'd seen them off sharpish, I thought. Good. Then I noticed the soaking bathroom rug, the pools of water in the corner, the sopping towel on the rack.

My downstairs neighbour would soon be pounding at the front door, insisting on an explanation for his dripping kitchen ceiling and ruined dinner. The Men In Black had been right. I was sorry I'd tried to get them wet.

Maybe, I thought suddenly, they'd been right about the rest of it too.

I was late and all the more depressed when I got to Uncle Bill's borrowed flat in Chelsea. The fact that Catherine was there almost made me cry or turn around and leave. How could I speak to her about what was driving me crazy when I knew she would almost certainly not share my fears?

While it would probably be good news to her, by contrast, I figured Uncle Bill might be as concerned as I was. At that point, my misery longed only for company, not confrontation.

'I didn't tell her you were coming,' Bill whispered, letting me in with a sheepish expression. 'She simply dropped by.'

I said nothing and went over to flop onto the couch, while Bill hustled around pouring drinks and Catherine patrolled in front of the mantle, occasionally eyeing me resentfully.

I was obviously in the doghouse but could not honestly be troubled to worry about it. This state of mind must have been written all over my face, which made matters worse.

'Why have you been so unavailable?' she asked finally after Bill had handed me a drink and refilled hers.

'Me?'

'Yes, you,' she snapped. 'We have...'

Bill gave her a stern look and she changed her tone.

'What happened to you over there?' she went on more gently. 'What did you find out? Uncle Bill is ready to burst with curiosity and so am I.'

'Well...' Bill made a dismissive gesture but his eyes betrayed him. 'One does wonder just how successful we were. You said it worked but...' He trailed off, not looking at me though practically asking with his back.

Settling in an armchair, Bill faced me again and smiled.

'He'll tell us when he is ready,' he said to Catherine. 'If he thinks it's any of our business.'

'Our business,' she gasped, turning to me in wonder. 'What is that supposed to mean? Whose side are you on?'

'Now, now Cathy, it isn't as simple as that,' her uncle said calmly. 'He has quite a lot to take into consideration...'

'You've remembered it, haven't you?' she insisted 'You know again what the "First Message" is.'

'Yes,' I sighed.

She studied my face for a long time and glanced at Bill, then back at me.

'Is it that bad?'

'I don't even know,' I said. 'I mean I can't honestly say. Depends on your point of view, your opinion for good or ill of mankind...' I shrugged helplessly.

'Are you afraid we'd be better off not knowing?' Bill wondered.

'That seems to be the official view so far,' I reminded them.

'I'm asking for yours,' he said.

'Maybe...'

'Dammit man,' Uncle Bill barked. 'I'm not interested in equivocation, some carefully weighed, considered opinion. You've had days, weeks for that, and it hasn't worked. Tell us your own view now, what you really think, in your heart and in your gut. If it's your opinion that we shouldn't be privy to the information, the Message, then I'll never ask you about it again. Nor will she in my presence, or I'll turn her over my knee like a four-year-old.'

'Oh really?' Catherine laughed. 'All right,' she then said solemnly after a pause. 'I promise, too. Well?'

'In my heart and in my gut... I believe you have a right to know,' I decided, head in hands.

They waited expectantly, but I didn't go on.

'Right,' Bill sipped his drink, relaxing back into his chair. 'Tell us in your own time. But one other thing needs addressing. We've been involved in this and have each had dealings with security matters in my case and the paranormal in Catherine's. Fine! But does the public have the right to know? That too, as your countrymen say, inspired by the duties of baseball umpires I believe, is "your call". So...?'

'I guess,' I said softly, reluctantly. 'Yes, they do have the right to know.'

'Good, I'd hoped you'd feel that way,' he smiled.

'So did I,' Catherine sighed loudly and sank onto the couch beside me. Both of them fell to looking at their shoes, the pictures on the wall, the liquid in their glasses.

'Your James Bond gambit really was a masterpiece,' I

told Bill, not for the first time but by way of getting started. 'The interrogation technique we devised worked perfectly. As we suspected, it must have been just what the General secretly feared.'

'Splendid,' Bill smiled. 'Splendid!' Then he gave an encourging nod. Catherine sat on the edge of her seat, half turned to face me, holding her breath.

'He told me... everything,' I said in an unconscious whisper. 'Simons and I heard the "First Message" together just as Dr. Merimak supposed we had.'

'And?' Catherine prompted very softly.

'They...' I swallowed hard and stopped, feeling myself begining to shake. 'They are coming. Coming soon.'

'What? Who...?' Bill burbled excitedly.

'When? How soon?' Catherine gasped.

'December 22, 2012.' I blurted it out, practically spat it out. 'I dreamt it later, remembered it even, getting the message and what it did to us. I know the General is not lying or mistaken. I don't have a blank spot now. It's as if the spell of the brain-washing has been lifted. But now I have this horrible nightmare vision of a nasty grey little bastard with big, black, watermelon-seed-shaped eyes staring greedily at my planet. I have premonitions of order breaking down all over the globe, of all personal, moral, religious, political bets being cancelled. Of conquest or domination, or just plain condescension, and the loss of all human pride and honour and independence. And no matter what I think personally or what I said a minute ago, shouldn't it be the UN who decides how or if the people of the world find this out? It's not my call, it's not!'

Catherine put her arms around me and Bill stood up and came over to pat me on the shoulder. We were silent for a long time, it seemed to me, and during the silence I realised that neither of them was as surprised, excited, or disturbed as I had imagined they'd be. The initial, specific information had taken them aback some and the nearness of the date, but that was all.

'Well,' Bill said at last, 'I think you'd better tell him about the German chap's communications and I'll fetch us the other half of these drinks and pontificate upon my theories about it all.'

'Schiller is a very respected computer expert, a humorous and intelligent man, and as secular as anyone alive,' Catherine assured me. 'He has been asked to write a programme, a sort of compilation of the world's religions, a distillation of man's most common beliefs.'

'That is, the things we most have in common,' Bill said. 'It's a subject that has fascinated me for years. Amazing how much just about everyone on the planet takes as given, things that are not concrete or of a factual nature. Creation myths are utterly universal and virtually the same everywhere.'

'A belief in some form of after-life is ubiquitous,' Catherine insisted. 'Basic moral values...'

'But they, the beings Schiller spoke to, told him humanity actually knows the truth.' Bill explained. 'The whole truth about our beginnings, whether we realize it or not.'

'Yes, that's the main thing. It is apparently part of the collective consciousness.' She spread her arms and dropped them. 'In each of us as a genetic memory, I suppose. Lost, like your own memory of the "First Message".'

'And Schiller is expected to remind us somehow?'

'That's what he believes,' Catherine said. 'And I believe him.'

'Incredible, isn't it?' Bill sighed, by now pouring not the second drink but my fourth and Catherine's fifth. No telling how many he had had before either Catherine or I had arrived.

'Yet, it is perfectly logical,' he went on, 'in its way and more or less acceptable in terms of faith and the established faiths themselves. What Schiller saw,' Bill went on, 'instead of any of the old illusions about spacemen, shamans, or angels, also tallies with my own theories.'

Okay, I was thinking after hearing more details Schiller had been visited by our now familiar messengers, in yet another guise. That of quite ethereal but recognizably human-seeming beings who wanted him to develop this computer programme containing details of all known religions, beliefs and mankind's chief prophecies.

'So Schiller's work, this distillation of basic elements and common threads, will hopefully contain the closest thing to the truth we can understand? And maybe trigger the hidden memories?'

'Or at least give us a starting place from which we might begin to understand or recall the truth,' Catherine said.

'To understand our origins at last, who we were then and why we're here now,' Bill enthused. 'To see our place in nature and the universe.'

'But who are they?' I asked. 'What are we to them?'

'I think, simply put, that they might be us,' Bill said. 'That just as the Men In Black are our fears incarnate, they, these beings, extra-terrestrials or angels or what have you, may be us as well. Our higher selves, our spirits, for want of a better word.'

'That's your theory and you're sticking to it,' I smiled.

'Well, part of my theory,' Bill nodded. 'It isn't complete yet.'

'But whatever the truth is,' Catherine unconsciously stroked my troubled cheek, then drew back quickly, 'the next name is that of a United Nations official, so maybe you, and the rest of us, even General Simons and the President are off the hook.'

'I'm damned sure not going back to New York,' I told them flatly. 'And Bill, you had best not, either.'

'No need,' Catherine grinned. 'Our man, Mr. Ngao Hatomba, is on holiday in Scotland.'

Chapter Twenty

Jonas Hatomba was a pretty fanatical fly fisherman, for someone brought up in a village on the west coast of Africa until he was ten years old. Apparently, he had only discovered the joys and frustrations of pursuing trout when he was in his twenties at Oxford and visiting a fellow student's family in the Highlands.

As it happened, we were not alone on the trip up north to meet the vacationing UN official. Though Uncle Bill stayed home, Schiller had joined us. To say I was not best pleased would be an understatement.

With all that had happened recently and all that would doubtless happen soon, I had a very strong desire to finally establish, or rather re-establish, my relationship with Catherine.

I knew by now that I loved her and needed her and I felt profoundly that she loved and needed me, too. The problem was going to be creating a romantic situation and getting her in the mood to admit it. Instead, we had a talkative boffin in the car all the way up to Scotland

I had a paranoia about flying with so many people out to get us. A small bomb would be very easy to plant on a domestic flight and would take out everyone on board, not just us. So, knowing our enemies were fully capable of such a thing, we decided to drive.

Though, as I say, I would have liked to be alone with Catherine, Schiller's company was impossible to resent. He had a good sense of humour and was a steady, reliable and fast driver during his spells behind the wheel. What's more, he was even distantly related to the playwright of the same name.

We spoke English for Catherine's sake, after a few jokes in and on the German languge. It seemed, too, that my paternal grandparents had come from near his own neighbourhood in Berlin, before becoming political exiles under the Nazis.

'My family stayed,' he said, 'as oppressor and oppressed. I'm part Jewish, you see. Perhaps that is why I got the message I did. I was told the greatest need today is to promote the spirit of unity and unity of spirit.'

This was something he kept reminding us of. That had been the real gist of his message from 'beyond'.

'Spiritual unity and unity of spirituality.'

'What was that once again?' I asked, smiling ironically somewhere outside Edinburgh.

Damned if he didn't go on to repeat it with a straight face for what must have been the twentieth time, before bursting out laughing.

Between Schiller's enthusiasm and Catherine's energy, I was getting back my own keenness to fulfil the quest, to find out what was really going on, what the point of it all was and who the senders of the messages really were.

'I've decided what we'll do when we locate the ambassador,' I announced.

'And what is that, pray tell?' Catherine asked glancing at me and then watching the road again as she sat behind the wheel.

'Well, he might not like his holiday being interrupted. If he hasn't been contacted yet, we might just encounter disapproval again, à la Petra. You and I are becoming somewhat notorious, Catherine.'

'So?'

'So,' I turned in my seat to grin at the gentleman in the back, 'we send in Herr Schiller, of course.'

What I didn't know was that Hatomba was positively looking for us, and that even if he hadn't been, an awkward reception was nothing compared with what did await us.

It was on the last leg, heading down the mountains toward the Spey valley on a lonely, narrow, winding road. A black Mercedes was following us and I began to wonder if it were the Men In Black, as it stayed back on the long straight road out of Braemar.

We recklessly speeded up on the roller-coaster road, losing our stomachs and feeling our scalps crawl as we crested blind hills, fearing cars coming head on. All the way they stayed with us.

Once into the Cairngorms, though, we had to slow down. Along the way were snow poles to mark the route in bad weather. There were passing places but the road itself was one lane.

For miles and miles no other vehicles or buildings were visible. On the heights around us snow still lingered, despite the warm season, and there were no trees and not even any sheep.

In Scotland, if there aren't sheep around, you know it's rough country. A break-down up there in those mountains would have been a nightmare. What we got, of course, was worse.

They came up fast, hugging the sharp turns and stuck to our back bumper like a burr on a sock. Schiller was at the wheel but this was no autobahn and I wished Catherine was driving. I thought they were going to ram us when, in true movie style, a guy leaned out of the passenger window with a Skorpion machine pistol.

'Duck,' I screamed and we did our best to. Poor Schiller had to watch the road, though, and as I curled up on the back seat and Catherine crouched in the space her feet had occupied in the front, bullets smacked into the boot of the car, shattered the back windows and passed through the front windscreen.

A large chunk was taken out of the headrest beside

Schiller's ear, then a series of tight turns got us out of the line of fire for a moment. They'd be reloading, I knew.

I was glad they didn't have an assault rifle and that the trunk of our car was full of luggage and computer gear, otherwise bullets would have gone right through the whole car, our bodies and out the other side, or only stopped on hitting the engine.

'You still have that Walther 9mm/k I gave you?' I called to Catherine, drawing my Browning.

'Yes,' she said and I saw her reach for her handbag and then heard the slide being cocked. 'Shall we lean out and let them have it?'

'No,' I yelled. 'Schiller?'

'Yah?'

'Pull up suddenly at the next stopping place after a turn. Catherine, we rake them with fire as they pass. Aim for the guy with the gun, or the door he is behind. It won't stop a jacketed 9mm.'

We came almost at once to the ideal spot, a space to pull into just after a blind turn. Our car screeched to a halt and we crashed into the front seat, dashboard and steering wheel respectively, but in an instant Catherine and I were up, aiming out of our windows and there they were, flashing by, the one with the Skorpion leaning out, looking forward. They saw us too late and got our full collective dose of twenty-one rounds.

It seemed to happen in slow motion, as is often the way of such things. The Mercedes swerved and lurched. I think the driver must have been hit too, but the shooter fell back limp and dropped the Skorpion into the road. Panicking and picking up speed they roared ahead and disappeared.

'Now we've done it,' Catherine said in a quivering voice. 'We've shot someone. We've riddled a car with bullets and we are driving a bullet-riddled car ourselves. If we don't go to the police, we are bound to be arrested before we've gone ten miles.'

'Let's worry about that when we are out of the woods,' I said, getting out to wreak and bury the Skorpion.

'Woods?' Schiller cried. 'I have not seen a tree in an hour.'

'It's an expression,' I told him. 'When we are off this damn mountain, I mean. And believe me, ' I said, 'they'll try again, and soon.'

I was right.

Getting to Hatomba seemed to be our safest course. We called Uncle Bill on our new mobile phone to warn him about the attack and he explained that Hatomba had been ringing us. He even seemed to be trying to decide whether to come to London.

Hatomba, it seemed, had received his message from the beings while up to his hips in the Spey and with a fish struggling on his line. We supposed he must have heard of us on the grapevine and so had tried to get in touch and got Bill instead. Bill informed him of our assumed imminent arrival in Scotland.

Going forward now worried me. It was heading toward trouble. I figured that our attackers' alternative ambush would be lying up there in readiness; that they would not even have to adapt a bit after the failure of their first attempt.

They would go with the contingency, as if it was planned, just as if the first one had never happened, as if they had just lost us. It would go ahead smoothly, I knew, and if they were any good, their wounded man would be treated by a trusted medic, the car and dead man disposed of quietly.

The cliff they chose was not as high as they might have hoped for but the best the mountain could provide. The spot was just before the end of the desolate high country and in distant sight of the valley with its farms and distilleries below.

They simply rammed us with a large truck. It sat in a passing place as we came over a rise and slowly approached. It seemed a normal sort of goods lorry, but as we drew near it moved forward, collided with the front of our car and rocked us backward, then began to push.

Our tyres screamed and smoke flew from our wheels as Schiller desperately tried to shift into reverse. By then, however, we were teetering on the edge, the ground crumbling beneath us for agonizing seconds and then we were over, falling.

Our car rolled on its side and tumbled, hit a boulder and flipped. For one clear moment we were fully airborne and then white light filled the car. There was no blacking out or blocking out, no lost time. One instant we were in the car falling off a mountain and in the next we were not. Just skidding on our hands and knees or rumps through the dirt, with heather, rocks and gorse bushes scratching us up and bruising us. Our clothes were shredded.

Still skidding along, I caught glimpses of the car below us, banging and shattering its way down the mountainside, its petrol tank exploding in an orange cloud of flame.

We were a trio of ragamuffins when at last we wandered into the riverside hotel where Hatomba was staying and asked for rooms of our own. The little village of Craigellechi had no clothing stores and it was too late to have the taxi we'd called from a farmhouse take us into a larger one like Dufftown or Keith to buy some. Everything closes early in that part of the world, though the light lingers late in high summer.

Hatomba was completely on his own and stood out a mile with his large frame and blue-black skin. At first as shocked by our appearance as were the hotel staff, he began to laugh in a voice that came right up from the soles of his green rubber waders, making his body and the fishing poles over his shoulder shake.

Just in from the stream, he needlessly introduced himself, as we did. After gaping at us, the hotel manager finally booked us in a few minutes later, and Hatomba visited each of our rooms with clean clothes for us to wear after cleaning up.

Catherine had, to my disappointment, taken a separate room without hesitation and my hope of a more pleasantly inspired and more consciously undertaken repeat of our last night in Jordan was in vain.

We gathered in the bar after a while, patched up, clean and odder-looking than ever. If in trying on the shirt and trousers Hatomba had given me, I had thought them too big by a third and too long by an inch or more and that I would appear a little ridiculous, I had not considered Herr Schiller's predicament.

He was in a bright blue pair of Bermuda shorts gathered around his small waist like the top of a lamp shade and belled out beneath, going well past his knees. I wondered why he had not left the T- shirt out instead of tucking it in until Catherine came down and I saw how much funnier it would have been on him that way.

She wore a dress shirt of the ambassador's that was a dress indeed on her. A school tie around her waist for a belt completed the ensemble. As her handbag was clutched in her arms on our miraculous exit from the car, she was perfectly made up and rather enchanting. As for me, I just looked like I'd lost a lot of weight in a hurry.

Hatomba gave another laugh as we appeared one by one and then ordered a round of drinks. Obviously not over the euphoria that accompanied seeing the beings and hearing their messages, he was in fine form and overjoyed to have someone to talk to about it.

In our little corner, tucked away from the rest of the customers as much to hide ourselves from view as to hold a private conversation, we three who had survived the car crash were silent and thoughtful for the most part, as Hatomba related his encounter. Only when he described the beings did Schiller perk up.

'They sound just the same as mine,' he said.

'Is that such a surprise?' Hatomba smiled.

'I understand from Ms. Frazier that it is most unusual,' the German insisted.

'Really?'

'It's the first time since this began that it has happened,' Catherine admitted. 'That two separate people seemed to see exactly the same sort of beings. Herr Schiller was the first who described them under hypnosis just as he had otherwise.'

'It will be interesting to see if I do the same,' Hatomba nodded. He and Schiller began to compare notes and found more things common to both of their experiences.

'Did they appear to find it difficult to make themselves seen and heard?' Schiller asked excitedly.

'Yes, they even said it was,' Hatomba confirmed.

'Did they move oddly?' I asked thinking of the Men In Black.

'No,' both men said almost at the same time.

'They were like us, then?' Catherine wondered. 'Quite human or something else?'

'Yes, they were very much human, not ghosts or space creatures or strange apparitions, but more than human, as well. Spiritual and spirit-like,' Hatomba shrugged. 'That is how I perceived them.'

'Not angels?' I asked, looking from one man to the other.

'Oh, perhaps,' Schiller grinned indulgently. 'One might call them that.'

'I was brought up a devout Christian,' Hatomba raised his eyebrows, 'and I would not have taken them for angels... I did not... but it is possible. They had no wings, harps or haloes,' he laughed. 'But in many ways they were more angelic than anything else. They did not seem to be extra-terrestrials in the science fiction way, although that word would also describe them. They were not of this world, certainly, but not, I would say, alien to it. Does that make sense or is it a contradiction in terms?'

'And they just came to you while you were fishing?' Catherine asked. 'Were there other fishermen around?'

'Some a hundred yards upstream, another walking along the bank. No one saw the light, the beings, or my reactions. No one seemed to hear anything.'

'What did they tell you?' I asked.

'To contact you,' Hatomba said, looking into my eyes.

Expecting another revelation or high-minded instruction, I was taken way off guard. Staring at him, I began to go very dry in the mouth and took a big swig of my drink.

'What did they want you to say to him?' Catherine asked.

'To ask him to pass on the "First Message",' Hatomba said simply and with a degree of puzzlement. 'They seemed at a loss as to why you hadn't done so already.'

Chivvying me along had not been Hatomba's only assignment. It was after the bar had closed and we had gone up to his room, so that Catherine could hypnotize him, that we heard more about that. I couldn't help wondering how it was that he was so cheerful when I found out about it.

'We are...' he said, pouring from a bottle of Glenfiddich, a souvenir from the distillery. 'We are each of us, as individuals and as nations and as peoples, to examine our guilt. To contemplate our transgressions.'

'What the hell does that mean? What does it involve?' I exclaimed.

'Obvious ones for nations or peoples would be the slave trade, the genocides on Armenians by the Turks and the Jews by the Germans. But do not suppose this is some racial or Third World, anti-imperial notion of mine. They made it quite clear that no people or nation is guiltless, any more than any person is. My people were enriched by the slave trade, not victims of it. We sold prisoners of our wars, the poor of our own homeland for money, goods and power. The Maoris of New Zealand drove out the Maorioris. The Sioux drove other tribes from the land the Americans stole from them. All over the globe from the beginning it has been the same. Everybody takes a turn and what is in the heart is what matters. Would not Shaka Zulu have conquered the world given iron ships and guns? Would Stalin not have gladly taken Germany and Eastern Europe with or without Hitler and fascism to defeat?'

'I'm no historian but I see the point,' I said.

'Despite my family's past,' Schiller began, 'I have never done anything politically to help make Turks and members of other immigrant groups, who've been in Germany for generations, full citizens. I have never even given money to charities...'

'The beings made it clear that we are all, every one, every group subject to guilt and obliged to examine ourselves. I am somehow supposed to lead the way, encourage this mass, collective and individual soul-searching,' Hatomba smiled. 'It is quite fantastic, but I truly believe it can be done and will make a tremendous difference.'

We gave ourselves a few moments to let this settle in before anyone spoke again. I was desperately trying to make sense of it all in the context of the other messages. I was too tired and too beat up to think clearly. For heaven's sake, I should have been dead. So should Catherine and Schiller.

We were probably in grave danger now and we were dressed like clowns in a hotel room in the remote Highlands of Scotland, our guns were in Hatomba's suitcase becaue of his diplomatic immunity. Later they would be mailed to Bill in case too much police interest resulted from the accident, or shell cases were found on the road. Worse still, if the attackers' car or dead man came to light.

And now I also had to deal with these beings, whoever and whatever they might be, insisting I make public their impending arrival.

The assessment of my personal and shared guilt was something I'd just have to take care of later, I thought, little knowing I'd soon have ample time for it. We were going to have to get to Inverness or Aberdeen in the morning, and risk flying back to London.

If Hatomba had the name of another receiver of messages, they could damn well be told to come to see us this time: I wasn't budging. It might be wise, I realized, to admit that there could be messages coming in regularly for years.

'Why don't we get on with the hypnosis,' I suggested, 'and then turn in?'

They got down to it quickly and everything went well. Once more there was no difference in the description of the beings, let alone the experience or the message. No name came up now either, but Travier and others, I recalled, had not got one either until afterward, so that didn't matter.

Saying our goodnights to Schiller and Hatomba a bit later, I walked Catherine to the door of her room.

'What do you make of all this?' I asked her.

'Things are changing,' she observed.

'Are they upping the stakes?'

'What?' she wrinkled her brow. 'Oh, in a way perhaps.'

'And this new image,' I pointed out, 'and the stated difficulty the beings had getting through, as it were.'

'It fits what they all said they saw under hypnosis...'

'But these last two...'

'While conscious as well, yes.' Catherine yawned. 'Uncle Bill would probably say they are harder to see now because they are not drawing on the subject's imagination any more.'

'Or they have decided to really and truly deceive us as to their appearance...'

'Maybe,' she yawned again. 'See you in the morning.'

Neither of us moved, her door was opened and all she had to do was step in. I had only to half turn and walk three feet to my room. For once, these things were harder than what we did do. For once contact, vulnerability, emotion and warmth were easier. I reached out for her just as she fell into my arms.

'Why didn't we die today?' she whispered.

'God knows,' I sighed. 'We just have to keep going until we find out.'

'Today was the first thing like that ever to happen to me. The MIBs were something quite different, and even seeing that strange flame from your empty rifle in New Mexico was not the same either. Today we disappeared, or flew or...'

'Were simply thrown from the car,' I had to say. 'I know it was more than that, but what it was exactly I can't imagine.'

'A miracle, a dematerialization.' Catherine shook her head. 'I can imagine it, I just can't believe it or forget it, or...' I kissed her and we held it for a long while and I began to slowly waltz her into her room.

'Wait,' she said, breaking from the kiss but not the embrace. 'I don't think it would be a good idea. Not tonight.' With a smile she separated herself from me and patted my arm. 'If I were you, I'd start thinking about how I was going to explain all this to the world, or even just to the press.'

Waking up in the morning, I felt pretty good. We seemed to be protected by a power far greater than my meagre security firm could provide, Catherine and I were finally drawing closer and I was beginning to believe that whatever was going on just might be for good rather than ill. That whoever the beings were, they didn't display a propensity for force. I couldn't fault any of the messages for positive intent and only people I rated as wrong-headed or plain bad seemed determined to oppose them.

I went down to breakfast, and despite my outsized borrowed clothes felt ready to face the world and anything it could throw at me. Anything, that is, except what it did throw.

I'd just sat down and ordered a big pot of tea with bacon, egg and chips soon to follow, when the police came in. This did not surprise me, as we had phoned them the night before.

Our story was that the driver had lost control of our car and it had gone off the cliff. All three of us had managed to jump clear before it hit the steepest bit. Let them prove otherwise. I had no intention of getting embroiled with them over our attempted murder, or of explaining how we had shot someone earlier. I only hoped the assassins hadn't screwed up and got caught.

'It's about our car, I'm sure,' I said when they asked me to identify myself. 'Please sit down and I'll give you all the details.'

We had worked out our story as we walked off the mountain to the nearest farm, so I had no fear we'd cross ourselves up. Schiller and Catherine would have to speak to the local authorities later.

'I don't know what you mean,' the uniformed young man said, glancing at a plainclothes type beside him. On second glance I realized this one was not local, but most likely Special Branch. I had to suppress a shiver. Had they found the bad guys' bullet-riddled car, the body of the gunman, or captured his accomplice?

'I have to inform you that you are under arrest and that

anything you say may be taken down and used in evidence against you,' the plainclothes man announced grimly. 'Come with us, please.'

'What am I supposed to have done?' I asked, choking back a frog in my throat. Murder. I just knew they were going to say murder.

'Violations under the Official Secrets Act.' They took me by my arms and lifted me from my chair.

'Wait, let me see your identification,' I said, confused and growing desperate. These could be the killers back for a another, more subtle, try. 'And the warrant.'

'Certainly,' the Scotland Yard man obliged and I looked very carefully at everything. It was all in order and the local cop, I learned in the ensuing fuss around me, was known to the hotel staff and had also checked the Special Branch man's bona fides.

As the others came downstairs, Hatomba tried to intervene. Catherine railed at them and found she too was under arrest. Schiller flapped around until he was informed that he was being taken to Inverness to be put on a plane to Germany by order of the Home Office.

Even Hatomba himself had been called urgently to New York by the United Nations.

They hauled all three of us off just as we were, in the same silly things we were wearing, me in handcuffs, no less. Schiller would be let go once he was in Germany, and he promised to continue his work on the faith and belief computations, as well as campaigning for our release. Hatomba did the same.

For my part, I was too amazed, amused, worried and perplexed to know what to make of any of it. Despite my security work in the United Kingdom, I had never signed the Official Secrets Act and I was absolutely sure Catherine had not either. Something very big and very shady was going on.

Chapter Twenty-One

As I sat in my cell, I kept thinking of how I'd tricked Simons and it gnawed at me that the irony would please him, that it might even have been part of the intention. I learned too, just after arriving in London under guard and still in cuffs, that Uncle Bill was also under arrest. He too was charged with crimes relating to the Official Secrets Act, which he at least might actually have signed at some point in his life.

The thing was, I knew that if they looked harder, on the other side of the Atlantic especially, they could have charged us with so much more.

'I can only suppose they do not wish to go that far,' my attorney explained while visiting me in jail. 'They would obviously have to incriminate themselves to do so, from what you tell me, just as you will to defend yourselves properly here.'

'How are Catherine and Bill doing?' I asked.

'Fine. As confused as you over all this, I dare say.' He tapped his pen on the table where the papers relating to the case lay. 'And like you they are certain they have not signed the Act, though the government insist the documents are extant and will be produced at your hearing.'

'Forgeries,' I groaned. 'When is Catherine supposed to have had occasion to sign the Official Secrets Act?'

'While investigating a haunted R.A.F. hangar, apparently.'

'As for Bill, I guess he probably did sign in his youth, but just what official secrets have we divulged or threatened to divulge? They don't recognize the existence of extra- terrestrials, don't regulate the paranormal.'

'All I know is that there is a D notice, a gagging order, on the whole thing. None of us can talk to the press or they to us.'

'Have you spoken to the government minister I told you about?'

'Out of the country, seeing the Tokyo transport system or something.'

'It's all rigged, I tell you.'

'I'm sure you are right,' my 'brief' smiled reassuringly. 'And I'll demonstrate that at the hearing. They can't have managed this flawlessly. They can't have the judge in their pockets.' He smiled awkwardly as if to say 'I hope'. 'It would have to be a conspiracy on a massive international scale...'

'It probably is,' I assured him sadly, a major depression setting in on me. So far only the American government, and especially extremists in its service, had been out to silence us, if not downright do us in. Now the Brits were involved and I didn't see a way out if they had decided to cheat from on high.

They could frame us with anything short of murder and we'd have to take it unless we wanted to confess, tell our story and hope the jury realized our shooting back had been in self-defence.

'The entire business is so extraordinary, I can hardly believe it,' my lawyer shrugged. 'A grand conspiracy would just about be par for the course, I imagine.' He smiled awkwardly again, and I suddenly realized they had got to him or that they shortly would.

'Any chance of my seeing Catherine or Bill?'

'I'll ask again, but I must say it seems unlikely...'

'Forget it,' I said. Why was I paying this guy, I wondered. With all the extra duties I'd had my people on lately, which I'd paid for myself, all my neglect of work, our various travels, the operation to snatch and pump Simons, I could hardly afford it even if the fellow had been the best legal mind since Clarence Darrow.

'It is worth trying. I'll see...'

'No,' I said. 'I don't think I'll require your services at all, as it happens.' Even if he was straight, even if I could find the money from somewhere, what was the use of getting the poor guy in trouble? Why get him harassed, threatened maybe? Why bring him to the inevitable crisis of conscience?

'You want another lawyer?' he asked almost hopefully.

'No,' I shook my head.

'Surely you're not thinking of conducting your own defence?'

'Why not?' I perked up. Why not, indeed? It might be fun and if I didn't stand a chance anyhow, why not indulge myself a little? Why not play Rumpole of the Bailey or Perry Mason just once?

'I had begun to think you were mad,' the lawyer said, gathering up his things. 'And now I am certain of it. Good day and good luck. You'll need it.' With that he left and I was taken back to my lonely cell.

Lying on my bunk, my arm over my eyes, I did not hear the door open or anyone approach the bars. Nevertheless, I knew I was not alone in the cell anymore. I didn't need three guesses to tell who it was.

'Sorry there's no place for you boys to sit,' I said.

'We will not be staying long,' replied the voice of the mouthpiece of the Men In Black. 'Do you see what your exertions have got you?'

'Come to gloat, have you?' I asked, with painful memories once more of my short-lived triumph against General Simons. 'Go ahead. Enjoy.'

'We are here to advise you,' the MIB spokesman insisted. 'There is yet time...'

'Can you get me out of here?'

'Well, I am afraid...'

'If I swear to be a good boy and shut up, if I promise to cease and desist, can you guys get me out?'

'That is not our function, not our...'

'Not within your power.'

'Do not underestimate our power,' he said heavily, darkly.

'Oh please,' I groaned. 'Enough of the drama, you useless little creeps.'

'We are here to warn you to co-operate with the authorities. If you do, surely they will let you out eventually. Naturally we cannot tip our hand. To demonstrate our power, our existence, would be counter to our purpose.'

'Oh yes and give away the existence too of what you are duty-bound to keep secret,' I laughed. 'You jerks couldn't move a flying dandelion seed, even if you wanted to, let alone make a blind bit of difference in the physical world.'

'Our kind have done more than you can imagine.'

'Yes,' I admitted on reflection. 'You probably have,but not with me. I'm on to you, and anyway I'm such a damn pessimist at heart that I always actually expect the worst. Ergo, you can't affect me much...'

'Most regrettable,' he allowed.

'So there,' I said, glorying in this small victory.

'Are you not even a little sorry for it?' the Man In Black asked with for the first time a hint of an emotion in his mechanically reproduced sounding voice. I sat up and looked at them ranged in a neat row at the foot of my bunk.

'I guess I am, to some degree, but what the hell is it to you? You can't possibly give a damn.'

'Our mission...'

'Oh, cut that out,' I said impatiently cutting him off.

'Our mission, as I say,' he continued simply and then I saw what he might have meant. Their mission was to frighten me and always had been. To frighten me not just away from looking into aliens or the paranormal.

'Why do I hate the water, why don't I ever go to the beach?' I asked suddenly. 'Why do I hate boats?'

'You were nearly drowned on vacation in Florida as a two-year-old,' the MIB said flatly. 'Your mother felt very guilty and never told you about it. But with our unseen help you remembered inside.'

'I see.'

'If only you were so sensible in regard to other matters.'

'Oh well,' I said and eyed them closely. 'So you don't have anything to do with outer space or mysteries or other dimensions. You just imply that, and have only appeared now because it is...'

'The truth,' the middle one in the row who did all the talking said quickly. 'We are of a world you cannot imagine, we have abilities beyond your ken, we will destroy you and those you love if you defy us. The unknown must be preserved. Man is not ready...'

'Put a sock in it, will you?' I lay back on the bunk and closed my eyes. 'Thanks for coming, guys, now piss off. And bring some fruit next time.'

Chapter Twenty-Two

All that happened next is a bit blurred in my memory and some of it makes so little sense as to seem almost Kafkaesque. Our hearing was closed, of course, and more than a bit of a farce. I saw Catherine and Bill but we were not allowed to speak. None of it seemed to be properly conducted, and I began to see more clearly than ever that we were being taken for a ride.

Because I was not let near other prisoners and I'd got rid of my lawyer, I had no way of getting a message out to anyone who might help us. I was not permitted to have visitors either.

There was now next to no question that we were all illegally imprisoned and that either they'd throw away the key or just keep us hidden for as long as they could, or as long as they needed to.

The fact that they were nevertheless going through some semblance of legal motions at least pointed to the latter. That they'd eventually take the political and legal embarrassment that would result, in order to have us out of the way now. They were buying themselves some time. What they were doing with that time I dared not guess and soon enough could hardly care about.

My morale plummeted still farther when I dwelt upon all this alone in my cell. We could be in jail for months, years even, I knew. So what if we might sue for false arrest eventually and win a fortune? If the 'First Message' were true, there wasn't a lot of time left, before the world was probably going to change beyond recognition.

What really sent my spirits into the depths was the

judge. A nasty old establishment stooge and haughty-voiced sour-puss. No bail was to be granted to any of us, the proceedings were to remain secret and we were still to be kept in solitary confinement. No trial date was set and the lawyer, still acting for Catherine and Bill, demonstrated his complete unwillingness to challenge anything. He was under the authorities' thumb, too. We were utterly beaten.

'It is my duty to try to dissuade you from conducting your own defence,' the dour old stick of a judge said lazily, looking down his long nose at me. From his expression you'd have thought he was examining a rather substandard maggot.

'Much obliged your honour, I mean, m'lord.' I half bowed. 'I'll persevere, however. It gives me something to do during my unlawful incarceration.' They had brought me all the law books I required.

'I would further advise you,' he leaned menacingly over the bench, 'to desist from such remarks. Otherwise,' he breathed heavily and rolled his watery old eyes, 'I may find you in contempt of court.'

'But m'lord,' I smiled and said helpfully, 'I can assure you, I hold this court in quite complete contempt.'

He fined me five hundred pounds, but I thought what the hell, let them try and collect it, let this whole sorry business leave as many tracks as possible. To that end I even got into a fight with a policeman. I didn't hurt him, of course, but got a sound thrashing for my troubles. I should also have got a criminal charge. As feared, however, nothing came of it. It really sank in then that I was buried.

About this time I came to the conclusion that my food was being drugged to calm me down or chill me out to the point of putting me in cold storage. By now I hardly minded. I sort of gave up. I even stopped marking off days with scratches on the cell walls in the traditional manner.

So it was that I was more out of it than usual when my erstwhile lawyer came to see me. It was in my cell rather than an interview room, and it was a strange meeting. He seemed rather sheepish, and I didn't exactly give him an exuberant welcome, much as I was glad to see anyone. His discomfort was palpable, and I tried to perk up enough to take in what was going on, what he was up to.

'I've been asked to tell you to be patient,' he smiled nervously. 'You'll be out soon and there will be no repercussions...'

'Oh there won't, eh?'

'It is only that for now it is best if you and the others are out of the way, protected from dangerous elements...'

'Why are you in with them on this?'

'No choice,' he whispered.

'I figured as much,' I yawned. 'You're still a damn coward though.'

'They want you to write a letter, as well,' he ploughed on, 'to Mr. Hatomba and Mr. Schiller, to assure them you are fine and being treated well and that the misunderstanding is about to be resolved.'

'It is?'

'Certainly,' he nodded vigorously. 'And your being here really is for your own good, you know.'

'And I truly appreciate it,' I said serenely. 'So, someone on the outside is kicking up a rumpus about this?'

'Not much of one,' he said, wiping his brow. 'An African UN official and a German computer expert, along with a few other crack-pots from here and there, are not going to be taken very seriously.'

'Naturally,' I admitted. 'Quite right too. They must be mad.'

'You understand that their efforts may indeed delay

your release?' he went on brightly. 'Add to the confusion?'

'How could I not?' I leaned over to give him a reassuring pat on the knee. 'Tell the people who had me arrested not to think I'm ungrateful.'

'Will you write the letter then?'

'I'm just too weary,' I shook my head sadly. 'Too, too weary. Isn't it strange considering how little exercise I get? I should be fresh as a daisy, but instead I'm worn to a frazzle. Dog-tired. Maybe after I've had a rest,' I winked, lying down on my bunk and rolling over.

In the night a light filled my cell, and I watched as the wall began to glow and burn as if it were wood rather than cold stone. As I watched from my bunk, half-inclined to call a guard, I realised that the wall was melting, dripping like candle wax and opening into a hole. As the flames died, fresh breezes wafted through and a gentle voice began calling my name.

Rising, I walked reluctantly to the wall and, looking out, saw a world of green fields and tall trees, though I knew the jail was in the heart of London. The weather was warm and pleasant and I longed to stroll on out through the hole in the jailhouse wall, but fear gripped me. From somewhere the voice of the speaker of the Men In Black whispered 'Don't' and I paused. No, I shivered, then determined not to obey them.

Running forward, I leaped out of the jail and suddenly found myself surrounded by people slapping me on the back, hoisting me on their shoulders and carrying me toward a streamer-covered rostrum in the distance. On it, waiting, stood a group of obvious dignitaries, who also flocked around me as I was carefully set down amongst them.

There was a transparent shimmering being taking my right hand and a being of pure bright light taking the other, a grey little fellow with big black eyes bowed in welcome as we passed and a white-winged angel, with halo shining, spread its arms and smiled.

'At last you are here,' said the angel. 'Among us where you belong.'

Ushered toward a dais, a hush fell over the vast assembly before us. Looking out at the crowd of thousands of all races and nationalities, more beings of every description, I smiled and waved, at which a great roar of delight and approval went up. The angel stood beside me and held up his hands and brought them to silence once more.

'Behold,' he cried. 'The true king.'

A mighty cheer broke from them like a tidal wave and in the next instant they were bowing before me. The angel conducted me down a set of steps even as lanes opened in the crowd and we walked among the people who wept for joy and reached out for a touch of the hem of my garment.

'What's all this then?' thundered a voice from above. 'Getting too big for our breeches, are we?'

Lightning flashed and crashed into the ground and darkness instantly descended and I began to run blindly as more lightning, seemingly aimed at my backside, shot down from the heavens. Dodging from left to right, I heard everywhere loud wailing and the gnashing of teeth, but no one was wailing or gnashing louder than me.

'Oi, you, enough of the bloody row,' a voice very nearby growled. 'Don't think playing mad or ill is going to get you anywhere.'

Jolting upright, I saw the night shift guard leering at me in the dim light.

'God almighty,' I muttered, coming awake slowly.

'No,' he sneered. 'But close.'

'There's no place like home,' I mumbled, looking around the cell.

'Having a nightmare, were we? Oh dear, oh dear, and tisk tisk tisk,' the guard clucked his tongue. 'Must have been something you ate,' he laughed, going out and locking the door behind him.

I almost wrote the letter the next day. Almost proposed that I'd go somewhere far away, under official supervision and be a good boy forever

Surviving that moment of weakness and coming out the other end made me feel better, though. I could take it. I could be the next Papillon. The next Bird Man of Alcatraz. Or form an escape committee of one and start tunnelling. They were not going to beat me.

That is when they came to take me to a new hearing, another bit of theatre that would only result in slowing the process and muddling the issue. For a moment, though, hope sprang up in my heart. I felt pretty alert that day and reckoned they had stopped drugging my food as heavily, perhaps in hope of me writing the letter they wanted. Maybe this would be a chance to get through to someone.

When I was led into the room and saw only the same collection of faces as before, a very miserable-looking Bill and Catherine more distraught than I'd have thought it possible for her to be, I sagged in my jailers' hands as they gripped my arms.

And there a few minutes later, after we had been called to rise, appeared the same mean old dinosaur of a judge we'd seen before. He may have been younger than Bill but he seemed a hundred years older. His nose wrinkled up at the sight of me and he sat down with an impatient sigh and a glance at the clock on the wall.

'I see you are still without a legal representative.'

'To the devil with advocates,' I grinned recklessly.

'I will not tolerate this glib and disrespectful attitude,' he warned sternly. 'I will not refrain from fining you heavily once again if it continues.'

'I do apologize, O Lord.'

'My lord,' he corrected me as if it were an understandable mistake. He and the night shift guard had the same high opinion of themselves, I noted, but remembering the course of my dream I could not be too hard on them on that score.

'My lord,' I said more soberly, 'I must protest at the irregularity of these procedures, our treatment and the apparent absence of any real charges against us. I say let us be charged with a crime and go to trial or let us go free.'

'We are not here in this instance to determine if you are to be charged with a crime.' The judge raised his thick eyebrows.

'We aren't?' I said stupidly.

'We are hear to decide if you are certifiably insane.'

CHAPTER TWENTY-THREE

Even in my drug-induced semi-stupor, I was so shocked I nearly fainted. What was this, the old Soviet Union? Were they that frightened of the messages? The last few had even gone back to the sort of philosophy or preachiness that characterised so many supposed alien contacts of the past.

Real, checkable, concrete and convincing stuff wasn't coming in now. If I'd been in my right mind, though, I'd have seen that that was exactly why they were afraid.

'Shame on the whole God-damned lot of you,' Catherine shouted suddenly, raising her head and surveying the room.

'That sort of outburst will hardly assist your case, Miss Frazier.' The judge wagged a regretful finger at her.

'We haven't got a prayer anyway,' I shouted. 'You are all conspiring to silence us and halt our investigation...'

'Conspiracies!' The judge gazed heaven-ward in exasperation and was about to admonish me again or to order my physical restraint when he seemed to pause, still staring at the ceiling. Then his face changed and he lowered his eyes, all self-possession left him, all his arrogance and impatience. His hands fumbled on the bench and he gaped at the assembly before him in what can only be described as acute embarrassment.

'If we may, m'lud...' began the prosecutor or whatever he was.

'Be... be quiet,' the judge said softly. Shutting his eyes tightly, he wrapped his arms around himself and rocked back and forth a moment in his chair, then stared out at everyone once more. 'What have I done?'

'I beg your pardon, m'lud?'

'These proceedings are at an end,' the judge announced in amazement. 'They are an outrage and should never have been instituted. The authorities are guilty of serious, no, quite blatant impropriety. Breaches of the law have taken place, and even I have allowed myself to be corrupted. No concerns for national secuity can justify this and as far as I can see, national security is in no way threatened by these people or their activities. You are free to go, and I shall gladly testify in your behalf in any action you wish to bring against the security services, the police or the Crown. Before you go, I would like to see you in my chambers, if you do not mind.'

Leaning over, he summoned the bailiffs and had an agitated conversation with them. They cleared the room and summoned a very junior policeman from out on the street, while we sat dumbfounded.

'I shall wish to have you arrest me in a few moments,' his lordship told the young cop and, rising, nodded to us and led the way into his chambers.

'I received this at my home this morning,' Judge Geoffrey Balham told us, handing Bill a letter. 'As this sorry business is not public knowledge, nor my involvement in it, I assumed that your accomplices had excellent resources.'

'It's from Hatomba, by God,' Bill exclaimed.

'Petitioning for us? Protesting...' Catherine conjectured.

'Seems to be appealing to his lordship's better nature,' Bill snorted, reading the letter. 'My word...' He lowered the single page and gaped at the judge. 'You?'

'What?' I asked.

'Mr. Hatomba knew my name because he was told it,' the judge said.

'Well, of course...' I shrugged. 'But...'

'It was his name,' Bill waved the letter at me and pointed at Balham. 'The beings finally told Hatomba the new name and it was Balham here.'

'And you've been contacted?' Catherine asked, some of her fire returning. I still felt pretty sluggish myself. 'You've received a message, a revelation?'

'Yes, just this very last few minutes,' Balham nodded, running a shaky hand over his pale and ageing face. 'Out there in the middle of it all.'

'Bloody hell,' I muttered. 'I kind of wondered...'

'I hope I'll be forgiven...'

'No sweat,' I smiled and hopped up to pat him on the back.

'Those fellows could easily con any patriotic chap,' Bill said gruffly. 'Think nothing of it, old boy.'

'Sure,' I went on. 'No hard feelings. As long as we're really free, all's well that ends well.' Just then I was too high on whatever they had been giving me and the relief, to care or be as righteously angry as I would be eventually.

'I don't mean forgiven by you,' Balham sniffed. 'Not simply you, that is.'

'Tell us about your experience just now,' Catherine said gently. 'What exactly did you see and hear?'

'Can't this wait till later,' Bill complained. 'I've a longing for fresh air, rest and a large snifter.'

'Me too,' I said enthusiastically.

'I have the feeling there won't be a lot of time,' Catherine shook her head.

'I guess not,' I agreed, trying hard to think clearly. One way or the other, the shit was shortly going to hit the fan. For all we knew we'd be locked up again, his lordship right along with the rest of us. Christ knows, we could already hear what must have been a king-sized commotion going on just outside.

Bill and I shrugged our shoulders and looked at Balham with slight nods. With a big breath and lifting his palms, he gazed back at us and at Catherine, smiling awkwardly. Obviously he was at a loss as to where to begin and how to describe what he had seen. This, of course, was the first time we had encountered one of the receivers of a message so soon after it had been given to them.

'Light?' I prompted helpfully.

'Shhhh,' Catherine hushed me. 'Nothing should be suggested. Let him tell it...'

'Ah, but there was light,' Balham insisted. 'That actually was how it began.'

'See,' I grinned stupidly.

'Shut up, please,' Catherine frowned at me.

'Sorry, I'm on drugs,' I giggled. 'First it was downers and then they made it some sort of speed.'

'And I was part of it,' the judge observed mournfully. 'Please let me be forgiven.'

'Let us not start that again.' I waved my hand.

'Do go on,' Catherine told him.

'After the light, a strange general light, there appeared balls of light that danced about the room and gathered at last round the bench. Time quite obviously stood still for everyone else because I could see you all out there frozen, as it were.'

'I understand,' Catherine smiled encouragingly.

'The balls of light formed into the shapes of men and women but not humans, not living or corporeal people.'

'What would you say they were then?'

'Spirits.'

'Surely not ghosts, old boy?' Bill barked suddenly.

'Shhhh!'

'No, but spirits,' Balham said thoughtfully. 'Some of

them dead, I imagine, but not ghosts. They neither floated nor walked, and they were neither flesh and solid nor completely ethereal.'

'Could you have touched them?'

'Oh yes, I think so, but they were nevertheless not very substantial in a physical sense. They seemed to have to exert considerable effort to be seen and begged my indulgence when they momentarily faded once or twice.'

'Remarkable! And...'

'Uncle Bill, please.'

'They told you to let us go, did they?' Bill carried on.

'No. They didn't even mention you or the bogus case before me.'

'Funny...' I began, but a look from Catherine stopped me.

'They advised me to prepare my defence.'

'Your defence?'

'Yes and asked me to inform the world at large that everyone must do the same.'

'Prepare our defence?' I whispered, mostly to myself. 'Militarily?'

'Legalistically,' the judge said. 'In terms of natural justice, moral justice, spiritual justice. We individually and collectively must think long and hard about what we have done and why. We must try to understand ourselves.'

'And become our own defence attornies in front of these beings?' I wondered despite Catherine's glare.

'Quite the reverse. If in military terms the old dictum or theory that the best defence is a good attack, then it applies here.'

'How's that?' Bill demanded, ignoring his niece.

'I gather,' said the judge, 'that we shall be acting as our own prosecutors.'

Silence reigned and each of us shivered a little, swallowed hard, or bit his or her lip.

'Whoever they are, they want to know us pretty damn thoroughly.'

'For us to know ourselves,' Balham corrected me. 'They seem to want to see what we have learned.'

'About what? Life?' Catherine asked. 'Ourselves, each of us?'

'Precisely.'

'Group and personal soul-searching,' I observed. 'It's linked to Hatomba's message.'

'My strongest impression from them,' the judge concluded, 'was that as far as they are concerned, shall we say, the unexamined life is not worth living.'

Only when we were about to leave anyway did someone knock at the door. Stepping outside, the judge conferred with them privately for a moment and then returned to us.

'Apparently,' he said, appalled. 'The Prime Minister is waiting outside.'

'Bless my soul,' Uncle Bill cried. 'What have we done to deserve that?'

'Are you sure?' Catherine gaped at Balham. 'Why, in heaven's name?'

'I never thought it would come to this,' I moaned.

Without further ado, the man himself walked in, begging our pardon, if you will, both for entering before being invited and out of regret over our unwarranted imprisonment. It seemed he knew nothing of it until that very hour. Well, that was his story.

'Please, sir,' Catherine rolled her eyes and settled an impatient look upon him. 'After all this, kindly refrain from insulting our intelligence as well.'

'If you insist,' he frowned and bobbed his head, pausing a moment at the effort involved in trying to be frank. 'You three and now his lordship are embroiled in matters of the utmost concern to every government on the face of the Earth.'

'Who isn't?' I observed gaily. A strange mood had overtaken me. 'Were your people the ones who tried to kill us in Scotland?'

'No, certainly not,' the P.M. exclaimed.

'He's quite right,' Bill allowed. 'You'd be dead otherwise.'

'I have a fax from your President,' the P.M. said to me. 'Here,' he handed it to me. 'It explains what he has recently discovered about that very matter and other attempts on your lives.'

'I see,' I said, after skimming over the text. I couldn't focus or concentrate very well, though, and took little of it in.

'The U.S. Secretary of State also sends his regards and wishes to meet with you later in the week.'

'And where will we be then?' Catherine asked. 'In jail still?'

'No, of course not,' the P.M. said quickly. 'That was a terrible error. But you understand we could not sit by and let you be killed.'

'Or let us find out more, or report what, as you say, is a matter for utmost concern for every government, etc.'

'Yes, regrettably...'

'But now we are free to go?'

'Yeees,' he said doubtfully. 'On condition.'

'That we stop...' I began heatedly.

'No, only that all of you undertake to say nothing of any of this business of your arrest and detention. Mr. Balham, you must not turn yourself in to the police, bring charges against others or speak to the press.'

'About the false arrests, etc?' Balham nodded.

'Quite,' the P.M. confirmed.

'Is that all?' Catherine asked.

'It is my request, and that of the President, that you delay making public any of your findings, conclusions or further communications from the extra-terrestrial sources you seem to be... monitoring, for want of a better word.'

'Delay?' Bill asked. 'How exactly do you mean that and why?'

'Why, only that things may be handled in the right way. We request that you consult us about subsequent contacts and related events and that, as I say, you take our advice, if not await our permission, before publishing anything.'

'Seems reasonable enough,' I shrugged. Anything was preferable to the cell or a bullet in the head.

'I'm not so sure.' Catherine massaged the back of her neck. She was as exhausted and emotionally drained as I was, just not drugged perhaps, and yet as sharp as ever and ready to deal with this high and mighty individual without flinching. God, I was proud of her and almost weirded out enough to say so right then and there.

'I am afraid I must remind you,' the Prime Minister said. 'That as responsible citizens of your respective countries, you should be happy to co-operate with your governments. In a democracy, it is a law-abiding citizen's duty to obey the directives of the elected officials responsible for maintaining order and security. We deem these matters to be Top Secret and, therefore, it is not strictly legal for you to know them.'

'Wait a bloody minute, young man...' Bill started.

'In law...' the judge chimed in, shaking his head.

'Of course, you are not breaking any law in the way you are finding out about these things. Indeed, some of them are not known to government either. But once you know them, your duty and responsibility is clear. Your legal and patriotic obligation.'

'And what if we are ordered to ignore these considerations by what can only be described as a higher authority?' Bill asked. As an old soldier, he was bound to be suspicious and worried when a politician began to run off at the mouth about patriotic obligations.

'I am not aware,' the P.M. said with dignity, 'of any extra-terrestrial beings having a mandate to order British or other world citizens around. Not yet at least.'

'Hear, hear,' I smiled with a degree of relief. 'He has a point, Bill, you have to admit it.' I wanted out of that jail and needed some guarantee of our safety, and anyway, I had long had my doubts about trusting these message-sending beings blindly. The Prime Minister's argument was as good a reason for a little caution as I had heard yet, and I did not feel like denying it.

'Perhaps,' Bill grumbled. 'But I'm damned if we're probably not discussing two different things.'

As soon as we were alone again the judge told us of the next person to receive a message. It would be a Russian woman, Valentina Vashinka, whose name, for some reason, sounded familiar.

Of course, his discretion was wasted. We were being listened to from outside the room.

Chapter Twenty-Four

We actually did get security cover once we finally went home. The same sort the damn Royal family gets. I had no doubt that these Special Branch boys were also there to spy on us, but I was glad to have them. It was bliss to relax a bit at long last and to avoid either bankrupting myself or my business by using my own people.

When I first put my employees onto finding Valentina Vashinka I assumed it would be child's play locating her. This was once again a famous person, even infamous, and the city she was supposed to be found in was European, but so far they had failed.

'Valentina Vashinka is an elusive character, boss,' my right-hand man assured me. 'Has her own security worries, especially now she's decided to try her hand in the new field of Russian multi-party politics.'

'Ex-K.G.B. and all that. Their top woman during the later stages of the Cold War and now a communist candidate for high office with underworld connections.' I nodded in agreement with him. 'Security worries indeed. But where is she?' I asked. 'We were led to understand she could be found in Berlin.'

'She should have been. She had several speaking engagements,' my second-in-command smiled. 'But just like you so often lately, she disappeared.'

I put in a full day at the office, having only been out of jail for twenty-four hours, and periodically chivvied people along in regard to digging up more information on Vashinka's whereabouts, but I wasn't particularly troubled over her not being found yet. The message receivers had always turned up for us or announced themselves, without our having to hunt them down much.

Even after a week of no new word of her, I was still not concerned. I didn't imagine this one would be any different from the rest. She'd surface or even call us when the time was ripe. Meanwhile, God knows, I was glad of a respite from it all, if one were being offered.

Catherine and I had been meeting most evenings, ostensibly, at first, to touch base, compare notes and keep each other up to date on any developments. Soon though, it was just to be together.

After an evening spent going over the whole thing, from the start to the present, it was late and I was too far over the limit to drive home, after sipping whisky while we worked.

'I know how you hate that couch,' she said with a yawn when we finally stopped.

'It is a bit on the short side,' I admitted with a hopeful grin.

We made love in her bed before sleeping and again in the morning, not desperately, not casually but with a gentle, delighted familiarity and comfort. At breakfast, we were more amused than embarrassed and she saw me off to work with a kiss at the door and jokes on domesticity.

As for her own work at this time, Catherine was at a loss. No other cases were of the least interest now and she could not afford to get involved in anything she might have to drop, needing as she did to be free to take up the line on the next message at very short notice. Going over notes and tapes, or swapping theories with me and Bill was about all she could do for the moment.

To give her a break and for the fun of it, I took her on a day trip out of town. I had a meeting with a client to discuss the upgrading of his company's security arrangements but I knew it would not take long. Afterwards,

Catherine and I would be able to drive off and have a picnic in the countryside.

It was on the way toward doing this, the business meeting having been successfully completed, that we had a mild sense of déjà vû and realised we were not far from the government minister's country home.

'Funny it began with a woman and looks like ending with one,' she observed.

'Who says it is ending? There could be dozens of other messages.'

'Oh, you know how Uncle Bill keeps insisting there will only be ten.'

'Well, there have only been eight, and Vashinka's will make nine.'

'There was yours. That was the first,' Catherine reminded me.

'That doesn't make Bill right,' I said and then changed the subject. 'Have you been back in touch with the minister?'

'No, not since we spoke on the phone ages ago, when she confirmed the lab reports regarding the formula. She seems to constantly be abroad on government fact-finding missions or some such things.'

'Maybe they're bullshitting us about that. Maybe they've shut her up,' I said. 'What do you say we go and see if she's down here at her country place?'

'Might as well, but I doubt it will do any good. She really is still supposed to be in Japan, I think. Saw her on the TV news the other day.'

Catherine was right. Indeed, no one, family or employee, was at home. Not even the dog. So to cut our losses and out of her work obsession we decided to have our picnic there, up at the stone circle. It was, we remembered, a beautiful spot and would be more so now that the weather was fine.

Spreading the blanket in the centre of the circle, after a pleasant climb in the sunshine, we ate our lunch and cleared the things away just enough to lie down and have a cuddle and a nap.

'I thought about you constantly in jail,' Catherine confessed with a sigh as she drifted off.

'I was too doped up to think of anything,' I confessed. 'I bet it was especially hard on Bill, though he won't say so.'

She didn't hear and it was just as well, as it hadn't been suitably tender, considering what she had said.

An hour later we woke, stiff but refreshed, packed the picnic things and folded the blanket. Rather reluctantly we started away, but simultaneously paused and looked around the stone circle one more time, absorbing the atmosphere, trying to make sense of all that had happened to us. Exchanging a smile, we turned again to go.

'Find her,' a voice clearly said above us. We froze. The sky was blue and empty even of a distant jetplane. 'Go and find her,' it said again.

Chapter Twenty-Five

Back in London, a bit shaken and wholly galvanized, I got in touch with my office at once and told them to assume Vashinka had been abducted. They should try to start to pick up a trail in Berlin. It was after I'd gone home to pack before going there myself, that the phone rang.

A strange American voice asked for me by name and instructed me to hold a moment.

'Look, what is this?' I said impatiently. 'I was just going out.'

'The Secretary of State would like to speak with you. I am calling from the United States Embassy.'

'Okay, okay,' I sighed, adding with some satisfaction, 'but tell him to make it snappy.'

He was on the line in a few minutes, apologizing for their part in our imprisonment, or protective custody as he preferred to put it, but I asked him to cut to the chase.

'Very well,' he said. 'As the President mentioned in his letter to you...'

'Wait,' I stopped him. I hadn't read it carefully or remembered much of it. Frantically I looked around the room for it, but knew I'd left it in the pocket of the trousers I'd come home from jail in. 'Give me the gist of it, if you can, I was not in the best of shape when I read the letter and it isn't handy.'

'The President also apologized...'

'Yeah, yeah, I'm sure. What else did he say?'

'It appears that General Simons has been behind the attempts on your life.'

'The President says that, does he?' I smiled. It was a case of what a pal of mine calls life imitating artifice. I'd conned Simons by telling him he'd been made a scapegoat and now, lo and behold, that is what he was.

'The President did not specifically say that, only that Simons may have more information about the rogue elements out to get you than he had been prepared to admit to us. However, in the last few days...'

'A definite link has been found?'

'Correct and...'

'What does he hope to gain?' I scoffed. I didn't believe it. Simons had told me the 'First Message' himself, though I had tricked him. Even if he was involved, he was not the only one, and I was willing to bet it was more official than they would ever let on.

'It is an obsession of the General's. He thinks he is protecting the independence of Earth's governments and leaders. Humanity's freedom and heritage.'

'Denying something is going to happen won't make it go away,' I laughed. 'He's no fool. So what gives?'

'It is all about options, for one thing,' the Secretary said after a pause. 'Maintaining stability and controlling public reaction.'

'Are you saying you disagree with the General?'

'Only as to methods.'

'I gathered from him that it was his desire not to harm me and that other elements, maverick or establishment, wanted Catherine and me liquidated to be on the safe side. I sincerely thought he believed I'd play ball once I was advised of the true stakes.' I hadn't thought that, but I wanted to put the cat among the pigeons.

'I can assure you that he now desires nothing but your demise, for personal and practical reasons.'

'I can understand that,' I said, 'but not a change of heart on the part of the administration or other authorities.'

'The change of heart is Simons'. He was not with the extremists from the start but he is now. Those...' The Secretary paused. 'Come to the embassy, please, and we can talk more freely than by telephone.'

'I'm very busy,' I told him, suspecting them capable of just about anything.

'Bring your own guards, bring Ms. Frazier and her uncle if you wish.'

'I have no idea if they are available...'

'She is expected to accompany you to Berlin...'

'How...? Bugs. My flat, my offices,' I muttered. It didn't surprise me.

'Come,' he said earnestly. 'Provide whatever precautions you like and I will be able to give you some information about Valentina Vashinka.'

'Give me an hour,' I said, hanging up at once to ring the office, then Catherine and Bill.

'Can't come,' Bill said. 'Too much thinking and writing to do. Want to finish what I'm doing. If I go out tonight at all old boy, it will only be to feed myself and my pet policeman. Ring me tomorrow, but not too early, what.'

'We are going to have to hunt Vashinka ourselves,' I said. 'We're going to have to take off right away.'

'Right. Good luck, one way or the other,' Bill insisted. 'I'll see you later.'

'You remember Dr. Merimak,' the Secretary of State smiled as we met at the embassy. 'He certainly remembers you.'

'Oh yes,' I nodded, not looking the man in the eye.

'What a shame Ms. Frazier's uncle could not come,' the Secretary smiled again, studying us.

'Thank God,' Merimak breathed. 'The old fiend.'

'He was acting,' Catherine said, her voice all steely.

'Not an accomplice to murder like some I could name.'

'You were not there...'

'I was at Petra when the bomb went off and killed two men.'

'I mean when they tortured me. But I had nothing to do with that bomb. It was Simons alone who...'

'Retired generals don't have the wherewithall...' I began.

'Let's be frank,' the Secretery said, holding up his hands to head off the simmering argument. 'I know you suspect the government of being hand in glove with Simons, or of controlling him altogether.'

'Amen, brother,' I agreed emphatically. We were in a secure room and had been searched for recording devices before entering. Outside I had a man with good media connections waiting to take us home in an hour. The Scotland Yard boys were there too, but I knew they'd have been ordered to hold the Yanks' coats if they wanted to grab us or knock us off.

'Tell them what is going on, Doctor,' the Secretary sighed.

'It's true that Simons has gone off the rails, that whatever his position with the authorities was, it has disintegrated. He even tried to kidnap me but I have been pretty wary ever since you and that old... Ms. Frazier's kindly, aged uncle "visited me".'

'Is that a fact?'

Simons and various people who agree with him and his methods, have disappeared.'

'Did the aliens abduct...?' I wondered.

'No, these people have not to our knowledge been carried off. They are holed up somewhere, more likely,' the Secretary said. 'Go on, Doctor.'

'The government is actively seeking now to contact the beings who contacted us when you and Simons heard the first message. I am responsible for the project and I can tell you it is well-funded and fully backed by the Administration. Personally, I can also assure you that the thinking in Washington, and I take it at Whitehall here in England, is that you are not to be harmed lest it anger the alien beings who sent the messages.'

'Any response on radio waves?' Catherine wondered.

'None whatsoever,' the Secretery shook his head. 'I am prepared to tell you privately that having you eliminated was indeed at one time virtually official policy. There were disagreements about it, but one school of thought and some half-hearted endeavour was along that very tack. Things have changed, however. Simons has changed as well and for the worse. To a degree, you are to blame for that yourself.'

'Petra came before I ever laid eyes on him, or remembered having done so anyway,' I pointed out. 'You can't say he didn't know about or assist in that.'

'Let us just say he was in two minds about harming you, but isn't now. While official circles are no longer divided on the issue, no longer inclined to allow your enemies free shots at you.'

'Most kind,' Catherine smiled.

'General Simons wants to hide the truth about the messages from the world. He wants any arrival of extra-terrestrials to be dealt with appropriately by government.'

'And you do not concur?' Catherine asked doubtfully.

'We no longer think hiding it for long is possible.'

'But if you were to succeed in contacting them through the efforts of Dr. Merimak here, you'd make a separate deal, see if they'd let you keep the people ignorant of their existence or let it out in your own way.'

'Yes, we would. We hope to do that one way or the other.'

'Through us,' Catherine said softly.

'If possible. Please assure them we will co-operate fully in any way we can but they must realise the terror and disruption to life on Earth if...'

'Maybe they are going straight to ordinary people because they don't trust you any more than I do,' I told him. I was not going to tell him we were not exactly in touch with these beings ourselves, if his thinking that we were protected us somehow. 'Or they may be doing so to subvert you on purpose.'

'That is one of our fears and a particularly strong one of General Simons and his associates,' the Secretary admitted. 'He fears conquest may be on the alien agenda. He wishes to force the world's governments to regard this as threat and to prepare to resist, trick, or somehow bribe the aliens.'

'Rather silly, in my opinion,' Catherine tossed her head.

'Perhaps,' the Secretary of State shrugged. 'He may also hope to threaten them. They may not come at all, he apparently reasons, if they have no friends here, if they would have to fight to come. If it would be quite costly for them.'

'But those in authority,' I asked dubiously, 'particularly yourself and the President, don't see eye to eye any longer with that attitude?'

'Some still do, but not the President or myself. Few people, of the very few world-wide who know of the matter, now think it is worth risking uncontrolled exposure by the press. Most of all, we believe it unwise to chance the alienation of the, er, aliens.' The Secretary smiled and lifted his hands in submission.

'So what is it supposed that General Simons is planning to do about it?' I asked. 'What was your news about Vashinka?'

'He has her. Judge Balham's chambers were bugged hastily from outside even as you entered. Simons was still on-side then, but split immediately afterwards over the change in policy that took place in a crisis meeting even while you spoke with Balham. He then disappeared with a few allies. As I say, however, he knew the name of the next receiver of a communication from the alien beings.'

'You may be entirely wrong in supposing them to be so alien,' Catherine said absently. 'Or thinking any deals could be struck.'

'We can but try,' the Secretary smiled knowingly. 'In my experience the oddest parties can come to some astonishing agreements.'

'What will you do if you locate Simons, his pals and the kidnapped Vashinka?' I asked. 'Go after him, rescue her?'

'Kidnapped is hardly the correct word.' He smiled that cynical, world-weary smile again. 'She is much more likely to be a willing accomplice.'

'My God,' Catherine gasped, sitting bolt upright and staring at me, then eyeing Merimak and the Secretary suspiciously. 'They're planning some sort of ambush for the "aliens".'

Chapter Twenty-Six

We were assured that the governments of the United States and Britain were not in league with Simons and that they would do all they could to capture him, but my real impression was that first and foremost they wanted to wait and see what would happen. They probably still hoped he might succeed, but thought it best not to actively aid him.

Catherine's instinctive verdict about an ambush was not far from the mark. Certainly Simons planned to disrupt the messages, discourage their senders somehow, cause the world's governments to take some action. Vashinka's message was surely going to be suppressed if he could manage it.

To cover themselves it did appear the governments were actively seeking Simons' hideout, promising to inform us of any developments. This kept me in London but it gave me no comfort. I suspected exactly what Catherine did, only it wasn't the 'beings from beyond' whom I feared would get it in the neck. Besides, we had been asked by them to go and find Vashinka, not just go on sitting around waiting.

Simons and his people weren't waiting. They were active, violent and ruthless. Catherine and I were at her place trying to relax, both dreading and praying for the phone to ring. My company had turned up nothing by this time, the third day after our hearing the voice and speaking to the Secretary of State, nor had any other official sources. By now our social lives had ceased to exist, so between that and being together we knew nearly any phone call would be important and pertinent.

This time when it rang it was both those things and a very personal shock. Catherine answered it and said curiously 'The police?' then I watched her turn pale as she listened to them. There had been a shooting and Bill was seriously injured.

We dashed out, illegally armed and accompanied by security personnel, driving frantically to the hospital, but by the time we arrived, the old fellow was dead. The policeman guarding him was in a critical condition, one of the attackers had been killed and another wounded.

For days afterwards, Catherine was very quiet and subdued. She organized the funeral on behalf of the family and cleared Bill's things out of the flat he had been borrowing, while I put even more effort into finding Simons. The first real concrete help came now from the British government, in anger over the wounding of the Scotland Yard officer and yet another act of violence related to this on their soil.

It was on the day of the funeral that I got permission to see the surviving assassin in his hospital bed. There was little hope of getting anything out of him but it felt like I was doing something and, after seeing Bill buried, I needed that very much.

As we walked down the corridor, the Special Branch sergeant with me nodded at one of the doors.

'Our man is in there.' And a moment later he paused in front of another door. 'And here is the filthy Russian bastard that shot him.'

'Russian?' I asked with amazement.

'Too right,' the sergeant confirmed. 'That was the language he called out in when he was delirious. Just now he isn't saying anything much, but we'll see about that.'

'If you need any help...' I offered.

'Wouldn't be allowed, more's the pity. Look,' he led me

farther down the hall, away from the armed and uniformed officer at the door. 'About the old bloke. The official story is a little different from what really happened.'

'I kind of figured that,' I smiled sadly.

'Maybe not how you think either,' the sergeant said before quickly giving me the details and then taking me in to see the Russian.

It was no use, the man was as silent as the grave and only stared back at us as if we were great objects of curiosity. His condition was too delicate to take rough treatment or I'd have been tempted to wring his neck just a bit, despite the presence of a policeman.

'Have no worries, sunshine,' the sergeant assured the prisoner. 'You'll sing a song of bloody sixpence yet. Soon as you're well enough.'

I had my doubts about that.

Outside I heard a stifled cry and a strange thumping at the bottom of the door. An instant later a nurse and a doctor entered hurriedly, drawing silenced Makarov pistols. We were caught flat-footed and gaping. The woman's pistol was trained right between my eyes, the man's at the sergeant.

We stood frozen as the man stepped over to the bed and shot the impassive patient in the temple.

'Turn around,' the woman ordered, and following the sergeant's lead I about-faced smartly, hoping against hope that we might be spared. A second later the cosh fell and I blacked out. Unlike the Special Branch man, I hadn't seen the cosh, and because you wouldn't hear a shot to your brain, for a millisecond as the fireworks went off in my head, I thought I had died.

When I came to, I was still in the hospital and Catherine's face was the first thing I saw. In my condition, lingering between consciousness and otherwise, I thought they must have got her too. Then I saw her black dress and decided again that it was just me who was dead.

Catherine touching my cheek, however, made me realize I was alive after all and had a throbbing headache. She was still in black from Bill's funeral and I was in the hospital where he'd died. The look in her eyes told me how close she felt she'd come to losing me and how she felt about it.

'What happened?' I asked. 'How come I'm not dead?'

'You were knocked unconscious.'

'By the bullet?'

'You weren't shot.' She explained that the guard stationed outside the prisoner's door and the Special Branch sergeant had only been knocked cold, the same as me.

'They were Russians,' I said, trying to get up, groaning loudly and lying back down. 'Unless the weapons were a false lead. Their faces looked Russian, though, and her accent sounded like it too.'

'You think it was the same people who killed Uncle Bill, getting rid of a loose end?' Catherine asked. 'If so, why not kill you then?'

'I have no idea, unless it was a different bunch, hired or government employed, covering up an embarrassing connection. Not one of our enemies. Maybe an underworld thing unconnected to us or Bill's murder.'

'How did it seem to you?'

'The wounded guy knew them,' I said, after thinking it over. 'And he expected what he got. Accepted it even, and without complaint. The look in his eyes said he'd have done the same if their positions were reversed.'

'That doesn't explain why no one else was killed,' Catherine said, sitting on the edge of the bed. 'If it was the same people, they certainly didn't wear the same kid gloves a few nights ago when they shot Uncle Bill and his police bodyguard.'

'I can't figure it out either, unless it was another miracle.'

'Did it feel like one?'

'I must say it didn't.' I shook my sore head. 'Can I leave here today or do I have to stay in for observation?'

'You can leave, they've checked you out.'

'It was artfully done, I guess.' I rubbed the back of my head and sat up very slowly. 'I can only assume this is the work of Valentina Vashinka's cohorts, but why would they let me off and not Bill?'

'Maybe they didn't think he was blessed, for want of a better expression,' Catherine suggested with distaste. 'His killing was to intimidate us or punish us, but like the more official circles, Simons and Vashinka are afraid to actually harm you and me.'

The next day on a crowded street I was passed a message unseen by my police bodyguard. I played it as casually as I could, and kept the small piece of paper in my fist until I got home and shut the door behind me.

'If you want to find Valentina Vashinka,' said the note, 'be at Marble Arch underground station at 6pm tomorrow.'

Armed to the teeth and nervous as well as very suspicious of the whole thing, I slipped out of my window to lose my guards and walked off alone into what could easily be a set-up. I had no idea who this might be, but it was the perfect bait and I was certainly losing faith in either the authorities or my own outfit finding Vashinka or Simons.

I ended up waiting a long time while they watched to make sure I was alone. After a while a woman passed me another message and, following its instructions, I walked to Hyde Park. Again they must have been watching to see if I was being followed.

The crowd scared me more than the park; it is easy to

murder someone in a crowd and disappear. Out in the open, with any people around, it's harder to escape unnoticed and much harder to get close, though this time I had to let them get just as close as they wanted.

At last a man in sunglasses and a baseball hat approached me. Young and fit, he seemed familiar. With a shiver and a tighter grip on the gun in my raincoat pocket I realized it was the killer from the hospital. Smiling awkwardly, he held both empty hands before him palms forward. His tight bicyclist's clothing could have hidden no firearms and only the thinnest knife.

'Let us stroll together,' he said in accented English. 'You can relax. I do not want to kill you or you would be dead now. My name is Uri.'

'Is it really?'

'No.'

'And the woman who is probably covering your back?'

'Irina will do. I repeat, we only wish to talk to you.'

'Maybe, and maybe you only want to capture me or deceive me.'

'My people are watching, not just Irina, and no one else will harm you,' he went on, ignoring my words of suspicion.

'Was it you who killed Bill...?'

'The old man?' the Russian asked enthusiastically. 'Yes, and I tell you he was something special.'

I stopped and turned to face him, fighting the urge to shoot him in the belly through my coat.

'Why?' I hissed.

'He had balls the size of...'

'I mean why did you kill him?'

'Orders,' he shrugged, as if it was tiresome but no more. 'Do you know he was the first to draw a gun when he saw us draw ours? He killed one of my men outright with a big old revolver even before we opened up.'

I could well believe it.

'I think they only said in the papers that the policeman did it for the sake of his family,' Uri went on. 'And so as not to admit the old man had a gun on him without them knowing. The policeman wounded our other man though. But that old man, he was advancing on us I tell you, not hiding.'

'He died going forward,' I smiled in spite of myself. 'I'm not surprised.'

'He was grinning at us,' the assassin shook his head in wonder and admiration.

'Why the order to kill him?'

'Who knows about why an order is given? We were to kill all three of you. He presented the easiest target on that night.'

'I take it your orders have been altered.' His story about Bill checked out. It corroborated the Special Branch sergeant's unofficial account. Only the surviving policeman and the killers could have known it. This guy was certainly who he said he was.

'What do you want to tell me?'

'You are looking for Vashinka?'

'Yes, it's no secret unfortunately.'

'Why do you want to find her?'

'She knows or will soon learn something I have to hear about. Those, in a way, are my orders.'

'And you will capture and torture her for this information if necessary?'

'No, if experience is anything to go by, she'll very much want to tell me.'

'I believe you,' he said incredibly.

'Jesus, you mean she's already...' I sucked in a breath, wondering if that was the reason for the sudden change of heart?

'I only know that she has sent a message to bring you

to her.'

'And then maybe I will be tortured for information myself, or given to General Simons.' She could be trying to sucker us. It could all be part of a trap.

'Those things are not part of my orders.'

'But if they were?'

He smiled and shrugged again as if to say 'business is business'. He was ex-Spetsnaz after all.

Chapter Twenty-Seven

I hated the humidity most of all. It was the sort of country where you break into a sweat drying yourself off after a cold shower. But we didn't have any showers. We were lucky just to have drinking water. It was the insects that seemed to get to Catherine the most, though.

Our former Spetsnaz companion and his ex-KGB girlfriend did not complain, but it didn't fool me. This was not their sort of climate either. A cold camp in the Guatemalan jungle doesn't even suit Guatemalans much. In the distance, on a hill with a lonely road leading to it, we could see a fine and very, very secure rich man's villa. We had been watching it for several days.

By a cold camp I don't mean the temperature, though at night it was more than chilly. I mean we had no fires. Not even a camp stove or heat tabs for warming our meagre rations.

Our greatest bit of good fortune was that the locals didn't like the rich former army officer and politician who had inexplicably built his villa in their remote territory. They would not have spoken to his guards of our silent forays to their homes to buy food or information. Our only other advantage was that the two Russians had been inside the villa once or twice.

In Uri's long-range rifle scope we had seen both Simons and Vashinka, the latter looking highly disgruntled. What was interesting was that the only emotion we saw Uri or the woman Irina display was at that. They were obviously loyal to Valentina Vashinka.

I would never have let Catherine come on a jaunt like

this, but with the other woman being involved and our needing an extra set of trustworthy eyes, I couldn't have stopped her. At least she was accustomed to roughing it, knew how to shoot and could keep still for very long periods of time, just watching and listening.

There were moments when I'd catch her fingering her weapon, a Galil assault rifle, and eyeing Uri, and I'd know she suspected he had killed her uncle; but I refused to confirm her suspicion and even insisted Uri did not do so.

In a way of course, full of years and going out in style, Bill had been lucky, and Catherine knew it. It's how he'd have wanted it. Still, it was best not to tempt fate or risk blood feuds.

'It's obvious,' I said to Uri, 'that Simons and his pals are not aware that Vashinka has contacted you to say she's become a prisoner and not a partner.'

We were sitting in our camp, Irina up on the crest of our hill, on duty watching the villa. I was due to replace her in half an hour. Our observation rota went on throughout the day, and most of the hours of darkness using a night vision scope.

Lying completly still up there under camouflage, seeing very little of interest, your eyes aching from being glued to optics of one sort or another was boring in the extreme. We had to relieve each other regularly.

'Perhaps.' Uri said. 'They are very much of the opinion that we are only gangsters and mercenaries. They would not expect us to risk our necks for her.'

'Maybe, but what if your fake reports of us still being in London under your observation are suspected?' Catherine asked. 'What if our leaving London was leaked by government sources from the U.K. or U.S.?'

'Then they will be waiting for us down there,' I said.

'Yes,' Uri admitted. 'But no one knows we have teamed

up and I think Simons will believe the reports my people are sending of your fictional presence in London.'

'If the controlled leak I arranged for with the Americans happens today as planned,' I said, 'properly timed with Uri's people's report of our sudden disappearance, Simons will never suspect an immediate attack. We will have complete surprise.'

'Even now Simons and his local fat-cat friends should be sending valuable people to watch airports in Guatemala City, the borders of El Salvador, Belize and Mexico.'

'What if they had people watching already, when we did cross over?' Catherine asked. 'What if they have other people in London than you? What if their connections, often the same as yours, report our weapons-buying trip in El Salvador?' She fixed Uri with a stare and took a deep breath. 'What if you are tricking us by pretending to be allies, but are part of a scheme to capture or kill us after all? There would be much less fuss about it down here than in London now, after everything else that's gone on there.'

'Then you are in very big trouble and I have been foolish to make a plan that leaves you two with so many weapons, bought not from my contacts but his.' Uri pointed at me and I nodded. 'You have test-fired and practised with them, you have selected your own ammunition and magazines. We could never take you alive without many people willing to die first.'

'Killing us stealthily, though...'

'Would have been easier and safer on the trail when you, Catherine, were so debilitated carrying your load of ammunition and water that you fainted with heat exhaustion, and he was so concerned he dropped his weapons and carried you a mile out of our way to bathe you in a stream.'

'Irina nearly fainted too,' Catherine snapped.

'Yes, the loads are too big for women soldiers, but we need the extra ammunition and could not count on water being near our camp. But the point is, if we wished to kill you, you would be dead.'

'Well, Uri,' Catherine smiled thinly. 'Don't think the same doesn't apply to you, even if we aren't professional murderers.'

'I know it,' he said simply.

'We have to trust each other a little...' I began.

'I do not trust you or anyone.' Uri cut me off. 'Even Vashinka may have set this up to bring you here, with Irina and me only as pawns.'

'That had crossed my mind as well,' Catherine admitted. 'And the only comfort in it is that you'll get shot alongside us.'

'But we have to co-operate or we are dead anyway,' I growled at them. 'Even if everything is perfectly straightforward, this whole business is dangerous and we will need each other. Any double cross and of course we've had it. I accept that. But I don't want to screw up and get killed, or get you killed, out of sheer paranoia.'

Uri grunted in vague agreement and resignation, then picked up his weapon and wandered down the hill with a small shovel.

'I'm just speaking my mind,' Catherine muttered. 'I sometimes think we should have let the government deal with this.'

'We discussed that,' I said. 'We agreed they'd probably never do a damn thing. Even if they tried, the Guatemalans would just play both ends against the middle, what with Simons' connections here and their own fears.'

'Maybe, but maybe not.'

'Okay, let's say the governments did get involved, it

would only come to a big stand-off anyway. Hostages, a siege or a pitched battle, a regiment of soldiers with air support blowing the villa to hell. We need Vashinka alive.'

'Our plan isn't exactly subtle, either.' Catherine rolled her eyes. 'There is no question that Simons expects us one way or the other, sooner or later. He'd have captured the person getting the tenth message and brought them here whoever they were.'

'Sure, I agree.'

'He obviously means to interfere with the process, prevent it if possible, to use it as bait for us and just maybe for the beings themselves.'

'That's right but it wasn't just anyone who is getting, or has already got the tenth message. It's Vashinka, with whom he already had dealings. Who has friends like these two who can fight for her. Vashinka who, despite whatever she may have done or believed in in the past, has seen or will soon see the beings, and wants or will want to make sense of it and, maybe, like the others, to change things on Earth for the better.'

'We hope.'

'Hey,' I grinned. 'You have to have a little faith.'

'You sound like Uncle Bill,' she snorted, then a wistful look crossed her lovely, but dirty and sweaty features. 'I found a journal he'd been keeping lately. And though I didn't have time to read much...'

'I've got to relieve Irina in a minute,' I said, because Uri was about to re-join us and I didn't want to be talking about Bill around him. It was best to change the subject. 'You know it's the aliens, as Simons and his pals see them, that Uri here really thinks Simons and Vashinka are after.'

'Yes,' Catherine sighed. 'Didn't I see it as an ambush immediately, myself?' She ran a hand over her dirty hair and smiled at Uri. 'Look, I was just voicing my fears a minute ago...'

'We all have them,' he nodded.

'And we are all going mad up here,' I said. 'That patrol of Simons, or rather his Guatemalan millionaire's, almost stumbling across us yesterday...

'And on this diet,' Catherine continued. 'we're going down hill fast. Worst of all we are boring each other to distraction.'

'Just as well we attack soon,' I smiled, glad she had made her peace with Uri.

The plan called for us to hit the place the next morning. We had needed the time we'd spent to acclimatize and reconnoitre the villa. We'd also had to allow time for the helicopter extraction to be arranged for us by accomplices in El Salvador.

Vital though this was, it unfortunately had to be taken completely on trust. If our chief contact, a man named Vargas, let us down, whatever Uri did or didn't do, whatever tricks Simons had in store, we were dead meat. Walking to Belize with armed men after us was a non-starter.

'Weapons check and plan review while we still have light,' I said, standing up to go and climb the hill to the observation post. 'At dusk, right?'

'Da,' said Catherine.

'Yes,' Uri grinned.

There was plenty to worry about all right, a million uncertainties regarding our companions, and Vashinka herself when and if we finally got to her. Again I fell to wondering if she'd actually been contacted yet, as I suspected, or if, as Uri thought, she was just suspicious of Simons.

Maybe she was still in with him, as Catherine feared, and luring us into disaster. But her name had come from the beings first and they had told us to go and find her. This whole crazy enterprise was part and parcel of the quest, completely of a piece with whatever was meant to be, for good or ill.

'What is she like,' I asked Irina as we exchanged positions on the hilltop. 'Vashinka? Is she a good woman?'

'She might be a very bad woman, especially to capitalists,' Irina smiled. 'Or anyone. But she is going to return my country to stability and prominence. She does not need to do this. She has money; she can use the present corrupt system to make much more. We are criminals now, but unlike some we do not like it.'

'You are at heart still good communists, you mean?'

'Patriots too,' Irina shrugged, 'whose country is a mess. Valentina Vashinka can make things better.'

'Better or like before?'

'No, much more freedom, and she will not bring back the Cold War.'

'And in the meantime she is a gangster,' I observed. 'Like many a politician in any country you care to name.'

'Yes,' Irina ducked her head and moved back from the crest. 'There were several cars leaving an hour ago. Fewer guards on the perimeter.'

'The plan just might be working,' I sent up an agnostic's prayer that it was. 'Irina,' I called softly before she had gone.

'What?'

'How do you feel about the possibility of Vashinka talking to beings from another world or dimension or whatever?'

'I don't know,' Irina stared at me hard and swallowed. 'It's not something I have thought about.' She started crawling away, whispering over her shoulder. 'If there are such beings, I hope they are friendly and have good sense.'

'Amen.'

Briefly we had no one on the hill watching the villa but sat around knees touching, a makeshift model of the place before us in the dirt. We had checked our weapons very carefully. Uri and I would take the Galils the women had been carrying, leaving Irina to use the semi-automatic sniper's rifle and Catherine with the M203 assault rifle/grenade-launcher combination weapon I'd been lugging.

The plan itself was of mixed authorship, but mostly Uri's, with input from me based on my security experience. We each took a turn relating the plan in English and affirming that each knew just what was meant.

'From what I have just been seeing up there,' I told the others, taking my turn at the review as well, 'they have bought the story sent from London and the hoped-for fake leak from Washington. They will not expect us until the day after tomorrow at the earliest, at the airport or border, and alone, with limited resources and largely indirect, non-violent choices. They will be ready for a burglar-style operation, or a large-scale attack which they would get wind of from the States or Guatemala City long before it happened. They will not be expecting us to hit hard and fast, as we plan to do, and certainly not in the wee hours of this very morning.'

Catherine helped the others through my more fanciful English expressions, though both were fortunately and completely fluent. The audacity of the operation and its quite deadly nature still shocked us all, particularly Catherine and me. But I knew the kind of man Simons' local benefactor and protector was, having been to Central America before.

I knew the kind of bully boys who worked for him, too. They were all violent, ruthless men, veterans of the cruel wars of oppression against the peasants and Indians of their country. And as for Simons himself, he had ordered Bill's murder and attempted mine and Catherine's often enough.

'We will approach the villa under cover of darkness and lie up until first light, just outside the perimeter from Vashinka's rooms.' I repeated. 'The women will be positioned to give covering fire and a smokescreen for our assault. The security is good against stealthy entry and once might have been good against guerrilla attack, but no more. They lack bunkers, sandbag emplacements and grenade baffles on windows. They do not seem to have light or heavy machine guns, just a now limited number of men with select fire rifles. Old H&K G3s and Israeli Galils like these. I wish we'd been able to bring a mortar but the grenade-launcher will do. Catherine was good with it in Salvador when we test-fired and practised. She'll certainly need to be good today.'

Uri went over details of our entry into the villa's grounds and if need be, getting to Vashinka's room, if the grappling hook up to her window did not result in her immediate descent. She would be expecting us, of course. She'd somehow sent the SOS that had called off the hit on me and Catherine and had summoned Uri, so hopefully she'd be keeping herself at the ready. Entering the villa to look for her would be a deadly business, though unlikely to succeed.

'When you leave the grounds of the villa with Vashinka, we continue covering fire,' Catherine took up the tale. 'As you fall back to our positions, we trade weapons again, leaving all but minimum ammunition with you.'

'Taking Vashinka,' Irina continued, 'who will have nothing to carry, we will fall back with half the water to the meeting point near the extraction site. You will rest and cover our retreat.'

'We ambush Simons' pursuit if need be, then hide the larger weapons, divide the remaining water and exfiltrate one hour after you,' Uri said.

We would only be armed with a couple of good old 1911A1 .45 Colt Automatic pistols by then, I was thinking with a touch of discomfort. If they caught us then...

'We rendez-vous, proceed to the pick-up point and fly away,' I smiled, suppressing my fears. 'Mere child's play.'

Each of us was lost in thought then and silently beseeching the gods, fates or whatever that the helicopter would indeed arrive.

Chapter Twenty-Eight

As the light grew we were all in our pre-selected positions. Hair-raisingly and painstakingly Uri and I cleared a path through the thankfully sparse minefield surrounding the villa. Now we had one hell of a high fence to blow a hole in. Uri's jerry-rigged bangalore torpedo would have to take care of that. If the patrols around the perimeter had been more frequent, we wouldn't have stood much of a chance.

With a stone digging into my hip, an insect making itself quite at home in my ear and my eyes glued to the luminous dial of my watch, I lay a yard or so away from Uri. Then at the appointed time I covered my ears, dislodged the bug and shut my eyes tight.

The explosions erupted a moment later and we were up and running in an instant. Dashing through the gap in the wire fence, we headed straight for the second-floor window of what Uri remembered as Vashinka's room.

There was no need to call for her, nobody could have missed the explosion. A vast flood of relief rushed over me as we entered the compound and saw her above us on the small balcony attached to her quarters. She called out a Russian word and Uri began to swing the rope and grappling hook.

Just then the first of Catherine's smoke grenades had begun landing to our left and right. A thankfully very still day, the smoke lingered, obscuring us from anyone's view on either side.

Vashinka disappeared into her room as Uri threw the hook, securing it in one go on the ledge of the balcony. I stood beside him, turning constantly, covering our flanks. An armed guard appeared suddenly out of the smoke, coughing and raising his rifle on sight of us. I shot him five times in the chest without a thought and heard a scream above us.

Vashinka had one leg over the ledge, wearing a tee-shirt, shorts and boots which she must have been sleeping in. A man had appeared and was pulling at her, another was leaning down to fire at as. A loud thump came and his face convulsed, the back of his head flew away in a mist as Irina's bullet struck him. The crack of her sniper's rifle followed a second afterward.

The man holding the now carefully still Vashinka paused, seeing his companion die. In that short time, with Vashinka making herself very small, he was hit by Irina's next shot and fell back from our view, releasing Vashinka who slid down the rope, burning her hands no doubt but saving valuable seconds.

We sprinted for the hole in the wall with her ahead of us, unburdened by weapons, Uri and I leapfrogging each other to cover our backs. Firing into the smoke to discourage pursuit, we heard the crack of bullets above and the smack of them hitting masonry. Catherine, from a distance and between grenades, had begun spraying the villa to keep heads down and discourage a group rush into the smoke screen. The single shots of the sniper's rifle also sounded, indicating the rash appearance of a bold spirit trying to aim his weapon from some window or other.

I never ran so hard in my life and, of course, shots were still coming our way despite the fine covering fire the women were providing. I knew, too, that unable to change positions much, they would be taking fire up there as well, counter-sniping and searching bursts from automatic rifles. But the smoke stayed with us and behind us all the way, explosive grenades occasionally being launched into the compound for good measure along with bursts of fire and the pinpoint shots from Irina.

We made the first line of trees and I collapsed in a heap, gulping breath and shutting my eyes against the pain in my chest and legs. The others had done the same, but only a minute or so later Uri was up and then Vashinka. For a woman well into advanced middle age, she was fit and so obviously as tough as hell that it frightened me just to look at her.

'We must keep moving,' Uri cried. 'They will be coming as soon as they can organize themselves. They will have jeeps, dogs, and a plane from the rich man's own airstrip will be up with one phone call.'

'You should have destroyed the plane,' Vashinka said, in English for my benefit or because she had been using it exclusively for weeks. 'At the same time as...'

'Too short of personnel,' I gasped, still not catching my breath as I reluctantly got to my feet.

'A timed bomb,' she said.

'Didn't have the chance to do it, or buy the gear,' I insisted almost apologetically.

'Will the helicopter pass over the field coming in?' she asked archly.

'Shit,' I muttered as we staggered through the trees, shots still cracking around us, chipping wood and hurrying us along like nothing else. She was right, we hadn't timed it so the 'copter could take out the plane on its way to pick us up, doing the job just as our first explosion went and still giving no warning.

'No,' Uri said, smiling sheepishly, and between breaths went on in Russian, which he translated after a bit. 'With a hired pilot,' I told her, 'to fly a risky mission is one thing, to bomb a private airstrip is another.'

'It was a matter of money?' she asked.

'We don't have much,' I said. 'Uri doesn't control your purse strings and my end of this is out of my own shallow pocket.'

'The pilot will not like being chased by an airplane either,' Vashinka pointed out.

'By then he won't have any choice,' I groaned. 'And it's a God-damn Piper Cub we're talking about, not a high performance jet fighter.'

She snorted in continued protest and disapproval, obviously giving us less than top marks for her rescue. Yet at the same time I suddenly realized there was a gleam in her eye and a touch of mischief. This critique was her way of saying 'Hello, and thank you very much'. I'd had a few commanding officers like that myself.

The firing had stopped by now and we soon met Catherine and Irina at the appointed spot, near where Uri and I would set up to interdict any pursuit. We passed over our weapons and took theirs. Dividing the water, we ran through our next phase while Vashinka rested. Catherine looked more excited than upset, but no less frightened than any of us, and that was plenty. The worst might very well be yet to come.

Sure enough, they did have the airplane up looking for us, but we could hear it coming and hide easily in the thick foliage. We knew that the women, on the move by now, would do the same. As expected, there were no police or Army helicopters up. Simons and his chums would not have reported our attack to the Guatemalan authorities, though I felt sure he had some of them in his pocket.

Uri's plan for the ambush worked well; they came into it nicely just as he intended, following a trail we'd left on purpose. I hit them first, with a decent field of fire but from a distance. They charged through the jungle at their ambusher in the prescribed manner, only to end up in a clearing where we could both have at them to even better effect.

In the ensuing fire fight I saw both a well-known retired Guatemalan officer much hated by the common people and many a human rights organization, and Simons, directing operations. Uri dropped the former leader of death squads in his tracks with a brain shot from two hundred yards. Others he wounded in the leg and I raked the area and dropped grenades into any bits of dead ground where they had taken cover.

Try as I might, I could not hit Simons though, and Uri seemed to be otherwise engaged. On cue I had to give up, blow off my remaining ammo as fast as possible and start running for it.

Uri covered me from his more distant position, and then we both just high-tailed it, dropping my now empty 203 and his sniper's rifle into the deepest part of the stream. Splashing along for fifty yards, we split off down a more narrow creek in the direction of our rendez-vous position with the others.

Chapter Twenty-Nine

After a while we scrambled up into the trees and paused a moment to refill our canteens. Pushing steadily for the meeting point with the women, we would not cross any more streams and would need to drink frequently. The humidity and temperature were rising with every minute that passed, but we had to move fast to link up and make the rendez-vous.

One of us coming down with heat exhaustion now, and we were all in danger of it, would be disastrous. Not even Vargas, let alone the chopper pilot, would want to stick around waiting over hostile territory.

The next few hours were miserable and draining, but eventually we came near our meeting point with Catherine, Irina and Vashinka. Now we had to be careful not to be shot by them. Any shouting and thrashing around in the bush trying to find the exact spot would risk being heard or seen by the still dogged pursuit Simons and his bunch might be putting up.

Uri started making a sort of whistling noise not unlike a bird but not a whole lot like one either. It was our agreed signal. We couldn't be far from where we needed to be, I reasoned, unless the maps were wrong or Uri's navigation or that of the women themselves. I began to get nervous, though none of these dire possibilities were new to me.

Then I heard the whistle, or something like it, about twenty-five yards to our right. We paused, sweating profusely. It was not impossible that Simons might have got ahead of us and either recognized this as a sign or had the women under observation. He could even have captured them and be waiting for us to show up. I watched Uri inch toward the whistling reply, worrying all the while and following him slowly.

Then we saw them and we crawled together. I put my arm around Catherine as we all huddled to quietly exchange information and discuss our next move. Everyone looked utterly done in. Our clothes were soaked in sweat and most of our drinking water was gone by now. They had not been in position for long before we got there, due to a slight navigation error and the airplane passing over on so many occasions.

'It seemed like we were having to take cover every five minutes,' Catherine said.

'I think they may have narrowed down the likely clearings where we could have a helicopter put down. If so, they may be watching these clearings from the air,' Irina told us.

'Impossible to cover them all with one plane,' Uri tried to give an encouraging smile.

Vashinka said nothing, either out of tact or because being twenty years older than the rest of us, she was even more exhausted than anyone else. I began to wonder if she could make it.

'Could they drop guys into each clearing by parachute?' I wondered out loud and then answered myself. 'I guess it would depend on whether they have that many men who can jump a steerable chute.'

'And how many clearings they think they need to cover,' Uri nodded.

'Simons is jump qualified,' I remembered. 'No doubt some of the others are, too.'

'They are short of radios,' Vashinka managed to say through her exhaustion. 'But they could signal in other ways.'

We hauled out our own maps and tried to figure it.

'How badly will they want you back? Or us dead?' Catherine asked Vashinka incisively.

'Now, after my obvious defection, he will want us all dead,' she replied wearily. 'He will particularly want me dead for personal reasons. He will feel betrayed, but mostly he must kill me because I know of his plans. He will need much more time to carry them out now because my people were to do much of the work. If I survive to give warnings he must think that it will be all the more difficult, if not impossible.'

'And what are his plans?' Catherine asked. 'I think I can guess but I don't have the energy, or the desire, to make a game of this.'

'Nor I,' Vashinka said weakly, her eyes closed as she leaned back against a tree, her breathing laboured. 'He intends to have the recipients of all the messages killed.'

We all just sat in stunned silence. Even Uri and Irina were surprised. Killing eight people, some quite prominent, all now public figures was crazy. All were linked in the press by now with extraordinary events, though there had been a mysterious universal agreement not to mention 'alien' contacts. Every one of them was nevertheless subject to considerable interest. Killing such people would not be easy.

'Simons may know everyone so far,' I said. 'Through his contacts in governments and military circles. Future ones would be only found by following us, so if we stop leading him to them, he can't hope to find the others. He can't expect to sort out all the new ideas, miracles and rumours around the world, and pick the genuine...'

'What others?' Vashinka asked, sitting up and looking at me.

'Any subsequent messages.'

'There aren't going to be any more,' she lay back against the tree and closed her eyes. 'Mine was the last.'

'Well,' I swallowed hard and shivered despite the heat, not really knowing why. 'He could never kill all eight people, even if we don't make it back to warn anyone. He hasn't got the resources, surely. Besides...'

'He could probably find like-minded people in every country in the world,' Catherine pointed out. 'Just as he has here.'

'I suppose so,' I sighed.

'Quite right,' Vashinka nodded wearily, her eyes still shut. 'And his job will be made all the simpler soon, though he does not know it yet.'

We stared at her so long and waited so expectantly for her to go on that she sat up with a start and looked at us for a moment to see if we had disappeared.

'We must gather all those who have been contacted together in one place,' she said.

'Did the alien beings tell you that?' I asked.

'My mother told me that.' Vashinka wilted again.

'Yeah, but...'

'When did she tell you this?' Catherine cut me off with a shake of her head.

'One week ago,' Vashinka said. 'My mother has been dead for twenty-seven years.'

'Was that the message?' I whispered dubiously.

'No, not all of it.'

'Better tell us now,' I said softly, trying to be delicate about it. 'Just in case. It gives it five chances of surviving because there are five of us and, anyway, I really want to know.'

'I was told by my mother and the others, some of whom I knew, some not, that this message is of supreme importance. That it should be heeded above all the others.'

'Right,' I said, suspecting a touch of ego in this.

'You understand,' Vashinka explained, 'that my mother was a revolutionary. A Marxist to her toes. Lenin had been her god and I have never known a better communist in my life. She died for her beliefs, defying Stalin.'

'Yes, I see' Catherine smiled. 'Go on, please.'

'I was told this: Contemplate the Universe, the world, nature and mankind.' Vashinka's voice came more strongly now. 'Wholly appreciate their beauty. Glory in their infinite vastness, find joy in their splendour.' She drew a ragged breath. 'And fully recognise what it means. Above all, remember who you really are.'

Our luck had turned bad. On the way to the extraction point, Uri had taken a fall and turned his ankle. The strongest and most experienced member of our party was now the weakest. He had had to lean on one of the rest of us for the last mile.

The chopper was late too. We had made it in time ourselves by only a few minutes. Now lying up under cover an hour later, we were all biting our nails with frustration. The airplane had been flying around just at the wrong time on top of everything else. It was gone at the moment, however, refuelling we hoped, or chasing our transport away, we feared, but we knew it would be back.

Wandering not fifty yards from where the others were waiting, I answered a call of nature and suddenly looked up, gasped and stared. In the middle of the jungle, only fifty yards away, there sat a building, a Mayan temple of some sort. Too fascinated not to explore even in the circumstances, I approached it

Covered in creepers and moss, earth nearly half-way up its side, it was easy to mistake for just another hill. Walking toward the temple in wonder, I was too absorbed to see or hear anything else, when from the stones themselves and the trees around me I distinctly heard, just as I had in England at the mysterious stone circle, a voice that was neither artificial nor human. 'Take him with you,' it said.

That is when, as I stood dumbfounded only a stone's throw away, Simons appeared.

Standing atop the temple, he aimed an M14 at me with one hand and held a flare gun aloft with the other.

'Gottcha, you sonofabitch,' he laughed. 'Of all the clearings it would be mine. There is a God.' He began firing one-handed and shot off the flare at the same instant.

I dived behind a tree, drawing my .45 from its old tank

crew style chest holster but at that distance I had little hope of hitting him. With a rifle like his it would be easy. He could cut my tree down if need be, or step left or right, and shoot me point blank.

He ducked as I took careful aim and emptied a magazine of eight at him, then he stood and levelled his rifle at me. Holding it in both hands now, the big 7.62mm battle rifle had been front-line issue in his youth and was deadly accurate.

'You tricked me but I bet you wish you hadn't now,' he called.

'Shove it, General,' I spat back, reloading for another forlorn go at him, a feeling of déjà vû coming over me, but no blue flames came out of the Colt .45.

'It isn't a pretty secret to know, is it? Well, I tried to spare you remembering it. I even tried for a while to spare your life, but no more. You are a fool and a traitor to mankind. An alien collaborator.' He aimed very deliberately at me and began to squeeze the trigger.

Simons got off one shot with the big semi-auto before Catherine blew him off the temple. She ran up behind me, breathing hard, pale green in complexion. In the distance we could hear the airplane coming. Someone on a high point somewhere had seen the flare and radioed its position, or a number assigned to the particular nearby clearing.

'Come on,' Catherine gulped, choking back vomit.

'Wait,' I said.

'It was from such a long way off before,' she said, 'and I don't think I actually hit anyone but this... this was so...'

'You saved my life,' I said urgently. 'Please don't say you regret that. Let's go.'

I took her hand, started away and stopped. Turning, I ran instead to the far side of the temple. Now from another direction in the sky, we could also hear, very faintly, a helicopter.

'No, please.' Catherine struggled to free her hand. 'I don't want to see. Don't make me look at him.'

By now, though, we were there, and at our feet lay General Simons, sprawled on his back, one leg at a strange angle, broken and looking like a new joint had formed in the wrong place. His arm hung by a thread where a bullet had nearly severed it.

'Help me,' he rasped sickeningly. That is when I noticed the body armour. The kevlar vest had stopped or deflected most of Catherine's burst. Simons was in a very bad way but he might live if given medical treatment soon.

'Get his legs,' I screamed frantically.

I didn't take time to stop the bleeding. I figured screw him, he could take his chances for now. I just wanted to get back to the clearing and onto the chopper. I grabbed his M14 though and we hauled, dragged and sometimes rolled him along with Irina appearing soon to help.

Beside the clearing, our helicopter's landing zone, we knelt tight-lipped. Just back in the trees we saw the plane circle high over head. If it lingered, our escape was cut off. The chopper's pilot could not or would not try to land, whatever Vargas threatened, assuming he'd even bother.

'We must get that plane,' Vashinka mumbled, still in a state of almost total exhaustion. 'Form a line. Uri, take the other pistol.'

Slowly she stood up, wavering a little and staggered out into the clearing.

I tossed my .45 to Uri and brought Simons' M14 to my shoulder. The two Galils would be best for this, but nothing we had was really much good for knocking down an airplane.

'Maybe we can drive it off at least,' I said. 'Remember to lead the damn thing, that is aim well ahead of it.'

Uri held the two pistols aloft, the women aimed the assault rifles, neither of which now held many rounds of ammo, and I checked the old semi-auto once more for any damage.

Seeing Vashinka, perhaps through binoculars recognizing her, as I'm sure she hoped, the plane glided down for a closer look and probably a clear shot from its side-mounted machine gun.

'Wait until I tell you to fire,' she cried, staring up at the sky.

Down it came, not power-diving but slowly, it seemed to us endlessly. And she stood calmly and watched it. From too high the machine gunner opened up and she didn't flinch. As it neared the ground and the stream of bullets walked towards her, she only waved at the airplane. The firing stopped for an instant, the plane levelled out and its belly sailed not a hundred feet above us.

'Now!' she howled.

We let loose with every thing and bellowed curses into the bargain, but of course the airplane flew serenely on, banked and started back for another pass. By now Vashinka was on her belly crawling for the tree line. Suddenly though, almost miraculously, the engine started cutting out. The gunner only had the briefest angle on us, firing just a few rounds before they turned away again, a fine misty cloud spraying out behind them.

We leaped up and cheered like characters in a World War Two movie. Vashinka was stumbling to us and falling. She's hit, I thought, and jumped to catch her but she was smiling and intact. She had used up her last reserves of strength.

'I am too old for fieldwork, comrade,' she said to me. 'But that,' she looked from me to Uri, 'is how to deal with an airplane.'

I was wrong about her strength being completely gone. There was still some left, after I had put her down beside Simons. As I we began to put a tourniquet on his arm's stump, bind his chest wound and deal with his broken leg, emitting a weak laugh and a Russian oath, she jabbed a bony elbow into his ribs.

'*Suchensin*,' she cursed him. 'We are alive.'

Chapter Thirty

We told the authorities in Belize that drug smugglers had shot at us while trying to steal our helicopter, but because our local contact, Vargas, had stolen it in the first place they had trouble believing us. The main thing was that we got General Simons to a hospital quickly. By now, you see, I had lost my anger and actually wanted him to pull through.

Catherine didn't need to have his death on her conscience either, even if shooting him had been done in the laudable cause of saving my skin. And somehow I knew his presence was going to be required. I'd been told to bring him with me after all, and he was as much a receiver of a message as anybody. Indeed, the first one was logically aimed more at him than me, when you thought about it.

Unbidden by us, the right words were spoken into the right ears by the right people and after only one night in an unfamiliar and much less commodious jail, we were released. Vargas and the pilot returned the helicopter to its oil company owners in Mexico and went underground fast. Uri and Irina stayed by Vashinka's side night and day, going with her and Catherine to London.

I remained with Simons in Belize until he was well enough to travel. The chest wounds had been glancing, the bullets, coming at him from an angle, having been partly deflected by his body armour. The arm that was severed by Catherine's gunfire had been lost but his badly broken leg was mending well.

'I guess a jaguar has got it by now,' I told him in regard

to the arm. 'It was just hanging there and it sort of tore loose while we carried you to the clearing.'

'No one had the presence of mind to go back and get it?' he grumbled. 'It might have been grafted on again.'

'We had other stuff on our minds,' I pointed out. 'Like airplanes with machine guns and little things like that.'

'Why did you save my life by taking me with you?' he asked, lying in his bed helplessly plastered up and very weak. 'I'd have died out there even if my erstwhile comrades had come to the clearing on foot and found me. If they'd even tried to carry me out,' he rambled on. 'By then they hated me, you know, for bringing all that had happened on them and...'

'I'm a great humanitarian,' I smiled ironically. 'What can I say?'

'You got arrested because you brought me straight here, instead of landing somewhere out of the way as you'd no doubt planned.'

'To hell with it, General, it all worked out for the best.' I leaned back in my chair and studied him. 'The big shots in Washington, London and elsewhere have decided to be helpful. They're going to facilitate a meeting of all the people who have received messages from the same source that sent the one we got. To try to make sense of it,' I explained.

Telling him the 'alien beings' had instructed us to have this get-together, I decided was not wise. He had amply demonstrated how frightened and suspicious of them he was, to the point of having killed and kidnapped people, so I held my tongue. Let him physically recover a bit more and hear it from an establishment figure he trusted a little.

There was never any question but that Big Brother would be listening very hard no matter what we did. A secret, truly private meeting between us was impossible. We could never keep the authorities from knowing, never guarantee a bug-free environment, never be sure that no one informed them about or let slip what was going on.

Mostly though, everybody was scared. In the end it was agreeed that the U.S. Secretary of State would chair the meeting and that it would take place on the American military base where the Bosnian peace talks had been held.

Maybe one of the reasons I forgave General Simons so readily was that there was a part of me that shared his concerns, just as some people in the various governments did. The history of our own planet was rife with examples of a technologically superior culture, purposefully or not overwhelming others completely.

Another fear pervaded the conference too, both amongst the message takers and the oh-so-anxious to assist and advise representatives of the UN and individual nations. Not that many countries, let alone people, were aware of the meeting. Only the larger nations with citizens present knew anything and only a very few select officials from these. The overall, almost palpable dread, however, was one of failure.

On the first day, I sat beside Catherine, and looked around the large circular table. Security on the base, especially around us, was so tight it squeaked. Of course, this was in place not only to protect us but to prevent the public from learning anything about the proceedings.

Press curiosity was high, but not intensive or frantic, due to the common practice of not revealing the extraordinary sources for the messages. Nor was the true nature of the confrence known by the outside world.

In addition, for the duration we had all agreed not to leave our large inner compound on the base and not to speak to the media about anything.

Looking at the faces of each of the others seated there, I recalled what they'd been like when I'd last seen them, what their interests were and how they had been contacted and given their messages.

No one else except the U.S. Secretary of State sat with us or entered the room at this stage but, as I say, we were quite assuredly being over-heard and the person perhaps most conscious of this was the British government minister.

I had not met her since that day at her country home, the day I first heard the voice and learned of my connection to the whole mystery and the 'First Message'. She looked no different, still confident, securely upper-middle class to her fingertips and obviously relieved to see that the others were as often as not people she could relate to. My feeling had been that she was there at the insistence of the Prime Minister and not by choice.

After formal introductions of everyone and a brief rundown of each person's particular message and interpretation, Catherine's and my own understanding of them were asked for. Then the updates began with the minister herself.

'I must admit that in the end I have been remiss in following up the progress of the scientists involved in exploring the viability and distribution of the formula,' she said, a little lamely. Only then did I see the tension in her face. 'Certainly things are happening. I am sure they are close to coming to a position from which they can present recommendations to Her Majesty's Government. From there, the government shall, in due course, make available their findings to our allies and, eventually, the world at large.'

'I'm certain there can be no question of that,' the Secretary of State nodded.

'So, to your knowledge, the formula has not at this

point in time been actively employed in cleaning up the environment?' Catherine asked the minister, a little amazed.

'It is early days yet,' the minister shook her head knowingly. 'Anything of this magnitude must be done in the proper manner. The thing has got to be proved beyond any doubt to be 100% safe. It must be checked and rechecked for side effects. It may, for example,' she smiled playfully, disarmingly, in full possession of herself now, 'it may be fine for someone from another planet or dimension, but not for human beings.'

'Yes, but...' I started.

'Monsieur Travier,' the Secretary turned to the burly Frenchman I had last seen in the company of a counter-intelligence expert intrigued by rumours of the 'First Message'. He looked worn now, pale and agitated. He obviously hadn't been diving in ages and no treasure-hunting expeditions had distracted him from rather more frustrating and sedentary tasks.

'Everywhere, despite the seemingly vast sums available,' he declared with a growl in his voice, 'we encounter lack of funds.' Throwing his hands into the air, he went on. 'The world is a very big and populous place, getting more populous every day. The organization itself costs an astronomical amount before anyone is helped to find a home at all. Private and governmental interference besets us at every turn. Quality low-cost housing for the poor is not something that appeals to everybody, especially rich landlords whose income depends on expensive squalid housing. The completely homeless are another matter that is in many ways far worse.'

'What would help?'

'Large-scale effort by the governments of each and every country, massive financial assistance from the industrialised nations. The will in high places, simply put, to do something.' Travier slammed his fist on the round table. 'A will which I am forced to say does not exist.'

'Thank you,' the Secretary of State said quickly. 'Mr. Halliday?'

'Well,' the American said standing up slowly. 'It's not good news.'

He didn't look quite as tanned and healthy as when we'd last met either, but happy enough within himself. Archaeology in the New Mexico desert and lounging around his pool had not been much a part of his life lately. He seemed as smug as ever though and I still didn't like him, but he'd come up to us that morning and been awfully nice about Uncle Bill.

'Please explain,' the Secretary of State urged him.

'I find the U.S. Food and Drug Administration uncooperative to the point of sabotage. The World Health Organization impotent and charities like Oxfam utterly handcuffed. We could feed every man, woman and child on Earth every day forever, for next to nothing within the month, yes the month,' he ground his teeth. 'And we are not being allowed to.'

Maybe he was exaggerating somewhat or grandstanding for Catherine, I thought, but then remembered he had married one of his researchers recently and that they were expecting a child. I reminded myself, too, what a small quantity of the fungus stuff he'd been told how to create was needed to grow enormous amounts of renewable food.

'I see,' the Secretary of State frowned, nodding profoundly and ignoring the shell-shocked looks on all the faces around him. He cleared his throat and ploughed on. 'Now Mr. Patel, please...'

My head had begun to reel and I was not alone in seeing that a pattern was emerging and it wasn't simply of conspiracy from the top, like the one that had suppressed the 'First Message'. This was also ordinary bureaucracy, greed, corruption, stupidity and laziness, along with an all, too, human suspicion of the new.

Patel had been branded a conman, he explained with a tremor in his strong voice. His sister's family had been threatened. His offices burned. Every meeting of people he organized got disrupted. In India, the western democracies and all over the Third World he had been thwarted, though time and again he had proved the reality and workability of his thought and image projection techniques.

In Patel's case perhaps there was an additional conspiracy from defence establishments, firms dealing in high-tech electronics, and any outfit with contracts to do work of any nature on satellites, which encompassed a very wide range of companies. Vested interests from top to bottom were against him, and only the powerless were on his side. Organizing them would have given him or them power, of course, but it was not being allowed to happen.

'I have been driven underground,' Patel said in the end. 'We distribute details of the hypnotic techniques and encourage people to gather together to use them. Some quiet arrangements have been made, images and ideas exchanged across vast distances. But actually employing millions of people? I am afraid it would take many, many decades for it to happen, for the techniques to be accepted, to compete against and defeat other means of communication, and create sufficient demand to give work to the masses.' Patel sat back in his chair, deflated and sullen. It was clear he felt he had failed, was being made to fail, and judging by the murmurs around the table, most of us agreed. The anxiety levels in the room were steadily rising, and even the Secretary of State was perspiring.

If anything, Haseem and Samara looked more hangdog and frustrated than the rest. The Arab had pretty much fled his country, having fallen out with its dictator and been accused of Zionist sympathies. The Israeli's political party had just been defeated in a general election and he was out of a job. Seeing him as too soft, the new government had rejected his efforts thus far, and were barely inclined to negotiate at all, let alone compromise.

'Peace, at this juncture,' Samara said emphatically, 'is more distant a dream than it has been since the modern State of Israel was founded.'

'I am an exile,' Haseem told us. 'Regarded as a veritable traitor in my country. There is no spirit of understanding between those who govern our two nations, and I see no hope of any developing in the near future.' He let out a sigh and shook his head with infinite sadness. 'To them, brotherhood and unity between us are totally unimaginable.'

A silence descended on the gathering and I found a deep depression coming over me along with a burning anger. Under the table I found Catherine's hand and held it for a moment. She glanced at me, smiling sadly. I nevertheless saw a cold determination in her eyes as she squeezed my hand very hard.

'That might be said to have been the last of the practical messages,' the Secretary of State crooned softly to the assembly after glancing over his notes. 'Ones of direct physical usefulness. There followed what may be termed messages of instruction. Information of a more metaphysical nature. Herr Schiller?'

'Are we just going to skip over the fact that nothing is being done?' I asked.

'Let us finish the review of the mesages, please,' the Secretary of State said soothingly. 'Herr Schiller.'

'Ja,' Schiller scowled at the important American,

looked uncomfortably at the others and went on with a shrug. 'It has been fascinating and I am constantly amazed at how similar all of mankind's belief systems are, at their core. How discernible a pattern there is to all our creation myths. It becomes quite apparent that there must be some hidden single source, some basic truth. Triggering the deep-seated common memory through my work is another matter. Sowing spiritual unity...' He mumbled that he had a great deal more research to do on so major a project, but like the rest of us he was distracted by his own growing outrage.

'After what I have heard today, however,' Schiller went on with a clenched jaw and eyebrows raised. 'I wonder if I will not be prevented?'

'Let us hope not,' the Secretary chuckled reassuringly, as if Schiller had merely been joking.

'It had better damn well not be prevented,' I muttered loudly, but Catherine dug a thumbnail into my wrist.

'Later,' she whispered.

'Perhaps Mr. Hatomba would like to tell us about his...' the Secretary of State began, still outwardly unruffled apart from the beads of sweat on his brow.

'Ach, Jonas is stymied in his own way,' Schiller groaned.

I knew they had stayed in close touch.

'Yes,' Hatomba said in his deep booming voice. 'I have duly spoken, both at home and around the world, while about my duties for the United Nations. I have been ignored, laughed at, threatened and accused of trying to establish a religious cult. My message has been called racist by some group or individual from every race on Earth. The recognition of collective or personal guilt is abhorrent to so many people and peoples, so many established hierarchies that I despair of it becoming any more common now than it ever was. The general run of humanity, as persons or tribes or nations, refuse to give up their cherished images of being either victims or members of a select and somehow superior group. All see themselves as more sinned against than sinning and few feel they have wronged anyone without considerable extenuating and mitigating circumstances.'

'And I, too, am nothing but a silly old ass,' Balham, the High Court judge, expostulated. 'Like the ambassador here, I am a mere eccentric, a crank or a religious nutter asking people to examine their own lives, to carefully contemplate their moral and spiritual errors. I too have found that man is more inclined to justify himself, no matter what, than to confess a guilt, admit a wrong, acknowledge a mistake. Soul-searching is not a popular occupation and even those inclined toward it by their natures fall far short of the truly important, particularly painful issues. All see themselves as well-meaning and only foolish now and again, merely misguided upon occasion, not quite themselves, or greatly provoked.' Balham rested his ageing head in his hands, leaning on the table limply. 'And I am no better myself, I assure you. No better at all.'

Why, I positively wanted to go over and comfort the poor devil. This was not the man I'd first seen sitting behind his bench like God Almighty. I had to avert my eyes and they strayed to Vashinka who, by order of message reception, ought to have her say next.

After a pause, but too short a one to fully let Balham's words sink in, the Secretary of State nodded at the Russian woman.

'I do not know what to tell you,' Vashinka shrugged, unlike most of the gathering, more fed up than angry. Nothing surprised her. 'Even though I am privy to certain information most of the rest of you do not posses, I fail to see the sense of what I was asked to disseminate by the beings who visited me. One of them was my own deceased mother, or an image of her. I have had less time to digest or reflect than the rest of you, less time in which to most probably fail, make a fool of myself and grow bitter, like many of you. Perhaps serious media coverage is the answer.'

'We will discuss that at a later date...' The Secretary of State tried to cut her off.

'Official sanction,' Vashinka spoke loudly over the top of him. 'And recognition. We require more resources by far. Above all, the publication world-wide of the 'First Message', must be undertaken at once, the one which puts all the rest into context.'

'If you will share your message with every one first,' the Secretary quickly asked her. 'Not everyone may have heard it yet.'

'Of course.' The ex-K.G.B. colonel shrugged and she cleared her throat. 'As you may know, I was informed in my message, that it is to be the last. It is also firmly in the category just described as metaphysical.'

I was intrigued to note that the tough old dragon was suddenly embarrassed and red-cheeked. Not, it seemed, from shame at what she had to report, though it was out of character by its nature, but because it gave her such happiness.

'Aside from their asking me to have us all meet,' Vashinka went on, 'the message I am to carry is this: contemplate and fully appreciate the beauty, infinite vastness and glory of nature, humanity and the universe. To have joy and faith in their splendour, to love them and to recognize what they mean. To contemplate also what the full implications of their incalculable intricacy really are. What this means, put simply, above all, is to remember who we are.' She let out a small laugh, shrugged her shoulders again and sank back into her chair. 'It is supposed to be the most critical point. I was informed that it is the one we must, beyond everything else, strive toward most devotedly.'

'As a matter of interest, and I think it's best we do this now rather than later,' the Secretary of State said almost casually, though I saw in his eyes the fear and excitement that told me it was of vital importance to the establishment. 'I would like to conduct a brief survey by show of hands. If only those of you who saw the beings who gave the messages could answer it will be best.'

'What about this "First Message"?' People shouted.

'Why are you changing the subject? We want to know what is going on.'

'Please bear with me,' he smiled patiently. 'My reason for doing this before all of you know the "First Message" will soon be obvious.'

Left out, because we had only heard their voices, Catherine and I sat and watched. General Simons was also not included in this, having only got the radio message which I'd overheard. We three had never seen the beings.

'Please hold up your hand if you felt the beings, whoever or whatever they may be, seemed benign, or friendly,' the Secretary of State asked.

All ten of those who had seen and heard them, in whatever guise, the minister, Travier, Halliday, Patel, Haseem and Samara, Schiller, Hatomba, Balham and Vashinka held up their hands.

'Fine,' the Secretary smiled again. 'Now, who thinks that it was not their true nature but a ploy, that the beings may be other than what they seemed?'

Nobody raised their hands.

'All right,' he nodded. 'Does anyone believe that this good feeling about them might be due to a plan on their part? A way of disarming us? Were you hypnotized or drugged, in our own terms, into reacting as you have? Is your trust in them unnatural, given that you are all persons of sophistication? Do any of you suspect your own feelings?'

There was a great deal of murmuring, but the unanimous verdict was that there was no doubt but that the beings were genuine and the impression they left in each of the people they came into contact with, was accurate. Indeed, a quick exchange of the impressions they left with everyone made it clear that, no matter what they had looked like or how they had presented themselves, the feeling was absolutely uniform and positive.

'Fascinating,' the Secretary of State stroked his chin. 'Now it is time to address what has been described as the "First Message". Before I have General Simons, United States Air Force retired, tell you what it is, I'd like to ask you once more to speculate beforehand by writing on the notepads provided, what you think these beings are and what you believe or suspect they are after.'

With his own hand, the Secretary went around the table and collected all the sheets of paper.

'Would you mind, General?' he said while glancing through them.

'Delighted,' Simons said with a glint in his eye. Still in a wheelchair, his leg in plaster and not yet having started the therapy that would enable him to use a prosthesis for his left arm, he looked pretty battered but excited nevertheless.

'Before you go on,' the Secretary of State interrupted, 'I'd like to suggest that silence be observed afterwards. That no exclamations be uttered and no discussions take place. Let us quietly go to our rooms and write down both our first impressions upon hearing the "First Message" and those found later after longer reflection. Shall we sleep on it? Reconvene in the morning after breakfast in our rooms?'

Nobody agreed, but those who didn't know the content of the "First Message" already were so keen to hear it that in the end the shouting of protests died down. The Secretary was going to get his way, I realized, and the authorities were going to keep us calmed down and isolated.

'Very well,' the Secretary of State said, placing his hands flat on the table. 'So we are agreed on that. A bit of solitary reflection this evening. Go ahead now, General Simons, if you please.'

'On a night eight years ago,' he intoned in a slow dramatic voice, 'a clear radio message from an undeniably extra-terrestrial source was received from deep space and bounced from unidentified places on earth and inner space, to the effect that they, whoever they might be, are coming.' Around the table people sat stunned. 'That's right, they're coming. They will arrive on December 22 in the year 2012,' the General grinned broadly. 'How do you like it now, folks?'

As silently as the rest, despite our inclination to talk frankly and angrily with the Secretary, we went to our suite, which was as elegant and spacious as you could hope for. It was also more full of listening devices than a Moscow 'foreigners only' hotel room at the height of the Cold War.

Even after we had closed the door behind us we seemed to mutually agree to say nothing for a while though not for the reasons of contemplation and attempted understanding the Secretary had intended. Catherine opened her handbag and took something out which she put in my lap. I'd been lounging on the couch and sat up to see what it was.

'Read that,' she said simply. 'I haven't let it out of my possession since Uncle Bill died but I think you'll find it interesting.'

It was the journal Bill had been keeping, a collection of thoughts on the quest, the meaning of the messages and where they might be leading.

Reading it made it clear that Bill,at least, was in little doubt as to who the beings were or why they were contacting us. Quite independently and from long before Herr Schiller's message had been received, indeed long before the advent of the computer, Bill had begun studying man's spiritual beliefs and mythology.

As I read on, I got the distinct feeling that he might really have something. It both frightened me and filled me with a strange excitement. Bill used to joke around or express bits of his theory but never gave many details, partly because for a long time he had not taken it seriously himself. Only just before he died had it become clear to him that he possibly had a grasp, though only a tenuous grasp, on the real truth.

I read most of that evening and finished it in bed before going to sleep. For a while I just lay there thinking and finally turned to Catherine beside me, who was making some notes about how to proceed the next day.

'What did you think of Bill's theory?' I asked.

'Ah,' she finished writing her sentence and put aside her pen and loose leaf-pad. 'I used to think he was too influenced by his one-time religious faith.'

'And now?'

'Unlike his verbal musings and occasional jests about it all, what he has committed to paper is devoid of prejudice or bias. The terminology, he admits, is influenced by being a westerner, his disdain for the church and his underlying spirituality, but I believe him when he says the theory itself is not a result of them. Still, I find it hard to accept. I feel it may be just a bit too convenient, too strange. Too unscientific as well perhaps. I also fear I can't be objective enough about something that meant so much to him. Perhaps I might simply be drawn to it for his sake.'

'Sometimes,' I told her 'you're so determined to be

objective that you ignore your not inconsiderable gut instincts?'

We kissed each other goodnight and I put Bill's journal under my pillow, intending to keep my hand on it while I slept. We had no hope of anything staying secret for long, but I wanted to preserve this for a little while yet.

Chapter Thirty-One

The next morning we went to the conference room with a determination to see positive moves to ensure that some action would be taken by the world authorities. It was this mood that the Secretary had suppressed earlier, but could not hope to contain for long.

We had no objection to his beginning by going over everyone's written speculations and reflections of the day and night before. Interestingly, the notion that 'they' were coming hardly affected anyone's view of who the beings were, and where exactly they might come from. A few people reported a degree of trepidation, but it was not born of General Simons' fear of conquest or cultural domination. All experienced once more the acute sense of embarrassment and shame at the particular aspect of the poor state of the Earth or of humanity that they had been told to help rectify.

Their ideas on the beings' origins still ranged from enlightened spacemen to the spirits of our own dead. It was still suspected that they might be people from some other earthly dimension or our very progeny, visiting us out of the future with the aid of time machines. As ever, only Simons saw anything sinister in it.

'Why do they wish to create this Utopia, if not to lull us and dull us into passivity?' he shouted over the hum of lively debate.

Once again we had been diverted away from our desired direction. All this not only prevented our uniting to demand concrete co-operation from the powers that be, but supplied their listening ears with useful information, necessary to their decision-making processes.

'And of course,' Simons railed on, 'they may wish to make the planet more comfortable, perhaps more suitable for them.'

'That might explain what we have come to term the practical messages,' Hatomba replied heatedly. 'But what of the other more moral or metaphysical ones?'

'Psy-Ops,' the General said. 'They want to freak us out. Yes, it's psychological warfare operations, ladies and gentlemen, and that's all it is. Obviously they have studied us and know what we are susceptible to. What our superstitions are.'

'Superstitions indeed,' Balham cried, pointing a long bony finger at the General. 'Let us not forget the kind of man we are dealing with in General Simons here. He is capable of murder and so he supposes that all other creatures are, as well. I say that it is absurd to ascribe bloodlust and subjection to these sort of beings, whatever their origins. And I point out that we have seen them and he has not.'

'Why would they wish to conquer us?' Schiller demanded angrily. 'Beings so apparently advanced, if you think them extra-terrestrial, which I do not, that they are capable of interstellar travel? What would be the point?'

'Lebensraum, Herr Schiller,' the General said with a gleam in his eye. 'Living space, slaves, even food for all we know.'

'Ach, you are too much influenced by the science-fiction films of your youth,' Schiller sniffed. 'And of recent times, too. You have no evidence that they are hostile, and next to none that they come from outer space. Thay have told us that communication with us is difficult; the radio message you heard was created by them to make things simple.'

'They don't have to come from outerspace,' Travier insisted, waving his arms dismissively. 'My experience was underwater. They may live under the sea for all we know. I do not see that it matters. Our assignments are what matters.'

'Hear, hear,' Catherine and Patel cried.

'You are right,' Schiller agreed.

'It is not because they were given by these beings either,' Travier went on, rapping his pen on the table at each salient point. 'But because they are good for humanity, because wherever the information came from it is available now. House, feed and employ people, my friends and clean up the earth.'

'Again I say why...?' Simons began.

'Why not, goddammit?' Halliday shouted.

'Calmly, everyone, please,' the Secretary of State said soothingly while growing agitated himself. This is what he feared most.

'The *why* is important too,' Samara insisted. 'Of course, it is fascinating but above all it may help reassure society that it is secure, and it may also cause us all to work harder at utilising the vital information the beings have gifted us with.'

'Absolutely,' Catherine agreed. 'Practical and intellectual steps on a massive scale must be undertaken at once.'

'Full discussions will take place...' the Secretary of State started to say.

'All governments, even my own corrupt one,' Haseem thumped the table, nodding vigorously, 'must be apprised of the probable source of this information and encouraged to act upon it. For peace, nutrition, spiritual welfare and everything else.'

'Eventually, yes,' our chairman allowed lamely.

'You are right, Mr. Secretary,' the British government minister came to his asssistance. 'It may be rash at this time to rush into any of this. World leaders must take a long hard look at this and come to responsible decisions regarding each and every aspect of it. I foresee a whole series of these meetings to assist in that process.'

'Very perceptive and sensible,' the Secretary of State smiled.

'No, no, no, Mr. Haseem is quite correct, governments must make all this available to the people at once,' Patel said emphatically. 'And interference by big business and fanatics must be prohibited.'

All around him voices were raised in loud agreement, fists were pounding the table, or shaken in the air as the Secretary of State sat smiling through it, though sweating more than ever.

'For now, let us restrict our discussions to who we think *they* are and why *they* are coming.'

More protests and grumbling ensued at this.

'I assure you, very soon everything possible will be done to address the messages themselves,' he said, holding up his hands, palms forward, appealing for calm. 'And I'm sure I speak not only for my own country but the governments of the world at large.'

There was a grudging pause. It was something at least.

'I don't see much ever happening, myself,' Simons pointed out gleefully, looking round the room, playing the devil's advocate. 'The governments and big businesses won't play ball,' he laughed. 'Not really.'

'What do you say to that, Mr. Secretary?' Catherine asked.

'I say that is a very pessimistic view.'

'Maybe this in itself will keep the aliens from the door,' Simons conjectured happily. 'If they see us obviously ignoring their instructions.'

'That makes a mockery of your other arguments that they have studied us and know our weaknesses so well that they can manipulate us,' Vashinka veritably hissed at him. 'What I do not see happening is ordinary people taking to the spiritual and moral advice given by Ambassador Hatomba, Chief Justice Balham, or anyone else. I have no faith in being listened to myself.'

'It all goes to show,' Simons interjected smugly, 'even if these beings are good guys, mankind just isn't ready for them.'

'I think that is a fair point,' the Secretary allowed.

'You know I don't agree with some of you who seem to believe every aspect of contact with these beings will be beneficial,' the General admitted with a sly grin. 'Hell, maybe I'm wrong, though. But from everybody's description of them one thing seems quite clear.' He paused and eyed the group. 'They're a holier-than-thou bunch of so-and-sos and damned judgemental.'

That shut everyone up instantly.

'Maybe that's why they're coming in the first place,' I said into the silence. 'Simply for that and no other reason.'

Again a bit of a furore started, challenges to explain and angry dismissals, but the Secretary called everyone back to order and turned to me.

'Elaborate, please. This may be of value,' he said. It was particularly what the authorities were after, and I knew it, but nothing else was going to be done until these points were resolved to some degree.

'I suppose you're referring to Uncle Bill's theory,' Catherine whispered to me.

'Yes, I think it is pertinent.'

'Please continue,' the Secretary of State urged me again.

'Some of you knew Bill Frazier,' I began, telling those who had not met him a little about him. Without naming names I also mentioned that he had died while helping to investigate the phenomena of the messages.

'Bill may have briefly been a Church of England vicar in his long life, but he abandoned organized religion totally and never regretted it,' I explained. 'He was a man of the world in every sense and, apart from while making jokes at his own class, without prejudice or rigid ideas. I guess you'd have to say he was very fond of the more than occasional drink, but he was nevertheless an accomplished scholar and a man of considerable experience. These are his findings after more time and thought on this subject than anyone else has either had or has been able to afford themselves.'

'Except perhaps me,' General Simons smiled.

'Yes, except for the General, who, unlike Bill, did not have direct and quick access to each new message as it came in, right up to the penultimate one. Bill realized early on that a pattern was emerging. Valentina Vashinka's contribution would only have reinforced Bill's theory, if he'd lived to hear it.'

'Yes,' the Secretary of State said over the top of various words of general agreement around the table. 'A pattern might be seen to have formed, to some degree. The beings might indeed be pursuing a particular direction. Go on.'

I took a drink of water and let the rest of the murmuring die down.

'For Bill, as for all of us, the first question was who are these beings? The second; where do they come from? At first the problem was that everyone of you he spoke to or heard about had a very different description and impression of what they were. Yet none very specific and some of the descriptions were not the same under hypnosis as while consciously reported.' I turned to Catherine for confirmation.

'All your unconscious memories,' she agreed, 'are of a

piece with one another. Among the conscious memories of the later message recipients, the majority do not even differ from what they describe under hypnosis.'

'Basically,' I said, 'you all saw more or less the same thing, whether you realized it or not. Some were told by the beings that appearing at all was difficult for them without the help of human imagination, which of course could be a source of confusion.'

Catherine nodded.

'Bill found that the way to understand who the beings were might lie in understanding why they are coming. Like a detective looking for a motive.'

'I found one,' General Simons smiled.

'Yes, but Bill dismissed the alien theory, because everyone's real descriptions defied it in every case. No one ever even saw a spaceship.'

Simons only shrugged and looked away.

'So, who could they be, Bill asked himself. Who would want to come here? And most importantly, safely assuming they are not extra-terrestrials who'd only just found us or the technology to visit earth, why now? And why give us this particular information? He had to look for the connection.'

A collective nod occurred while I took another sip of water.

'Why the individual feelings each of you were imbued with? You,' I asked the minister, 'what was it you said you felt most? As if the President, the Prime Minister and the Pope were coming to visit, and your home was a mess. Wasn't that it?'

'Yes,' she confirmed almost reluctantly. 'So?'

'And Travier felt ashamed that there were not enough rooms for everyone.' I watched him nod, feeling a slow excitement grow in everyone present. 'Halliday was humiliated at the idea of there not being enough food to go around. Patel, that so many people were idle and unfulfilled, not busy. Haseem and Samara, that the constant war-footing their countries are on was like a disuniting feud between siblings in front of company.'

They too nodded, and I took a breath, glancing around at the now very attentive faces, none more intrigued than the Secretary of State.

'By this time, well before the "First Message" had been recovered by me and shared with him, Bill had come to the conclusion that company was indeed coming. Important company. Though in retrospect we can all agree that that was obvious...'

The rapidly delivered murmurs were of assent, the keen looks asking me, even defying me to go on.

'So, to re-iterate, the real issue is not who they are or where they come from, but why they are coming at all, right? Consider, as Bill did, the arrival of the messages of a moral and spiritual nature. Bill had long been conducting a study not unlike Herr Schiller's and had basically concluded that all human societies have 'known' that they were created, that certain laws applied to our behaviour and that breaking them was wrong in the eyes not only of men, but of whatever or whoever had made us. That, too, is pretty obvious. As Herr Schiller says, there are amazing similarities in how we believe we were created and why.'

'Ja, as I've said, I am coming to the conclusion that there is a common root. A basic single spiritual belief held by all humanity. It is my understanding that we possess an inner knowledge, even memory, of who we are and where we come from. Go on, go on!'

'So did Bill, and what is more he came to wonder if where we came from is not the same place that these beings come from. That who they are is who we are. He theorized not only that they may be our creators...'

Suddenly the buzz of voices, some in agreement, others in doubt or wonder, filled the room so loudly that I could not be heard. The Secretary of State himself shouted everyone down, aided by those most anxious to hear me out.

'Continue,' he said at last. 'What were Mr. Frazier's conclusions?'

'He felt, given the sorry state of the Earth and of humanity, and considering the nature of the messages the beings have sent...' I swallowed hard, watching their faces '...that they are not so concerned about creating a Utopia here, as the General termed it, as with avoiding too much embarrassment, maybe even trouble when they arrive. Or more pointedly, as Bill put it, when the boss gets here.'

Bill's proposition was tossed around and examined from every angle. No one could deny that it made sense in the context of the messages, considering where they seemed to lead and given the point they seemed to be making. Actually believing that Judgement Day loomed near, however, was another matter.

Over the course of the on-going conference many other theories were suggested, but none very seriously. Somehow it always came back to the same thing, Bill's notion and its consequences. In their hearts, perhaps, everyone who had seen the beings instinctively recognized the truth of it.

By the end of the meetings, or that round of them, we all discovered we had been drafted into semi-official positions with our respective national governments. Everything was couched in the most encouraging and positive terms, progress was virtually guaranteed on all fronts, more meetings scheduled and sub-committees formed. At last, we all were made to feel, things would begin to happen.

Chapter Thirty-Two

Even though we had little choice but to go along with the programme, we honestly expected to see some action taken and strove toward helping the authorities to plan the best possible ways to proceed. However, months later, we were still banned from speaking to the press, veiled but very real threats having been made to anyone who might transgress. And as time went by, we began to lose faith in the establishment.

All along, from the first discussions about Bill's theory and its general acceptance, I had perceived a sense of relief on the part of the government authorites. If it were 'religious', it didn't worry them, wasn't part of their remit, wasn't even real. Spacemen they could do business with, future technocrats they could relate to, borrow from, scientific discoveries about parallel dimensions they could conceive of and accept, but this was nonsense. We were not serious people anymore, the project, the messages, they might well be thinking, were just the work of some kind of cult we had formed.

I tried to ignore that feeling and carry on helping Catherine, who had been given the chair of the group after the Secretary of State had returned to his regular duties. We did a lot of flying around the world and kept busy, or seemed to, but it was taking its toll.

We had re-married, and the work was now a major part of our lives. We found ourselves in a position, indeed had been manipulated into it, where the work mattered because it simply had to. To believe in ourselves at all now we had to believe in the work as officially laid out.

On the parcel of land we'd bought in the English countryside as a retreat stood an ancient stone circle like the one near the British government minister's home. Sometimes when we were able to take time off and get away, one or both of us would go and sit there and hope for some new message, some fresh advice, but none came. The voice didn't speak to us again.

Whenever possible we escaped to our cottage, and as an unspoken, shared discouragement set in, this became a more regular occurrence. So it was one day, with the ususual sense of peace we felt while there, as I was mucking out the stalls of the stable where we kept a couple of horses, I suddenly felt the hairs rising in a familiar way on the back of my neck.

'Why are you here?' I asked without turning.

'To congratulate you,' said the funny-horrible spokesman of the Men In Black.

'What?' I wearily faced them, seeing them arrayed in the usual row, oddly sitting on the top rail of the gate.

'You and Ms. Frazier have been most wise,' the middle one said. 'Most wise.'

'How's that?' I wondered, shovelling up a big pile of fresh manure.

'Co-operating fully with the authorities, of course. Seeing sense generally.'

'Why would that bring you around?'

'You are safe. We like you to be safe. We wish you to take no more chances.'

'I don't know what you mean, you little shits,' I hoisted the shovel and flung the horse dung at them with all my strength, slipping in another pile for my troubles. They vanished and Catherine stuck her head in from the garden a moment later to see what I was shouting about but I did not tell her.

'Fell down, that's all,' I lied. 'Got my jeans mucky.'

Days went by and I still didn't say anything about the MIBs. Just as we never talked about our feelings of having sold out to the authorites. Then, lying awake in bed one Saturday morning before getting up, newspapers unread on our laps, both of us rather quiet and thoughtful, Uncle Bill came in. The room had exploded in light and music-like sound and he just stood staring at us in astonishment.

'What's going on?' he demanded.

'Bill,' I cried stupidly, staring back at him. 'You're dead.'

'Never mind that,' he said. 'Has everyone here gone mad?'

Behind him a group of equally semi-solid-looking beings stood watching anxiously.

Catherine slipped out of the bed and approached the shade of her uncle with graceful caution, her nightgown flowing behind her. In fact, she looked more like a ghost than he did. Bill gaped at her in wonder.

'So you see him too,' she said to me, over her shoulder, some of her professional curiosity and scepticism returning.

'Of course he does,' Bill groaned impatiently, glancing back at his companions with an apologetic shrug. 'Don't study me Cathy, just listen.'

But we did study him. We had at least twice been saved by miracles, we had been troubled by the MIBs, though mere figments of our imaginations perhaps, and we had heard voices, but this was altogether different. These at last were the beings we had been told so much about and now, apparently, Uncle Bill was one of them.

'Were... were you right?' I asked him. 'Your theory...'

'More or less,' he said distractedly, as if he was in a hurry. 'I want you to come with me, just for a while. It's very important.'

'Come with you?' Catherine whispered.

'Just for a while.'

I got out of bed too and put on a pair of slippers, but it was not a physical journey he was talking about. As we were drawn into a circle, the other beings formed around us. I could not help but look closely at Bill and the rest. Some were familiar too, and smiled or nodded. Others, somehow seemingly of a slightly more ethereal nature, came forward as the room dissolved and disappeared and we went away.

'Why didn't they listen to us?' one of them asked.

'Were we not understood? Was the information impractical or too difficult?' They sounded quite concerned and disappointed.

'No, I think it all came across okay,' I answered lamely.

'But why has no-one used our help?'

'Those you spoke to tried,' Catherine said. 'Please tell us who you are.'

'But... but...,' Bill stammered, sounding rather hurt. 'I'm your old Uncle Bill.'

'Yes. I mean...'

'A little thing like death doesn't change that.'

'And you others?' I asked.

'Just friends and family for the most part,' Bill told us. 'The rest are what you might inadequately call ang...'

'Any word you might understand,' one of the hazier ones explained, 'that could describe us even a little, would only be misleading and trigger invalid preconceived notions. What we are is both inconceivable to you and utterly simple.'

'What do you want?' Catherine asked calmly, fascinated and yet serenely peaceful. Oddly, I felt just the same.

'To show you something. To seek your help.'

'Tell us,' another of the more purely spirit-like ones

asked again. 'Why have no changes occurred despite the messages we sent? Were they not useful? Does no-one care that we are coming? Does no one understand the significance?'

'They are weak. We are weak. Our leaders are flawed and cynical and often self-serving,' I told them. 'They did not listen or did not believe. We have been misled and as individuals we can do very little. Vast funds, enormous resources are needed and without the assistance of our governments it was impossible. You have over-estimated mankind.'

'Would they reject us then? Reject our help?'

'Some don't trust it...' Catherine began.

'The dark-hearted or troubled ones, yes, but we tried to watch over you as you resisted and overcame them.'

'Can't you go to the people in charge?' I pleaded. 'Can't you appeal to somebody with power and influence in our world, who might...'

'They can't, old boy,' Bill said. 'The rest of us aren't much better. You have to do most of the work just to see us. You have to be able, and in some way inclined. And they, we rather, have trouble understanding you. We soon forget, as people forget the bad or dull or uncomfortable from the past. It's natural and happens to everyone after the initial review stage is over.'

'What's that?' I wondered.

'Going to be different for you lot, however,' Bill said, not answering me. 'And there's the rub, what! Going to be less leisured, less, well, gradual so to speak.'

'What do you mean? What will be?'

'Remember my theory?'

'Sure, but...'

'Very silly terms, very inadequate understanding, over-complicated and too narrow, but along the right lines, if I say so myself.'

'You mean somehow, that it is all going to go bang in our natural lifespans? The end of time?'

'As you know it, yes,' Bill nodded. 'But one way or the other, Doomsday comes in everybody's lifetime. This'll just be rather collective...'

'Please do not be frightened,' several of the beings hastened to assure us.

'For every individual it will be as it has always been,' one of the less solid beings went on. 'That will not change.'

'What can we do now, though?' Catherine gasped. 'Save the world? Save humanity?'

'No,' another one of them said. 'But you may help to prevent the greatest suffering imaginable. Please observe.'

'Observe what?' I asked because we were standing in a sort of fog and my mind was spinning. The greatest suffering imaginable, I thought.

'A preview of the end, old boy,' Bill whispered.

In that instant the images this triggered in my head were horrible. I saw a glowing red meteor racing through space toward the Earth like a tracer bullet. I saw it strike and the planet shudder. I saw in close-up now the terrible destruction, the massive tidal waves washing away whole cities, volcanic eruptions blowing up like H-bombs and great clouds of dust and ash filling the sky and blotting out the sun. I saw the polar ice caps creeping over the surface to freeze formerly temperate lands and elsewhere forests turn to deserts. Closer still I saw death come to people in a million ways, each more grotesque than the last. I began to shake and felt an anguished cry rise within me.

'Ready?' asked Bill.

'Observe,' said the wispy being again.

I opened my eyes and realized I had been supplying all

this myself, that they had as yet shown me nothing, that only milliseconds had passed. Beside me Catherine, too, looked on in wonder and tightly held my hand.

A sharp, sudden pain struck us and was gone as quickly; all our senses were now employed; we were not merely 'observing' but seeming to live the things before us, watching from afar and yet in it, as ourselves, as in a dream. We were crossing a beautifully illuminated bridge, going toward a humming source of power and strength while all around us others were being drawn along too.

We were frightened and uncertain and very, very perplexed, but the closer we came to the central point the less these feelings seemed to matter, though they did not quite disappear. Voices ahead cried out names and so did others all around us. Some called our names and in the near distance I saw faces I knew and loved and people waving.

In a leaping, dancing crowd we came together shouting in joy and amazement, utterly awed and uncomprehending. Yet in the back of our consciousness a nagging doubt remained, a guilt and a need to examine it.

Yet above all there was a surging, shocking, enormous realization, relief and calm, exhilaration, wonder and familiarity. A homecoming of warmth and happiness wrapped around us and from everywhere emanated the bright, glorious bursting of beautiful sound and colour and an overwhelming sensation of unity.

Then the world, our world, re-appeared and though we were no longer part of it we stood with it around us and the anxiety returned. With the aid of those close to us we looked inward as well and we saw clearly how we were and how the world was. We realized all we had foolishly forgotten, rejected and ignored.

From above an infinite magnificence, intelligence and

comprehension, an all-encompassing enthusiasm and love seemed to fill the sky, the crowd, the Earth and each of us. A sort of ultimate union of infinity and harmony enveloped totality. Creation was one with its creator; nature, ourselves, everything was one, once more whole again. Happiness of unbelievable intensity, yet combined with complete serenity, descended. But it was marred again by our doubt; the knowledge that something was wrong; that the cosmic reunion was tainted by a shameful secret that was not secret. We had lost our gifts, lost our honour. We had now forgotten ourselves, had not recognized our own.

A downward-floating, darkening sense of indescribable grief weighed upon everything, a sense of harrowing despair and self-loathing as big as the universe. We began to shudder and weep with rage and humiliation and the knowledge that we could have done better. That we might at least have remembered and loved and tried harder. Everywhere this total, all-pervading and abject mortification swelled and exploded. The infinite sadness, disappointment and sense of rejection vibrated through the battered Earth, the pain of it so deep and unknowable it seemed to quake and shatter in a never-ending soul-rending sob throughout creation.

Inside myself I was free, though; I was being cleaned and cleared and understood. I was confident. I knew my unforgivable failings for what they were and felt them forgiven. Inside myself I forgave them. I saw and felt and knew this for all the countless others as well. But the echo of the shame and pain and horror went on, elsewhere, somewhere and forever. It was unforgettable, unbearable, unimaginable in its depth and breadth. As if a mother's heart had been broken many trillions of times and for eternity.

With the horror of this suffering still chilling and gripping us we again stood alone with the ethereal beings and Bill and the rest. As shaken as we were, they turned to us and spoke anxiously and desperately.

'We slipped ahead just a little to try to prepare, modify, perhaps mitigate...' one being began to explain.

'Defer and tone down some of the negative and hurtful...'

Now all the beings began talking at once as the mist returned and faded, leaving us in our bedroom again, the less solid beings themselves slowly fading.

'All at once...'

'The shock and disappointment...'

'The guilt'

'Your independence was planned, freewill part of the gift, part of the lesson, but this... the Earth as it has become...'

'How could it be foreseen?'

'How can it be borne?'

Then they were gone and only Bill and the other more solid ones remained, though also fading now. Helpless and still deeply embarrassed, they lingered awkwardly, trying hard to remain visible to us.

'Will they be in trouble?' Catherine asked, obviously hardly knowing what she meant herself. 'Will we?'

'They mean well,' Bill said. 'They may be quite correct. They know such a lot more than I do. But there's still hope.'

'Hope?'

'Use what means you can, tell people the messages, help them prepare. Use what some call the collective unconscious, Mr. Patel's people, ordinary communications. Don't be afraid. It is not too late.'

'But if we fail, who will suffer?' I asked. 'The beings, you, us?'

'No, not them, not us, not you.' Bill said sadly.

'Who will be punished if we fail then?' I tried to grasp his arm and couldn't hold or feel him. 'If Humanity itself so badly fails?'

'Yes, who?' Catherine asked desperately, as first his companions then Bill slowly disappeared. 'Who will feel that terrible, eternal pain? Who is to be saved?'

'The one who could feel it,' he said. 'Who would feel responsible, who gave so much and asked so little.' Bill's voice came faintly. 'The one who, for pity's sake, must be spared...'